THE
INSIDER'S GUIDE
TO THE
TOP TEN BUSINESS SCHOOLS

Also by Tom Fischgrund

Match Wits with the Harvard MBAs

Fischgrund's Insider's Guide to the Top 25 Colleges (editor)

Barron's Top 50:
An Inside Look at America's Best Colleges (editor)

THE
INSIDER'S GUIDE
TO THE
TOP TEN BUSINESS SCHOOLS

Tom Fischgrund, *Editor*

Fifth Edition

Little, Brown and Company
BOSTON   NEW YORK   TORONTO   LONDON

FIFTH EDITION

Library of Congress Cataloging-in-Publication Data

The Insider's guide to the top ten business schools / Tom Fischgrund, editor. — 5th ed.
    p.   cm.
  ISBN 0-316-28385-1
  1. Business education — United States. 2. Business schools — United States. 3. Master of business administration degree — United States. I. Fischgrund, Tom.
HF1131.I57 1993
650'.071'173 — dc20   93-12610

10 9 8 7 6 5 4 3 2 1

RRD-VA

*Published simultaneously in Canada by
Little, Brown & Company (Canada) Limited*

PRINTED IN THE UNITED STATES OF AMERICA

Dedicated to my parents, Cis and Herb

CONTENTS

III BUSINESS SCHOOL TIPS

PREFACE TO THE FIFTH EDITION

As American business has changed, so have the top MBA programs. The internationalization of business, the increased complexity of the marketplace and the workplace, an emphasis on quality and the customer, more stringent standards of ethical behavior, and new management techniques and tools require executives today to be able to operate in a far more complex business world. To meet these needs, top MBA programs have expanded their curriculums with international programs, developed new offerings in entrepreneurship, placed greater emphasis on human resources management and ethics, and made the MBA computer literate. Yet the basic missions of the top MBA programs have not changed. The top schools still strive to develop business managers who can think and lead.

The original edition of this book was written ten years ago and has gone through three major revisions. This fifth edition has been significantly revised. Since education at the top schools is dynamic and continually evolving, each of the school profiles was reviewed and completely rewritten or revised to reflect changes in the programs. In addition, all the data and information in the appendices were updated. A new section was added that provides insights from top business school administrators into why an MBA is still valuable in today's business environment and how to get into a top program. The end result is an up-to-date and accurate in-depth insider's guide to the top ten business schools.

An MBA from a top ten program continues to be a very valuable degree. The education, the training, the contacts, the credentials, and the job placement record of the top schools underscore this value. Going to one of the top ten is a major investment in time and money, but one that is well worth it and that will continue to pay back rewards over a lifetime.

ACKNOWLEDGMENTS FOR THE FIFTH EDITION

IN preparing this edition, I sought and received the cooperation of all the top ten schools. The school profiles written by recent graduates are new and everything is updated. As always, the opinions and viewpoints expressed in the new write-ups are those of the individual authors of each profile. The opinions and viewpoints expressed in the book as a whole are those of this author.

I would like very much to thank the following individuals and schools for their cooperation:

Allan J. Friedman, Director of Communications, University of Chicago Graduate School of Business

Richard Laermer, Director of Public Affairs, Columbia Business School

Elaine Ruggieri, Director of Public Relations and Special Events, The Darden School, University of Virginia

Loretto Crane, Director of Communications, Harvard Business School

Jean Thompson, Associate Director of Admissions and Financial Aid, Kellogg Graduate School of Management, Northwestern University

Tim Renn, Director of Communications, Kellogg Graduate School of Management, Northwestern University

Rod Garcia, Associate Director of Admissions, MIT Sloan School of Management

Kathleen Hulik, Director, Media Relations, The University of Michigan School of Business Administration

Cathy Castillo, Director, News and Publications, Stanford Graduate School of Business

Paul Argenti, Adjunct Professor and Director of Communications, Tuck School of Business Administration, Dartmouth College

Patricia Wetherall, Assistant to the Director of Communications, Tuck School of Business Administration, Dartmouth College

Christopher Hardwick, Director of Public Affairs, The Wharton School, University of Pennsylvania

INTRODUCTION

An MBA from a top business school continues to be a golden passbook. Graduates from these schools earn starting salaries of sixty thousand dollars and more, move rapidly up the corporate ladder, and have an unmatched blend of skills and confidence. An incredibly large number of today's corporate and business leaders are graduates of the top business schools.

It is not difficult, then, to understand why MBAs are so popular and competition for business school admission so intense. Harvard alone receives over 80,000 admission inquiries and 6,000 completed applications for an entering class of 803. Similarly, Wharton (University of Pennsylvania) receives almost 40,000 inquiries and 5,400 applications for its 760 enrollment slots. To satisfy this tremendous demand, many schools are developing part-time and evening business programs. As a result, more than 60,000 MBAs are awarded each year from business schools in the U.S.

While the number of MBA graduates continues to rise, the demand for MBAs in general remains flat. Therefore, it is increasingly important to get an MBA from one of the top ten business schools. These top schools have purposely limited the size of their class enrollments to maintain the quality and integrity of their programs. At the same time, this ensures that the limited number of students that graduate each year will be in great demand. A degree from one of the top schools can be worth as much as $10,000 to $15,000 more the first year than a degree from a lower-rated school.

However, not all the top business schools are the same. They have different teaching methods, different areas of specialty, different strengths and weaknesses, and different personalities. For example, Harvard uses the case method, trains general managers, and has a "West Point" mentality. Wharton, on the other hand, uses a combination of case method and lecture, focuses on finance and general management, and has a quantitative orientation.

Given this diversity among the top business schools, students should choose a school according to their academic needs, career goals, and personal interests. For instance, if a student is interested in finance and doesn't particularly want a high-pressure environment, the student should know which school would best meet those qualifications.

Deciding which of the top business schools to apply to has always been difficult because the information available is quite limited. The schools themselves send out brochures with very sparse and basic information. There are a few guidebooks that publish one-page summaries that are brief and restricted to general statistics. While these sources are valuable in providing such specifics as number of students, average GMAT scores, and course requirements, they fail to provide the in-depth information needed to make a well-informed decision. It is important to consider the academic, professional, and social environment of each school. For example: What is the school's strongest academic area? How competitive are fellow students? How much studying is required?

This book has been written specifically to provide this information for anyone who is considering applying to business school, anyone who is currently enrolled in or about to begin an MBA program, or anyone who simply wants to know more about the top ten schools. It presents all the necessary inside information on each of these schools.

Each school is described and reviewed in depth by a recent graduate of that program who knows all the intimate details: the strengths and weaknesses, academic requirements, social climate, and anything else you might wonder about. More specifically, this insider's guide will focus on seven areas for each school:

1. *The Program*

   a. What's it really like?
   b. What courses are required?
   c. How large are classes?
   d. How are classes taught — case method, lecture, or combination?

e. What is the overall academic orientation (academic specialty)?

f. What is the reputation of the school? Is it deserved?

2. *Getting In*

a. Who gets admitted to the program?

b. Are there quotas?

c. What is the school looking for in prospective students?

d. Are interviews necessary?

3. *Academic Environment*

a. How is grading done?

b. Do many students flunk out?

c. Is it hard or easy to flunk out?

d. What are fellow students like: friendly, competitive, cutthroat, etc.?

e. What kind of interaction takes place in the classroom?

f. Is there a lot of pressure?

4. *Social Life*

a. Is there life at business school?

b. Is there time to socialize?

c. What do most people do?

d. What kinds of demands does the business school make on the student?

e. What is it like to be married while going to business school?

f. What is it like to be single while going to business school?

g. How good is housing? On campus? Off campus?

5. *Recruiting and Job Search*

a. What kind of placement record does the school have?

b. What kinds of jobs do most students take?
c. How is recruiting conducted?
d. Is recruiting held on or off campus?
e. When does recruiting begin?
f. Do most students have summer jobs between the first and second year? What do they do?

6. *On the Job — First Years Out*

a. What does business school train you for?
b. How adequate or inadequate a preparation is the MBA program for a job?
c. How useful is the degree?
d. Is there much job switching after a year?
e. Do salaries meet expectations?

7. *Summary Overview*

a. What are the major strengths and weaknesses of the program?
b. Is there a general feeling that getting an MBA was the right decision?

The decision to go to business school represents a large investment. If you are enrolled in a full-time program in one of the nation's top schools, the direct out-of-pocket costs can reach $25,000 a year. When you consider that it is difficult to work at the same time that you are going to school, then the cost per year from lost salary and direct costs could reach $60,000. Since almost all of the programs are two years, the total cost of a business school education can reach $120,000. In addition, business school means an investment of two years of your life. Much could be accomplished in the working world during that same period.

Therefore, if the decision has been made to spend the enormous amount of time and money going to a top business school, then make a wise choice. Gather as much information as possible on the top schools and then decide which school is right for you.

SELECTING THE TOP TEN
BUSINESS SCHOOLS

PICKING the top ten business schools is like choosing an economic policy — everyone has a strong opinion and is convinced he or she is right, but no consensus is ever reached. A number of ratings by business school deans, high-level company executives, and corporate recruiters provide some insight into rankings, but as with any nonquantitative rating, the final decision must be somewhat subjective.

Still, there is a remarkably high degree of consensus among the ratings as to which schools are in the top ten. It is clear that the top programs are recognized as superior not only within the academic community by business school deans, but also by recruiters and employers who have had direct experience with top ten MBA graduates. Moreover, it is evident that the top business school programs have maintained high ratings over time.

The top schools have well-defined philosophies, clear mission statements, and well-developed programs. Still, all the top schools continually strive to refine and improve their programs, which solidifies even further their position in the top ten. Based on the best information available and the most recent ratings, the following schools are included in this guide (in alphabetical order):

CHICAGO
COLUMBIA
DARDEN (VIRGINIA)
HARVARD
KELLOGG (NORTHWESTERN)
MIT SLOAN
MICHIGAN
STANFORD
TUCK (DARTMOUTH)
WHARTON (PENNSYLVANIA)

We hope the following chapters will be helpful to you in making your decision about business school and will aid you in your future success in one of the top programs. Then good luck in getting today's "Golden Passbook" — an MBA from a top business school.

OTHER TOP MBA PROGRAMS

WHILE only the top ten business schools are listed and reviewed in depth in this guide, some claim that there are fifteen schools in the "top ten." It is true that many other graduate business schools have excellent programs. Therefore, here is a list of other top MBA programs based on available rankings, subjective evaluations, and reputation:

CARNEGIE-MELLON
CORNELL
FUQUA (DUKE)
INDIANA UNIVERSITY, BLOOMINGTON
NEW YORK UNIVERSITY
UNIVERSITY OF CALIFORNIA, BERKELEY
UCLA
UNIVERSITY OF ILLINOIS, CHAMPAIGN-URBANA
UNIVERSITY OF NORTH CAROLINA, CHAPEL HILL
UNIVERSITY OF TEXAS, AUSTIN
VANDERBILT
YALE

I

THE TOP TEN BUSINESS SCHOOLS

Insider Profiles

────────────── *Chapter 1* ──────────────

THE UNIVERSITY OF CHICAGO
GRADUATE SCHOOL OF BUSINESS*

THE PROGRAM

« The fabric of Chicago's past is as richly colored as a patchwork quilt: Mrs. O'Leary's cow and the Great Fire of 1871, the infamous stockyards, Al Capone and the Mob, Boss Daley and the Machine, the 1968 Democratic Convention and the Chicago Seven, and, of course, the Blues Brothers. Besides all of this great folklore, Chicago boasts two of the country's top ten business schools. With "Sweet Home Chicago" playing in my ears, I loaded up my car and a U-Haul and headed for the South Side of Chicago. Passing the U.S. Steel factories and refineries in Gary and Hammond, Indiana, I wondered if I had made the right choice. Maybe a small, quaint Eastern school would not have been so bad after all. As I got off the Chicago Skyway at the Stony Island exit, I came face to face with how the proverbial "other half" lives. Poverty, unemployment, and lack of education are ubiquitous; abandoned automobiles and empty liquor bottles stand as testaments to the lack of hope in the South Side's ghettos. I took a deep breath, however, and my anxiety level declined precipitously as I drove down the Midway Plaisance onto campus — it was like entering a completely different world. The gorgeous, gray limestone Gothic structures with their gargoyles and spires, the rich history of Nobel laureates at the university, and the outstanding reputation of the Graduate School of Business (GSB)

*BY K. PAGE BOYER, MBA

*and its faculty all served to confirm my decision. Now all I had to do
was find the bookstore before classes began.* »

According to university tradition, over a century ago, when the
University of Chicago was just being formed, a prominent eastern
educator wrote that establishing a major institution of learning in
Chicago was "the next thing to putting it in the Fiji Islands." From
its inception, the university has defied tradition and has revolution-
ized higher education. Distinguished graduate education is the hallmark of the University of Chicago, with its four graduate divisions
and six professional schools. The University of Chicago Graduate
School of Business, established in 1898, is the second-oldest business school in the country. Sixty-two Nobel Prize winners have been
associated with Chicago as students, professors, or researchers, including eight on the present faculty. The GSB gained the distinction
in 1982 of being the first business school in the world to have a
Nobel laureate on its faculty. John D. Rockefeller, the university's
founder, said of the university, "It's the best investment I ever
made."

The University of Chicago Graduate School of Business is probably the most laissez-faire in orientation of the top ten business
schools. Every aspect of life at the GSB is free market in tone:
students bid with allotted points for courses, professors, and job
interviews. Students also help to determine which faculty members will receive tenure, based on quarter-end evaluations. The
GSB recognizes that students are paying dearly for their education;
consequently, course evaluations have a great deal of impact. The
typical GSB student is tremendously intelligent, highly motivated,
and very individualistic. It is not unusual for students to learn as
much from each other as they do from the professors and curriculum.

The traditional class size at Chicago is approximately 460. Particularly because Hyde Park (the area of Chicago in which the GSB
is situated) is surrounded by relatively tough neighborhoods on three
sides (Lake Michigan bounds the fourth), the GSB makes every
effort to help to integrate B School students into the university and
the city of Chicago. The LEAD (Leadership Exploration and Development) program is an effort to make "ice breaking" a little less
stressful by dividing the incoming class into twelve cohort groups.

LEAD is a required course for all first-year students that explores topics that are essential to leadership, such as self-awareness, negotiation skills, ethics, communication, and team-building.

Extensive annual planning is one of the keys to the success of LEAD. Each spring a group of students reviews and evaluates the previous fall's LEAD course and develops a new curriculum drawing on the expertise of the GSB's leading faculty and other resources of the broader business community. The following fall LEAD is then led by the second-year students who themselves played the central role in developing and delivering the new curriculum. In addition, members of the GSB faculty and staff act as advisers to each cohort group. In the long term, the LEAD program is designed to promote a stronger sense of community and school spirit, as well as to enhance the traditional GSB curriculum.

The school year at the GSB literally begins ten days before classes start in late September with Orientation period. Second-year students voluntarily give up a week's pay from their summer jobs to come back to Hyde Park and help to make the transition a little smoother for the incoming class. They organize and execute every aspect of Orientation, including, perhaps, a Cubs game at Wrigley Field, an evening at Second City (the comedy club where John Belushi and other *Saturday Night Live* original cast members got their starts), a cookout on the Quad (short for Quadrangle — the center of campus), or a boat cruise on Lake Michigan. In the midst of the bread and circuses during Orientation, academic counseling sessions are provided to aid first-year students in selecting courses and professors and to answer the plethora of questions that all first-year students have. Academic review sessions are also offered in calculus, and professors from each area of the curriculum give presentations on their courses. All students should plan to purchase personal computers through the GSB. An introductory summer computer course at a local college might be helpful for those not yet living in the computer age.

« *My first academic experience at the GSB occurred in the middle of Orientation. I decided that a low-key review of calculus might be a relatively painless way to ease myself back into a scholastic frame of mind. I walked into Stuart Hall and looked around for room 101 (at least 50 percent of a student's GSB career will be spent in Stuart 101 or 105). I was about twenty minutes early; I had planned on putting my book bag down and waiting for everyone else to show up. To my dismay, the room was packed with students (keep in mind the fact that these reviews were voluntary, as well as the fact that we had all been out fairly late the night before, "Orientating"). It was at this moment that I realized review sessions were set up like tennis classes: beginner, intermediate, and advanced. Having taken a fair amount of calculus in college, I figured that the intermediate level would be appropriate. I was wrong. The performance levels expected and demanded at the GSB from day one are what win the University of Chicago MBA so much respect from the corporate world. »*

The demographics of an incoming class at Chicago are relatively stable from year to year. The age range tends to run from twenty to the midforties, with a mean age at entrance of twenty-seven. Approximately 10 percent of the class already hold advanced degrees. The composition of the class is roughly 77 percent men and 23 percent women. International students make up 22 percent of the class. Approximately 98 percent of the class have some work experience under their belts (mean years of experience: 4.4). Only ten years ago the ratio of students with and without work experience was virtually 50 : 50; the strong trend at the GSB has been away from admitting students directly out of college. Chicago's reputation as a quantitatively oriented school is attributable, in part, to the composition of its classes: 54 percent of the class majored in business or economics, 18 percent in engineering, and 10 percent in math and science. The remaining 18 percent of the class are scattered among the social sciences and the humanities. Every region of the United States is represented, but more than 50 percent of the GSB entering class hail from the Northeast and Midwest (30.4 percent and 21.7 percent, respectively). Getting away from dry statistics, the net of all this is that the consistently high quality and dramatic diversity of the GSB student body make Chicago an energetic and challenging environment in which to pursue an MBA.

« Unlike most undergraduate experiences, B School is a study in opposites. By the end of Orientation, I had begun friendships with some of the most unique and talented people I had ever met. Most of my B School friends had very different backgrounds. Our class had a

line manager from General Motors, a forest ranger, a female army sergeant, and a billionaire's son. The one common thread was intellectual curiosity and ability. It seems to me that the "grapevine," or network, both during and after the GSB experience, is the most valuable facet of the program. My classmates provide a wealth of information on any industry or locale about which I could possibly have questions. It is a thrill to receive holiday greetings from Caracas, Rome, and Japan . . . not to mention Brooklyn! As an alumna of Chicago, I can now take advantage of a very active, aggressive network that runs across all industries from East to West and beyond. »

One of the most attractive features of the program is its flexibility. In sync with the tremendous diversity in backgrounds and experience levels of the student body, ranging from a recent college graduate to a practicing CPA to a seasoned chemical engineer, the curriculum provides an individual with the opportunity to structure a tailor-made course of study. The GSB prescribes three core areas from which a student must select eight courses (of the twenty-one required to graduate): (1) Foundations Core, (2) Breadth Core, and (3) Policy Studies Core. In each area, however, a student has a variety of courses from which to choose. There is only one course — LEAD — that all students must take to graduate.

The majority of the GSB community believes that business may be viewed as both an art and a science. While there certainly are qualitative aspects to business, the fundamental tools, or building blocks, are quantitative: modeling, formulation, and forecasting, for example. The goal of any enterprise is to maximize profit — you hardly have to be a brain surgeon to figure that out — at the point where marginal cost equals marginal revenue. One would be hard-pressed to formulate an argument that says $2 + 2 = 4$ is not quantitative. Once the student has developed the fundamental measurement and management tools, he or she can turn to mastering the nonquantifiable nuances. More likely than not, the refining stage is going to occur in the real world, rather than in a hypothetically constructed case-study course. To quote GSB literature: "Essentially, the Chicago philosophy holds that it is wasteful to try to provide a pale substitute for business experience. What the university can do well is develop the student's critical, analytical, problem-solving, and decision-making capabilities." At Chicago, the professors, not the sometimes less than informed students, give most of the lectures.

Although the foundation of the GSB is academic excellence and a discipline-based approach to training tomorrow's business leaders, recent innovations have enriched the curriculum and bridged the gap between the classroom and the business marketplace. In addition to the LEAD program, the GSB offers four popular management laboratory courses and a new concentration in Total Quality Management.

The management labs are two quarters in length and involve student teams working to solve real company problems for client sponsors. The goal is to accelerate the process by which students learn to manage themselves and others in an organizational setting. In the New Product Laboratory, the oldest of the four lab courses, students and their faculty mentors become extensions of a firm's own capabilities in new product development.

Total Quality Management was designated as a field of study within the GSB in 1991. Drawing on ideas from several disciplines — including management science, marketing, behavioral science, and economics — TQM aims at the continuous improvement in quality in every function within an organization. Nine courses are offered in the TQM field at the GSB, including a management laboratory course. A recent survey of the twenty leading business schools in *Quality Progress* magazine found that the GSB is the leader in the number of quality-related classes offered and in class time devoted to quality management in introductory management courses.

The GSB's focus is not on creating generalist middle managers; Chicago creates specialists. Chicago's alumni/alumnae body comprises Wall Street mavens, high-powered consultants, and marketing gurus. Like graduates of the other top ten B schools, the GSB's graduates occupy the top echelons of their chosen professions.

The University of Chicago is renowned for its strength in finance. A number of GSB faculty members have served on the President's Council of Economic Advisers and on the Federal Reserve Board. Approximately half of the GSB's graduating class accepts finance-related jobs. The lion's share of cutting-edge research in finance is done by the faculty members at the GSB. However, Chicago's role on the frontier of research is not limited exclusively to finance. In recent years, the marketing faculty has been rising dramatically in stature, both within and outside the GSB. Whether you attend Chicago or one of the other top ten business schools, you will read articles by some of the GSB's finest, such as Stigler, Fama, Peltzman, Miller, and Hamada, to name just a few. The majority of Chicago's faculty are involved in outside consulting in both the public and private sectors, in addition to their teaching and research activities.

The University of Chicago operates on a quarter, rather than a semester, system. That translates into taking almost a semester's worth of material at other schools in a ten-week period at the GSB. It is very easy to get behind in one's work and very difficult to catch up. Most classes, of which you take three or four per quarter, meet twice a week for an hour and twenty minutes each. Being on the quarter system means that midterms roll around by the fourth week of the quarter. Missing one class on this schedule can prove to be hazardous to your health. Besides the usual midterm and final, some classes require projects, papers, and/or case presentations. A common mistake made by first-year students is to lie back early in the quarter and then realize, too late, that they are never going to be able to recover by the midterm. By the second year, students figure out how to get the reading list before the quarter begins, so that they do not start the quarter two classes — or one week — behind.

The GSB offers four MBA programs: (1) the Campus/MBA, (2) the 190/MBA (this evening program for people who work full-time is called "190/MBA" because it is held at the downtown facility, located at 190 E. Delaware Place; a new, larger GSB Downtown Center is under construction, and completion is expected in early 1994), (3) the Weekend/MBA, and (4) the Executive MBA for mid-career business executives. The last two programs are also held downtown. Most B School students finish the Campus/MBA program in six quarters; a typical student will take three quarters of three courses each, and four courses during each of the remaining three quarters.

Although graduation seems like a virtual impossibility at the beginning of the first quarter, the much anticipated event (for both the student and the student's loan officer) rolls around very quickly.

Convocation is held the second week of June in Rockefeller Chapel. Although most GSB graduates will agree that the two years of their lives spent at the University of Chicago were as close to boot camp as they ever want to come again, most will readily affirm that their Chicago MBA was well worth the effort.

GETTING IN

THE most challenging intellectual exercise one can undertake is to try to figure out how to get admitted to the GSB — all other cerebral gyrations pale in comparison! The full-time Campus/MBA program receives 30,000 inquiries annually and roughly 3,000 completed applications, out of which a class of approximately 460 is ultimately assembled. Almost every applicant is well qualified for a place in the entering class, and each year the competition for admission intensifies. To whom, you may be asking, should the bribery check be paid? Unfortunately, it does not work like that. Seriously, though, there is living and breathing proof in each entering class that one need not have 4.4 years of work experience, a GMAT score of 650, and an undergraduate GPA of 3.54321 to be admitted to Chicago.

The GSB evaluates each applicant on the basis of the following indicators of past — and forecasters of potential — performance: personal essays, history of extracurricular involvement, educational record, letters of reference, performance on the GMAT exam, employment experience where applicable, and any unique factors that may help introduce the candidate to the admissions committee. From a purely quantitative standpoint, there are no arbitrarily fixed cut-offs in terms of a candidate's GPA or GMAT score, nor are there any quota requirements.

The students in a typical GSB class are the exact opposite of wallflowers; the challenge becomes getting a word in edgewise in any conversation, because Chicago has an abundance of leaders and very few followers. People come to Chicago to stretch their limits. Most of my classmates had good jobs, but wanted more for themselves. The quantitative reputation of Chicago may conjure up images of pocket protectors loaded with pens of every hue found in nature. In reality, very few GSB students have calculators clipped to their belts. Rather, the one generalization it is possible to make is that the people admitted to Chicago have all demonstrated their academic and leadership prowess to the admissions committee's satisfaction. The GSB seeks candidates with a high probability of success in both an academically demanding program of study and a business career. Admissions officers also look for interpersonal skills, communication skills, and maturity. It is quite common for a student to look around after a few weeks at the GSB and think, "The admissions committee *must* have made a mistake in letting me in here — my classmates are so much more qualified." However, the admissions committee very rarely makes a mistake; they just happen to see potential in a candidate that a candidate may not yet be able to see in himself or herself.

« *It started to become abundantly clear to me that an MBA could offer me the professional capabilities and contacts I needed to be able to jump effectively on the fast track. In today's complicated business world, an undergraduate degree in economics or business — let alone the liberal arts disciplines — simply does not bestow the skills and sophistication needed to compete. Consequently, to play it safe, as well as to ensure that my plebeian existence did not last any longer than absolutely necessary, I submitted applications to thirteen business schools. I decided to hit the top ten and a few backup "safety" schools. The thought of another year in limbo was just the incentive I needed to sit down and do all those applications! Given that my undergraduate GPA and my GMAT score might as well have been carved in stone, my applications were the final frontier for selling myself to the admissions committee. Two weeks and continuous cups of coffee later, I took all thirteen applications, with their respective renditions on the theme of "What I want to be when I grow up," to the post office. As it turned out, I had a choice of five B schools. I selected the U. of C. to supplement my liberal arts background with quantitative expertise. In retrospect, I am glad I did.* »

Given that, aside from a few very high or very low standouts, almost every applicant's GPA and GMAT score look like a carbon copy of every other applicant's, you should look for a point of difference to exploit in your essay. Why, for example, do you want to attend the University of Chicago's MBA program, instead of Dartmouth's, Harvard's, or Stanford's? What nonquantifiable skill and/or personal characteristics do you have to bring to the party? Any applicable demonstrations of leadership, business or pro bono experience, or academic accomplishments should be brought to bear on the above questions. You, in essence, bear the burden of proving to the committee how you would contribute to and benefit from the Chicago MBA program. Standardized test scores and undergraduate transcripts are but two pieces in the overall decision process. Personal essays and letters of recommendation are required, while interviews either on campus or with alumni off campus are strongly encouraged. However, all should be used as selling tools.

Chicago works on a rolling-admissions basis, which means that the admissions committee reviews applications as they are received. Common vernacular translation: the early bird gets the worm. Here is a candidate's chance to demonstrate that he or she is capable of meeting deadlines. Applications are available late in the summer; November 1 is not too early to turn in an application.

Letters of recommendation provide relatively unbiased testimony on the candidate's behalf. Strong letters from a college professor and a former employer can help in supporting a candidate's contention that he or she can contribute to a business program. If the college professor or former employer also happens to be a GSB alum, all the better; you've hit the jackpot if they also happen to be large contributors to the Alumni Fund (see bribery)!

The application homework assignment is to put together the strongest case possible in favor of your admission to the GSB. And be nice to yourself — leave plenty of time.

At the GSB, current students are actively involved in the admissions process. The deans' student admissions committee includes 150 first- and second-year students selected by the deans and the admissions office staff who volunteer their time to assist in the school's recruiting efforts.

ACADEMIC ENVIRONMENT

THE Chicago MBA program is similar to your first job out of college: you will be overworked and underpaid. No, it's worse than that. You actually pay the GSB to be overworked! Looking back on it, the GSB experience is rather like the Peace Corps ad: "It's the toughest job you'll ever love." I remember sitting with friends over a beer during our first quarter and our saying to each other: "Obviously, GMATs and GPAs are not reliable indicators or accurate measurement tools for determining how intelligent an individual is. Otherwise, why would we be paying for this kind of abuse?" The atmosphere among and between students is generally very enjoyable and constructive. Be prepared, though, as of the moment you first arrive on campus. The hard work and long hours required to make it through any U. of C. graduate program create a general atmosphere that is charged with intensity.

« *It was a drizzly day in April when my sister and I took a road trip to Chicago to play "In Search of Housing." I had breezed through Hyde Park briefly the previous November for an on-campus interview, but unfortunately had not then been able to stay to soak up some of the culture. Now, after walking around campus all morning looking for housing, we decided to stop and have a hot dog and soda outside the bookstore. I remember very clearly my sister saying, "The tension here is so thick you could cut it with a knife . . . and I'm not even enrolled!" The view that greeted us that day included all the medical interns going in and out of the U. of C. Hospital and Clinics with their slip-on-shoe-guard fashion statements, as well as all the students coming out of the bookstore, having just purchased their spring-quarter texts. After having written a check that size, no wonder they looked anxious.* »

It must be remembered that seventy-five hundred of the eleven thousand students at the University of Chicago are graduate students. The typical prankish nature of a college campus does not really exist at the U. of C.; it is a tremendously academic atmosphere. The B School is no exception. The students at the GSB are not so much competing with other students as much as they are competing with themselves. The high individual standards and expectations of excellence are what make the MBA program what it is. Chicago's quantitative rigor provides students with superior critical and analytical skills. The GSB's contention that developing a student's problem-solving and decision-making capabilities, rather than attempting to simulate business experience in the classroom, should be the first priority, has received wide applause from some of America's Fortune 500 companies; salary and placement statistics confirm this approval.

The typical student will have one to three classes per day (an hour and twenty minutes each) Monday through Thursday, and it is reasonable to estimate that a student will spend three hours preparing for each class nightly. Most GSB students put in twelve- to fourteen-hour days as a rule — not an exception — six to seven days a week. Many incoming students opt to submit a substitution petition for courses in areas in which they may already be very well versed. A substitution approval permits a student to replace the introductory-level core course with a more advanced course within the same core area. The three cores are as follows:

Foundations Core

(Courses in all areas required)

- Microeconomics
- Financial Accounting
- Statistics
- Behavioral Sciences (recommended but not required)

Breadth Core

(Courses in four areas required)

- Financial Management
- Industrial Relations and Human Resource Management
- Macroeconomics
- Managerial Accounting
- Marketing Management
- Production Management

Policy Studies Core

(One course required)

- Business Policy

Given that a student must take twenty-one approved courses to receive an MBA, an individual is left with twelve elective courses plus the LEAD program after he or she completes the eight core requirements. The University of Chicago does not accept transfers of credit for course work taken at other institutions. However, one of the advantages of attending a world-class university is having other graduate divisions available within the school. Only fifteen of a B School student's courses must be taken at the Graduate School of Business. This leaves a student free to elect courses at the Law School, the Pritzker School of Medicine, the Divinity School, or any of the other graduate divisions within the university at large. The GSB also offers students the opportunity to "concentrate" (an approved sequence of three or four courses) in a specific area of study. Many GSB students choose to concentrate in finance *and* marketing, for example.

« During my final quarter at the GSB, I decided that I wanted to take a finance course that would be more applications oriented. The course I selected was Business 335, Applications of Financial Theory. The course is structured to be taught purely by the case method; students work in small groups in order to analyze and present the cases. The breadth of material covered is outstanding. The course attempts to put into practice the theory developed in the Investments and Corporate Finance courses, namely, capital budgeting, cost of capital analyses (net present value), leasing, valuation, regulation, capital structure, dividend policy, corporate governance (the inherent tensions between stockholders and debtholders), signaling, and a multitude of other relevant issues. I found it fascinating to learn how stockholders can vote to issue more debt in order to finance risky projects; in essence, the stockholders can gamble with the current bondholders' money. The risk to outstanding debtholders is increased — without a concurrent increase in their potential reward — because if the firm fails to remain a going concern, stockholders will be paid with the liquidated assets before the bondholders see dime one. Because of this class, finance was no longer just "academic." »

The prevailing attitude at Chicago is that the case-method approach is appropriate for the "softer" areas of the program like marketing,

behavioral science, and corporate policy. However, when it comes
to the "hard" disciplines — finance, statistics, accounting, management science, production, and operations — the case-method format is less frequently used except in some high-level applications
courses. In most GSB courses, the material is quantitative enough in
nature to make the lecture method much more efficient. Many of
the first-year courses are taught on a lecture basis and typically range
in size from fifty to eighty students. During the second year, some
of the smaller, seminar courses lend themselves to a case-method
approach.

Chicago's course offerings are broad and varied enough in both
subject and teaching method to offer everyone, regardless of background, the opportunity to create a very individually rewarding program. In theory, students sort themselves out according to
proficiency in each of the core areas. That is to say that, in theory,
CPAs should not be sitting next to novices in the beginner-level
accounting courses. However, in practice, beginners are sometimes
"fortunate" enough to occupy a seat located amid a row of CPAs.

« I decided that the best way to tackle the GSB curriculum was to
work from the "MBA Blueprint." In other words, it seemed most
logical to dig in with the required courses and get them out of the
way. So, like half my class, I naively signed up for the first three core
courses on my list: Microeconomics, Financial Accounting, and Statistics. What had not occurred to me was that some of the CPAs had
figured out how to leverage their strengths during the first quarter by
taking the same beginner-level accounting course as the bona fide
beginners, in order to set a floor under their GPAs. On a dreary, gray
December morning, I headed over to take my Financial Accounting
exam. I had the sinking feeling that I was in for some heavy-duty
trouble. I realized that my game plan was, in fact, flawed when the
professor (who literally wrote the book on accounting) handed out the
final exam and I did not have the slightest idea how even to begin
three out of the four exam questions. Although it was a struggle, I
still passed the course. The U. of C. MBA program is not for the weak
of heart. Incredible frustration and disappointment are fairly common, since most GSB students have never before had to work for B's
and C's. Lesson to be learned: business school at Chicago is no
vacation. »

The intensity of the GSB program will depend upon how hard you wish to work, as well as when you take certain courses. On average, it is advisable to let the "quant jocks" take the core courses the first quarter. The competition is slightly reduced in later quarters, because the curve is not artificially inflated by advanced students. The first year is the most difficult of the two for most students. The University of Chicago requires that a B School student carry a twenty-one-course grade point average of at least C (a 2.0 GPA). The average GSB student will have no problem maintaining a consistent B and C grade point average. (Chicago has done its fine-tuned screening, so if you are in, you are probably able to do the work.) In any case, it is very difficult, once admitted, to flunk out of the GSB. The roughly 1 percent attrition rate at Chicago is attributable to students who voluntarily leave the school. Also, academic counseling is always available . . . and encouraged; it is much better to ask for help early in the quarter, while there is still time for an academic turnaround.

For the student who is a little more driven, the amount of incremental work required jumps — almost in quantum terms — to maintain a B+ or higher average. There is no grade inflation at Chicago. A's and B's are very difficult to attain. If a steady flow of A's is in your plans, you should not expect to meet too many of your classmates or to spend a whole lot of time playing; your nights and weekends will basically be preordained. On the upside, classes are in lecture format (with notes to study) or involve group work (so you can call on your fellow students for help). The downside in lecture courses, though, is that the grade rests on two exams, at best. Usually there is a midterm (0 to 50 percent of your grade) and a final exam (50 to 100 percent). If you operate well under this all-or-nothing type of scenario, then you are going to love exam week.

The GSB uses the following course marks: A, B, C, D, Pass, F, I, W, and R. A, B, C, D, and Pass are grades given for courses taken for credit. As always, F (Fail) indicates unsuccessful balancing of work and play. An I (Incomplete) is given when a student has work outstanding to be completed by a given date and has filed the appropriate form with the dean's office detailing the arrangement. If the completion date is missed the I may be converted to F. A W indicates that a student has dropped a course after the fifth week of the quarter (due, perhaps, to the unsuccessful balancing of work and play). A student may take two elective courses under the Pass/Fail grading option. A student must file to take a course Pass/Fail by the end of the fourth week of the quarter. No Pass/Fail course may be used to satisfy distribution or concentration requirements. A student who elects a Pass/Fail course is ineligible for the dean's Honor List in that quarter. The key reason a student chooses Pass/Fail is that it reduces pressure, because the grade of Pass does not enter into the calculation of GPA. When corporate recruiting heats up, the Pass/ Fail option seems to increase in popularity.

Most GSB students are not straight out of school. They are giving up good salaries for no money now and better salaries later; they are at the GSB to learn. If you choose to miss class, which rarely happens, it is your loss (both financially and educationally). Academically, Chicago is *a lot* of work, but you get out of the program exactly what you put in.

SOCIAL LIFE

SOCIAL life at the GSB? Okay, this is where a good sense of humor is helpful! As a second-year student advised me when I visited the U. of C. for a tour of campus, "If you are not married when you come to Chicago, stay that way. If you are married when you come to Chicago, you may not be by the time you finish the program." Despite students' very limited resources and very real time constraints, though, it would be hard to find a group of people able to party longer or harder — and still be able to perform at the levels set by the GSB — than students at Chicago. Every aspect of life in Hyde Park is intense: the neighborhood, with its myriad socioeconomic gradations, the incredibly strenuous academic program, the fever-pitched, maniacal interplay of corporate recruiting, and . . . yes, the wild abandon with which GSB students party. But, as with every other endeavor at the University of Chicago, even partying takes on a cerebral hue.

« *Friends of mine who had gone to undergraduate party schools, either huge state schools or small, isolated private schools, could not refrain from chuckling with me at what the University of Chicago calls its Frat Row! You can drive down the purported Frat Row at the U. of C. at 11:00 P.M. on a Saturday night (just after final exams, even!) and not know that you have arrived at Mecca. »*

Social life, as most know it, does not exactly exist in Hyde Park. Nonetheless, the Pub (a campus favorite — actually, the *only* campus watering hole) becomes overrun with B School students on Thursday nights. A few brave Law and Divinity students may be talked into playing a game of pool or — at least — splitting the cost of a pitcher. As far as any sort of nightlife is concerned, the Pub and a few other local establishments (Jimmy's or the infamous Tiki — which does serve fairly good chicken wings at 2:00 A.M.) are about it. Most B School students start holding private parties in their apartments by the beginning of second quarter.

« I often found myself at a classmate's party standing with a group out on a fire escape in bitterly cold Chicago in the middle of February, drinking beer and eating M&Ms. It was always tremendously entertaining to me to think that these same people would be leading some of America's Fortune 500 companies into the twenty-first century. My fondest B School memories occurred outside of the classroom, because that is when I had the opportunity to really get to know my classmates. Whether it was accepting a dare to get up and ride in the saddle of a metal campus sculpture at 1:00 A.M. on a winter night, sharing an umbrella at a Miles Davis concert on the Quad in a pouring rain, or sitting at a Thanksgiving dinner given by friends for those of us with "work to do and no money to go home," my classmates are what made my GSB experience the success it was. »

Hyde Park offers much more opportunity for fun on the non-nightlife front. The Henry Crown Field House has indoor tennis, squash, handball, and racquetball courts, a 200-meter Pro-Turf indoor track, four basketball courts, a complete weight-training facility, saunas, and batting cages. There are also two indoor pools on campus. A run or bike ride along Lake Michigan is always enjoyable. The Court Theater, Smart Museum, Oriental Institute, and Museum of Science and Industry are all within close walking distance from campus and offer wonderful ways to spend an afternoon. The works of many great architects and sculptors are viewable at the University of Chicago, including Eero Saarinen's Law School and Ludwig Mies van der Rohe's School of Social Service Administration, just south of the Midway. On the north side of the Midway are Frank Lloyd Wright's famous Robie House and Henry Moore's *Nuclear Energy*, a work done to commemorate the spot where Enrico Fermi and other University of Chicago scientists achieved man's first self-sustaining nuclear chain reaction in 1942, ushering in the nuclear age. Rockefeller Chapel is a beautiful Gothic cathedral, whose seventy-two-bell carillon makes a tower tour well worthwhile.

As far as B School–sponsored groups and clubs are concerned, there really is something for everyone. The difficulty arises in having to pick and choose with what you wish to become involved. The Business Students Association (BSA) is the big kahuna of student groups; it sponsors speakers from business and industry, publishes an outstanding student paper, and organizes various social activities. There are professional interest groups based on job function (e.g., Banking and Finance, Investment Banking, Management Consulting, Marketing, Oil and Energy, Real Estate, Venture Capital), geographical and special interest (e.g., Asian Business, African American MBAs, Canadian Business, European Business, Women's Business), as well as many more. For those not intent on homesteading in the Reg (the main library on campus is the Joseph Regenstein Library), there is more than enough to keep you busy. In the fall, an International Food Fest highlights the diversity of the student population, while the Winter Formal (held recently at the Field Museum of Natural History and the Shedd Aquarium) highlights the social skills that many of us may have forgotten. In the spring, a Booze Cruise on Lake Michigan and the GSB *Follies* are other highlights. Students write, produce, and direct the *Follies*, spoofing life at the GSB.

If you manage to do all of the things available in Hyde Park, there is always Chicago to tackle. You can get anywhere downtown by car, train, or bus within twenty minutes. Obviously, some forms of transportation are safer than others. The I.C. (Illinois Central) train is fantastic; it is clean, uncrowded, and safe, even fairly late at night. The Jeffrey Express (the #6 bus line) is generally crowded and not very safe later in the evening, but it runs more frequently and is less expensive than the I.C. Once downtown, Chicago's nightclub area — Rush Street — is like a second home to some graduate students. The clubs are all lined up next to each other, allowing bar-hopping with ease. If you love pizza, then Chicago's deep-dish pizza is a must. Chicago is famous for its blues, great sports teams (Bears, Cubs, Bulls, White Sox, and Blackhawks), and politics — Republicans have their hands full in this town.

Chicago is a city of neighborhoods, each with its own unique identity. There are ethnic delights to be found at every turn: Swedish bakeries, Greek gyro shops, Irish pubs, and Polish butcher shops. A real treat for new arrivals to Chicago is to go downtown on St. Patrick's Day, when the city dyes the Chicago River Kelly green! During the summer, one can enjoy the famous Taste of Chicago — a week-long food fest held in Grant Park — as well as the Blues Festival in mid-June, the Fifty-seventh Street Art Fair, and the Jazz Fest, held just before Labor Day.

For the most high-minded, Chicago boasts the world-famous Chicago Symphony Orchestra, the Lyric Opera of Chicago, and the Chicago Opera Ballet Company. In keeping with the subject of favorite pastimes of the rich and famous, it should be mentioned that a lovely time may be had scoping out the Chicago Board of Trade (CBOT), one of the world's oldest and largest futures exchanges, and the Chicago Mercantile Exchange (the Merc) — the world's premier financial futures exchange — where they make the proverbial market in pork bellies!

For the first quarter or so, the single students tend to socialize together, and the married students do likewise. Soon, however, most distinctions between single/married and B School/non–B School (i.e., other U. of C. graduate schools) tend to disappear.

« *It just so happened that my last final exam at the GSB occurred on St. Patty's Day. One of my close friends was working diligently, trying to put the finishing touches on his honors paper; I had turned mine in that same day. I called this particular classmate and his wife to see if they were in the mood to celebrate the completion of yet another enormously successful term. It turned out that he had to keep cranking on his paper, if he hoped to make the deadline; that certainly did not stop his wife, a friend of ours from the Law School, and me from celebrating!* »

There are advantages and disadvantages to being either single or married when trying to get through the MBA program. The advantage of being single is that there are no competing demands on your time; you can, theoretically, study continuously. But being married provides a great excuse to take a night off — an excuse single students would love, on occasion, to be able to employ. Someone who comes to the GSB unmarried can devote 100 percent of his or her life to the MBA experience. The flip side to that blissful scenario is that single people do not generally have any source of income or any built-in emotional support system. Yet again, it takes two very mature, supportive people to remain together under the duress and demands of the academic program.

Married and single students are both usually assigned to university housing, which tends to be relatively good. Much of the housing in Hyde Park, both university-affiliated and privately owned, is turn-of-the-century brick walk-ups. During the first year, most married students live in married-student housing; this provides a great opportunity for spouses of students to meet each other and plan get-togethers when their spouses have to study. Single students live either in university apartments or in I-House (International House). I-House gets a split verdict: some students say that living there (very much like living in an undergraduate dormitory) is a wonderful way to meet classmates; others claim that the lack of privacy, common bathroom facilities, and never-ending B School chatter are unendurable. During the second year, many students choose to rent privately owned apartments. For entering students who have worked and saved for a few years, there are plenty of condos, both in Hyde Park and on the North Side. Assuming you can locate a parking space (all parallel parking in Hyde Park), you can proceed to unload all of your boxes from the Ryder truck and settle in for a great couple of years.

RECRUITING AND JOB SEARCH

IT has been said that B schools are nothing more than very costly placement agencies. Given the way many students approach the program, such criticism leveled against top MBA programs is partially justified. The balance between learning and recruiting is very delicate; students begin the corporate mating dance as soon as they arrive on campus.

By the second week of the quarter, all students must submit updated résumés for inclusion in the *Résumé Book*. The *Résumé Book* is literally a book of students' résumés and is mailed to four hundred of corporate America's finest, to arm recruiters with all the information they could ever wish. LPFs (Liquidity Preference Functions), hosted by recruiting companies, also begin during the first few weeks of the quarter. A company will come on campus and make a presentation to students concerning the opportunities available to MBAs within their firm. LPFs provide students with the chance to ask questions about the company in a noninterview environment. They are a wonderful forum for informational interviewing — without risk of corporate retribution. Following the presentation, the sponsoring company will host a cocktail party of sorts — hence, "Liquidity" Preference Function. LPFs are generally held on Thursday afternoons — very conducive to continued partying over at the Pub. Friday's catch-up plans are torpedoed once again.

The bulk of recruiting activity occurs on campus. At the start of every academic year, students are given 1,000 nontransferable points with which to bid for interviews. If a Merrill Lynch interview costs 300 points, for example, then a student bidding for this type of position may be able to "buy" only three or four on-campus interviews. The GSB interview bidding system runs on the school's mainframe computer, and since all students are required to own a computer, they can bid on interviews at any time from their home. Every week students sign up for campus interviews via a computerized closed auction. Interview slots are "sold" to the highest bidders. One week of schedules is available for bidding at any given time. Students can access the mainframe via their modems and bid directly from their personal computers for interview slots. A student can retrieve up-to-the-minute status reports on preliminary schedules; students may not bid more than their total wealth. An account will be debited as many bidding points as the "market clearing price" dictates. The market clearing price is the number of points bid by the highest unsuccessful bidder. Although interview schedules are limited, there are other ways in which a student may get to speak with corporate recruiters.

« *Most companies put on presentations at the GSB to discuss available opportunities at their firms. These "LPFs" are a field day for the very aggressive, recruiting-obsessed student, because such informal gatherings provide a chance to circumvent the bidding process, as well as to rub shoulders with company representatives. If a student is unable to obtain a slot on the recruiter's schedule, he or she certainly has other occasions to make contact, and can often pick up a free meal in the process.* »

These presentations offer students a chance to supplement what they've learned about a company from the corporate literature available in the Career Services Library. Students get a more accurate sense of the corporate culture in particular by speaking with employees of the company. Presentations and LPFs help students decide how many points, if any, they want to bid for a given interview. Given that students have limited resources — bidding points — they must choose their targets carefully.

The University of Chicago GSB's office of career services is excellent. The office offers an array of career management services, including an extensive career library, a comprehensive interview training program for first-year students, individual counseling, a résumé referral service, and a variety of career management workshops. Beyond those services, during the most recent academic year 230 U.S. and multinational companies came to the GSB to interview students for full-time positions; approximately 90 companies recruit first-year students for summer internships. In total, more than 10,000 interviews were conducted on-campus last year.

Interviews for first-year summer internships are held during spring quarter and, as mentioned, are limited. There are always more first-year students looking for positions than there are positions available through on-campus interviewing. As with permanent employment, the top three industries for internships are commercial banking, investment banking, and consulting. The lack of a confirmed ten-week summer internship soon creates an undue amount of stress; many students become unnecessarily preoccupied with finding work, to the detriment of their studies and peace of mind. A number of students try to land a summer job with the company they would like to work for after B School, which creates even more anxiety.

« *After having run the numbers for carrying the cost of my apartment in Hyde Park, as well as paying rent again for an apartment in Manhattan, L.A., or Washington, D.C., I decided that it made more sense to go to school during the summer and graduate a quarter early, as did 15 percent of my classmates. To be honest, it seems that many internships of a ten-week duration do not permit one to move much beyond the position of photocopy engineer. When all was said and done, I fared as well as, if not better than, most of my classmates in the search for permanent employment. Going to school during the summer, rather than having an internship, did not disadvantage me in the least. As a matter of fact, I found most employers quite receptive and sympathetic to my choosing to get through the program and get on with my life. I finished the program in March, which permitted me to take some vacation time as well as to get a jump on starting work. I took a job as an assistant executive at an advertising agency. By the time the rest of the MBAs showed up in August or September, I was already a permanent fixture . . . and I knew where the water cooler was located.* »

Recruiting for full-time positions begins in November and continues through mid-March. Second-year students interview on campus, have call-back interviews (usually at corporate headquarters), and pursue employment opportunities on their own via a barrage of letters both to companies that are and companies that are not coming to campus. There is no way around the fact that recruiting requires a tremendous commitment of time and energy. But more than 90 percent of the class have firm offers by the time they graduate. To leaf through the GSB's *Placement Report* is like taking a stroll through a capitalist candy store. The top three industries by number of hires for the most recent class were commercial banking, with 15.8 percent of the class (median salary, $55,000); investment banking, with 15.2 percent of the class (median salary, $52,500); and consulting, with 14.6 percent of the class (median salary, $70,000). Starting salaries ranged to a high of $104,800. Offers in Chicago were accepted by 22.7 percent of the class, 21.8 percent headed to New York City, and 9.3 percent made tracks to the West Coast.

In addition to the extensive career management services offered to current MBA students, the GSB offers lifelong career assistance through a full-time career management professional who is devoted exclusively to serving the school's alumni and alumnae. Services available to alumni and alumnae include individual career and placement counseling, seminars and workshops offered nationally, and a newsletter that lists available U.S. and international jobs submitted by companies and executive search firms.

ON THE JOB — FIRST YEARS OUT

An MBA from a top business school provides knowledge, skills, confidence, contacts, and accelerated career advancement; it is an easily understood credential. As such, corporate America compensates MBAs fairly well for making this investment. The broad range of knowledge that an MBA possesses permits him or her, moreover, to be much more innovative and entrepreneurial than his or her non-MBA counterparts. The fact that the large majority of America's corporate top brass hold MBA degrees speaks to the career-enhancing aspects of an MBA program.

« At a recent party held in Chicago for the "best and the brightest" (alumni and alumnae from the top five business schools were invited), I realized how tightly knit my personal and professional circles have become. Not only were my classmates from the GSB in attendance, but there was a good-sized contingent of MBAs from my company, as well as a group from my client's company. It is this network of professionals that makes an MBA from a top business school so valuable. A vivid — and humorous — demonstration of this network occurred when I noticed one of the women at the gathering sitting against the wall, painstakingly organizing all of the new business cards she had collected that evening! »

What an MBA from Chicago provides, first, is a heuristic framework for decision making. Chicago MBAs have both the theoretical and applied training necessary to make decisions in a complex business environment. Moreover, with the proliferation of MBA graduates over the past decade, the price of entry into attractive industries is an MBA from a top ten school; without it, one is competitively disadvantaged for the most sought-after occupations.

« *It has been my personal experience that MBAs from Chicago can define, analyze, and solve a problem more effectively than non-MBAs, and more effectively than most MBAs from other schools. It is the focus on process that gives Chicago MBAs an upper hand; when faced with a problem, they determine what to minimize or optimize, subject to what constraints, and within what tolerances.* »

The biggest danger facing newly minted MBAs is unrealistically high expectations. The danger is greatest for those who have never worked full-time before; graduates who have held permanent positions, it is to be hoped, know enough to temper their expectations somewhat. The world in which GSB students live is an insulated microcosm; you will probably never be surrounded by so many gifted people at a single time again. The work environment is not generally composed of as many quick, motivated, would-be movers and shakers as is B School.

In addition, an MBA per se does not entitle one to the respect and cooperation of coworkers . . . that will still have to be earned. Depending on the industry in which one accepts an offer, the resentment felt by non-MBA coworkers can effectively stall even the brightest shooting star. What MBAs possess is general information, not job-specific knowledge. An insensitive, highly egotistical MBA can very easily blow both his or her legs off by walking into a hostilely predisposed environment and attempting to convert the non-MBA heathen coworkers (who, coincidentally, have seniority and a knowledge of the ropes). If you possess a Chicago MBA *and* a modicum of sensitivity, then you will be unbeatable. Common sense will help guide you through the minefield of corporate politics. An MBA can facilitate or obstruct one's path, depending on how you use it.

Chicago MBAs are goal-driven individuals. GSB students demand and expect a great deal of themselves and those around them. Most are used to being top performers in whatever they undertake: academics, sports, or business endeavors. Frustration is the most common ailment afflicting MBAs. Salary expectations are generally met; it is job-responsibility expectations that are frequently underdelivered. The job switching prevalent during the first few years of employment is not driven predominantly by money concerns; rather, job switching occurs primarily because people stop feeling challenged and productive. It is very difficult for an individual who is accustomed to calling the shots and being in control to have to deal with boredom or lack of opportunity to demonstrate his or her capabilities — conditions indicative of an inexperienced boss or manager. Even a very seductive starting salary will not alleviate the inherent problem of being underchallenged.

A close friend of mine developed the following acronym for the GSB *Follies*, succinctly summarizing the tangible benefit — and sometimes blinding pitfall — of the program: MBA = Money Buys A Lot.

SUMMARY OVERVIEW

INDIVIDUALS who believe in the free enterprise system in its pure, unadulterated form should know that the "Chicago School" is its greatest defender. The free market ideal permeates life at the University of Chicago; both the GSB and the Law School, for instance, maintain that a single life can have a dollar value assigned to it. If the marginal cost of an action exceeds the marginal benefit, then the action should be rejected. The "Chicago School" philosophy is seminal in formulating inextricably linked social, economic, and environmental policies concerning such issues as corporate responsibility for acid rain or global warming; trading rules for dealing with the Third World debt crisis and Pacific Rim competitors; and judicial precedent for corporate bailouts and insider-trading violations. Clearly this thinking impacts the way America does business.

The academicians and theoreticians practicing at the University of Chicago possess some of the finest minds in the world. Chicago's program is excellent in all areas, exhibiting particular expertise in finance. Chicago-trained MBAs are not second-guessers; they survey the available evidence, weigh costs and benefits, and act. As business becomes more and more globalized, having a consistent rationale for your actions helps to minimize your risk exposure to exogenous shocks.

The camaraderie among students is one of the GSB's high points. The program requires a tremendous amount of work, but it is also a great deal of fun. The quality of the students who attend Chicago fosters a very stimulating and challenging environment. The toughest part of the Chicago MBA program is getting admitted. Once that is achieved, career opportunities abound. The growth experienced during two years of active involvement with the GSB is phenomenal. Maintaining a parity level of enthusiasm and excitement is the real challenge facing a Chicago MBA on graduation.

Chicago is a great town in which to live. Whether one prefers the blues, sports, theater, art, or nightlife, Chicago has it all. The social activities at the B School are also terrific. Hyde Park, on the other hand, does not provide much in the way of nightlife. A night out for pizza with friends or Harold's chicken at home in front of the TV is about as hot as Hyde Park nightlife gets. The lack of available outside activities in Hyde Park is the biggest complaint of most GSB students.

An additional drawback of the MBA program — or any top ten professional program, for that matter — is the tendency for students to lose perspective. There is so much focus placed on corporate recruiting from the outset of the program that students barely have a chance to get acclimated to their surroundings and academic load before LPFs and bidding for interviews begin. Focus on the job search is of such an intensity that studying is sometimes subordinated to recruiting. It is *very* easy to get caught up in the recruiting frenzy, at the expense of the education and contacts you are supposedly at the GSB to obtain.

Finally, money oftentimes becomes the major, if not exclusive, focus of a student's employment selection process. Don't get me wrong; I did not choose to invest the money and effort I did in Chicago's MBA program so I could go off and undertake volunteer work in Uganda. The negative image of MBAs portrayed in movies such as *Wall Street* is indicative of ills and misplaced values on a non-career-specific societal level. Nonetheless, MBAs are more visible, and generally more highly paid, than society at large. The ranking of priorities — with dollars being right at the top of the list — oftentimes leaves MBAs dissatisfied with their careers after only a few months on the job.

All other things being equal, an MBA from Chicago is a very valuable and prestigious asset. Chicago's unwavering insistence on strong analytical and critical skills is what prompts corporate America to bid up GSB graduates' compensation consistently. The broad, quantitative expertise possessed upon graduating from Chicago — in areas ranging from finance to statistics to marketing — is highly relevant to employers. You must remember that prospective employers are, in fact, the consumers of MBAs. If corporations do not see MBAs filling a need within their organizations, then there will be an MBA glut. As with any form of capital investment, therefore, the long-term appreciation or depreciation in value will depend on continued demand for the Chicago MBA.

Chapter 2

COLUMBIA BUSINESS SCHOOL*

THE PROGRAM

« Before attending Columbia, I pictured the school as several dispersed buildings near a poor area of New York that is part and parcel of an overwhelming city. My parents and their Connecticut friends considered it scary at best. To my surprise and theirs, Columbia is a spacious campus designed as an urban academic village filled with buildings you are likely to see in Princeton, New Jersey. Names such as Plato, Aristotle, and Sophocles are etched into the facade of the enormous library. Gigantic urns sit on pedestals, and oddly shaped fountains keep the pigeons cool. Shady trees like elms and sycamores provide cover for a large population of squirrels and probably a few other rodents. Outside the Business School is a pleasant little green whose centerpiece is a modern, DNA-like sculpture that seems to perplex and delight us quantmongers. While the university is far from bucolic, the campus atmosphere is inviting, friendly, and, to my family's delight, safe and secure. »

Refusing to rest on its Ivy League laurels, Columbia Business School is on the move. The charge is lead by Dean Meyer (pronounced Mayor) Feldberg, who has rallied support from students, faculty, staff, and alumni. He has brought together these various groups to support his vision of making Columbia the premier school for international business. The dean has improved the quality of life, revised the curriculum, raised $65 million, and built solid relation-

*BY DAVID RAY, MBA

ships with alumni, alumnae, and the business community. No constituency is outside his reach. In every speech or interview, Dean Feldberg never fails to mention that Columbia is destined for preeminence. The foundation for this vision is supported by Columbia's traditional strengths, including a diverse student body, a topnotch faculty, and a world-class city.

As gateway to the business world, New York is a living laboratory attracting superior educators and employees. It is a city boiling over with opportunity and burning with the itch to grab it now. For the price of a subway token, students conduct original research on major companies, attend countless presentations, and visit the best in art and entertainment. The Business School's culture is vitally linked to New York's rhythm. You are very likely to rub elbows with distinguished alumni, alumnae, and other business barons who enjoy maintaining links with academia. The Board of Overseers, which reads like a *Who's Who* of international business, ranges from financiers and entrepreneurs to corporate chiefs and public servants. The list includes Henry Kravis, founding partner of Kohlberg Kravis Roberts & Co.; Howard Clark, CEO of Shearson Lehman; Ben Rosen, Chairman of Compaq Computer Corporation; Arie Kopelman, President of Chanel, Inc.; and Senators Frank Lautenberg of New Jersey and Robert Kasten of Wisconsin. And surprisingly, the southern novelist Eudora Welty is a graduate of the school.

At the heart of this global network and reputation is the faculty, who teach well and conduct path-breaking research. Nuggets of wisdom are imparted daily by adjunct professors drawn from nearby industries, while disciplined insights into quality, turnarounds, finance, and marketing are offered by the faculty gurus. Be sure to catch Bruce Greenwald, the Phil Donahue of finance, who can handle a class of one hundred students like a private tutorial; or the impeccably dressed Safwan Masri, fashionable hotshot of operations management. There is also cash king John Whitney, who recites Emerson while discussing the finer points of crisis management. And if you are lucky you can crowd in with 400 other students to hear the ninety-two-year-old undisputed quality expert Dr. W. Edwards Deming inspire students to discover his renowned "system of profound knowledge."

The student body is as diverse as the city itself. A typical class hails from forty-one states, sixty countries, and more than two hundred undergraduate institutions and may include lawyers, medical doctors, engineers, scientists, consultants, writers, musicians, professional athletes, and a fair share of bankers. More important, Columbia attracts students who are well-informed, confident, and street-smart. Many of your classmates' life-styles and interests could never endure a hiatus from a big city. Two years is a long time to spend in essentially collegiate environments. Such pastoral settings as Hanover, Palo Alto, or Ann Arbor are fine for some, but not those of us with high-rolling spouses, part-time careers, or an insatiable desire for fun after dark. It is not so surprising to find a student lugging her cello to class to make the 8:00 P.M. curtain at Lincoln Center or to find yourself seated in the audience.

A glance at the sixty student organizations demonstrates that Columbia Business School is a melting pot for people with a variety of professional, recreational, racial, and religious interests. Everyone has some affiliation with a club, and if you can't find one that suits your needs, then you can easily form one. The newcomers reflect the evolution in business attitudes and issues — "MBAs for Greener Business," the "Derivatives Club," and "Gays and Lesbians in Business" (GLIB). Columbia Business School, like New York, is the ideal environment for inspired individuals with initiative. When you add a number of students from the nearby School of International and Public Affairs, the crowded halls and cramped telephone booths bubble with ideas and nervous tension, making diversity another of the school's greatest strengths.

Leveraging these assets, Dean Feldberg is transforming Columbia Business School into a powerhouse by favoring new ideas as well as "Ivy" tradition. Upon arriving, he urged students and faculty to improve the school's quality of life by taking advantage of the depth of skills held by the students and placing them in charge of allocating resources. But the most visible change is a new core curriculum. Throughout the core courses, the faculty infuses information on four unifying themes: globalization, ethics, quality, and human resources. For example, a finance course may discuss conflict of interest and professional misconduct in the securities industry, or a management course may espouse the benefits of corporate social responsibility. According to Vice Dean Geoffrey Heal, the cross-disciplinary program is for "poets as well as physicists." While the jury is still out on the new curriculum, everyone welcomes the change.

Core classes range in size from fifty to seventy students, depending on the professor's popularity. By the second year, classes get smaller in areas of concentration. Sometimes upper-level courses are called seminars, but don't count on intimate groups. If the professor is a star, these courses will certainly be packed. Moreover, right-brainers are indispensable in group projects, case studies, and any other activity that requires original thought and imagination — skills not so immediately available to the quantmeister set.

In its academic orientation, the Business School uses a myriad of cases, lectures, texts, and publications to get its message across. Many professors bring in experts or ask the executives-in-residence (knowledgeable corporate superstars) to teach specific cases. Some professors require class participation, while others rely solely on lectures. Prior to selecting courses, discerning students carefully read the course evaluation guides, which break down professors' strengths and weaknesses. Warning: no matter how wonderful a course's title may sound, don't be fooled. Unless it is totally unavoidable, most students take the professor, not the class. The courses with the hottest professors are quickly closed, leaving the unlucky or dawdlers to suffer through twelve long weeks with plodding teachers. While the administration has weeded out many of the poor professors, there are still a few underachievers worth avoiding. If there are any questions or problems during the selection process, you will ultimately be sent to Student Services, headed by Assistant Dean Gail Berson, whose power in the school's informal structure is unrivaled. She's tough-minded, efficient, and well able to laugh at herself in the middle of chaos. During the orientation spiel, Gail gleefully suggests that cash donations or airline tickets to warm places will magically improve your lottery number. Not!!

Enticed by the high-paying jobs on Wall Street, Columbia Business School graduates overwhelmingly favor finance when determining a major. Nearly 70 percent of the most recent class hold a degree in this field, but most double-major in marketing, management of organizations, or international business. A major constitutes five courses in a specific field. Double-majoring is common, since one course may sometimes be applied to two majors.

While Columbia Business School is best known for finance, international business has gained equal respect. This is consistent with Dean Feldberg's mission to graduate "globally competitive students." Using symbols to emphasize his point, the dean recently installed several clocks above the school's Hermes logo to remind students that whether they're in New York or Arkansas, they are competing with those in Tokyo, São Paulo, Paris, or London. In conjunction with the School of International and Public Affairs, the school just formed the Chazen Institute of International Business. Through a $10 million gift by Jerry Chazen, CEO of Liz Claiborne, Inc., the school now has the muscle to strengthen its international network. Sponsored activities include student summer internships, language study programs, international speakers, and funding for faculty research and travel abroad. There are already several courses dealing with the worldwide aspects of accounting, marketing, and Japanese studies as well as student-led educational trips to South America, Russia, India, and Japan. The school feels so strongly about its global web that it has audaciously titled a new brochure *Columbia Is International Business*.

Another innovation is the expansion of concentrations. The school now offers majors in Management of Organizations and in Environmental, Media, and Construction Management, reflecting departments that continue to grow and offer students some of the best professors skilled in both research and real-world experience. And for the student interested in less traditional areas, such as public and nonprofit careers, there are some great courses, including one that develops a real budget for New York City. These and other disciplines are taught well, and the students who attend Columbia for reasons other than the finance curriculum are well served.

GETTING IN

THE number of applications to Columbia inversely fluctuates with the bad press on New York City. Since Los Angeles and Washington, D.C., have recently taken a beating, applications to Columbia have shot up 12 percent. The constant is that the Admissions Office is able to offer admission to well-qualified candidates who consider Columbia to be their first choice. On average there are roughly

3,300 applications for 750 spaces; 45 percent of the applicants in this pool applied from places outside the United States, which is one reason why interviews at Columbia are not mandatory. On-campus interviews for candidates who live in the Northeast Corridor are by invitation only; however, the school offers information sessions on Mondays and Thursdays at 1:00 P.M. After watching the videotape and listening to the Q&A, candidates often attend a couple of classes. Don't be shy! It's a great opportunity to see how the students think and act.

« *Without doubt, my greatest nemesis has always been the standardized test. The thought of picking up the number two pencil and filling in the blanks for the GMATs almost killed me. Who cares about the migration of the tsetse fly on the reading comprehension section? Nevertheless, I paid my $500 for Stanley Kaplan and took several practice tests before the real marathon. But once again my scores did not reflect my gallant effort. With this obvious blemish on my record, I pleaded my case in the application by emphasizing my strengths (accomplished pianist, college class president, community activist, and owner of a successful costume jewelry company). As it turned out, I was accepted with the condition that I attend math camp — an intensive calculus class taught at the Business School a few weeks before classes began. The class was filled with people who shared diverse backgrounds. Sitting next to lawyers, athletes, and copywriters, I realized that Columbia had purposely selected a diverse, well-rounded student body, which made the learning process infinitely richer.* »

One unique feature of Columbia Business School is that students are admitted three times a year. While the majority start in September, more than 250 students begin their first semester in January or May. Since the school is open for business year-round, international students, working students, summer jobless students, and students in a rush can finish their MBA in sixteen months versus the usual twenty months. On the other hand, while the flexibility is ideal for many, the constant flow of new blood probably dilutes traditional class bonding. The offset is that it provides a wider scope of contacts and experiences for all.

No matter when you wish to start, no duds need apply. The

"Admissions Office's Mission" clearly states that Columbia does not want "dull, mundane, or pedestrian people." While a few investment analysts have squeaked through, most applicants are leaders with unusual backgrounds who develop and tolerate quirkiness. The dean is looking for students who, he says, "can roll up their sleeves and hit the ground running." This means that students must demonstrate strength in academics, professional promise, and personal qualities. Sounds familiar, huh? During the next few years, the Admissions Office will be aggressively recruiting U.S. students with language skills and international experience. This fits neatly with Columbia's goal of being the quintessential international business school.

If you haven't worked in London or don't speak fluent Japanese, no need to worry. Columbia wants well-rounded, smart people with solid work experience. There are no quotas, but Icelanders may have a better chance than New Englanders. A typical class consists of 30 percent international students and 30 percent domestic minorities. Women make up one third of the population. And 98 percent of the applicants have at least one year of work experience, but most of the students have been working for three or four years.

While professional accomplishments are important, previous academic experience and personal qualities are equally weighted. Great recommendations are paramount, so preferably choose someone who knows you well and speaks in superlatives. The essays are another chance for the Admissions Office to see your human side. Most applicants treat this section conservatively, yet Assistant Dean of Admissions Debbie Felix encourages originality. When describing a failure, don't bother saying you work too much and have no time for the opera. Tell them you were kicked out of law school. Honesty generally scores Brownie points in a big way.

ACADEMIC ENVIRONMENT

DEAN Meyer Feldberg would agree with former mayor Ed Koch, who once said that in New York "You have to walk a little faster, talk a little faster, and think a whole lot faster." The dean welcomes students at each orientation with a reminder that Columbia is *not* in Hanover, New Hampshire. The beat of New York City, exhilarating and often overwhelming, reflects the pace of Columbia Business School's academic program. Besides classes, your weekly calendar is jammed with endless group meetings, corporate presentations, review sessions, informational interviews, and a plethora of extracurricular activities. This produces a manic energy. By the time you have managed to find your equilibrium, you've completed the program and look back with a sigh of relief and pleasure.

Of twenty courses required for an MBA degree, there are nine full and two half required core courses, but students can be exempt from one or more of these by passing placement exams. Studying for these exams is well worth the effort, since passing allows students to move into smaller, more specialized classes. Much like boot camp, the first year is highly structured. In the first term, core courses are determined for you. These are Statistics, Accounting, Managerial Economics, Managing Human Behavior in Organizations, and either Marketing or Finance. As this is a heavy quantitative term, students are rarely seen without their HP-12C and spend enormous amounts of time solving difficult problem sets and attending Friday review sessions. When you are not studying on weekends, a little voice warns that you should be. The second term is also a grind. (In fact, the entire program can be a grind if you want to work your tail off.) You have to take Global Economics, Decision Models, Accounting II, and Operations Management along with either Marketing or Finance and one elective. By the middle of this term students have spent enormous amounts of time on group projects and are skilled users of the school's computer software. For the right-brain students — those who excel in qualitative subjects — the first year is daunting but manageable. Besides review sessions, peer tutoring is readily available, and faculty and students are always willing to make the impossible seem clear.

« *Back in my carefree undergraduate days, I never dreamed of pursuing a graduate degree. The whole thought was intimidating. I equated "graduate studies" with "writing dissertations about the national decline in productivity." Of course, it wasn't anything like that. Two things became immediately apparent. First, all the courses tied together. Unlike undergrad, where I would typically wander from art history to physics, here even disparate topics such as statistics, microeconomics, and marketing all had common threads. The flow of the courses did more than just expose me to new skills. They constantly refined and honed them as well. Second, the courses were interesting and tangible. Since I worked for several years before school, I was constantly reflecting on how I could have done things differently armed with the knowledge I was now gaining.* »

The most successful students understand that learning is the primary goal. These students take difficult courses with excellent professors without concern for grades. Generally these classmates get the interesting jobs. However, many unfortunate students become obsessed with grades and class rankings. The object of their quest is the mistaken belief that placing "Dean's List" on their résumé is a ticket for a first-class job, because a few investment banks and consulting firms use this as a measuring stick. But consistent with Dean Feldberg's mandate to improve Columbia's quality of life, the school no longer gives Dean's List status to first-term students.

The school tries to deemphasize grades by replacing the ABC method with H for Honors, HP for High Pass, P for Pass (or Perfect), LP for Low Pass, and F for Fail. By the time grades are posted, they generally take the shape of a classic bell curve, with the mean being HP. Very few LP's are awarded, and F's are virtually nonexistent. Fewer than 1 percent are dismissed for academic reasons, so students should not freak out if they can't deal with first-term statistics or managerial behavior, whichever is their scourge.

« *For me, the first few minutes of each financial services class were terrifying. The thought of having to talk in front of my peers for the required fifteen minutes sent chills down my spine. I spent three weeks listening to students with backgrounds in financial services (I had spent the last three years in the music industry) speak glibly about brokered deposits and municipal bond insurers, and cringed when I considered the contrast I felt my contribution would make. To my surprise, however, when called on I managed to sound vaguely coherent. Having survived the first ordeal, I became more courageous. In fact, each time I spoke and presented, I became more comfortable until, by the end of the semester, I found that I actually enjoyed and looked forward to giving presentations.* »

There are plenty of places to turn if you are having trouble in a class. Most quantitative courses have regular Friday review sessions taught by professors, doctoral students, or MBA wunderkinder. Private tutors are also available and free for several sessions. Despite having a reputation for being research-driven, Columbia professors like to teach, encourage office-hour visits (most will even give out their home phone numbers), and are very willing to answer questions or discuss career moves with anyone who makes an effort to seek them out.

SOCIAL LIFE

WHEN it comes to social life, the Business School doesn't try to compete with New York. Rather, it encourages students to be part of the city. During the orientation boat cruise along the Hudson River, you realize that through the forest of tall, brightly lit buildings there lies enough entertainment to swallow you up. Putting aside the *New York Post* headline that reads "HEADLESS MAN FOUND IN TOPLESS BAR," you venture forth to discover some of the best music, theater, restaurants, and architecture the world has to offer. Even on a student's budget, you can have a great time wandering the city without feeling guilty the next morning. On the other hand, you can feel guilty, too. The choice is yours.

The school actively promotes events that take advantage of the city. From the "Fall Fling" and the "Spring Ball" to the rugby team's notorious "Pub Crawl," you can find yourself in the hottest clubs and hippest dives in town. For those who prefer higher culture, the school offers discount tickets to opera, theater, music, and dance.

To supplement the New York scene, Columbia tries to create a sense of community by offering draft beer and soggy chips every Thursday at "happy hour." Reminiscent of undergraduate fraternity parties, the weekly event attracts diehard partygoers as well as many students from other grad schools. For all its faults, the infamous happy hour is the best opportunity for students to meet one another outside of a classroom context.

« *One question people would always ask was what I thought of my classmates. Were they the stereotypical superaggressive, hard-driving, coldly calculating, unfriendly sorts that one should never show fear to? Well, I wondered the same thing before starting school. After the confusion and isolation of the first few weeks, things sorted themselves out. Some students were complete grinds (I never saw them), some were superintellects (I envied them), and the rest were a lot like me. We all found the work exhausting, but the friendships and shared experiences (happy hour, Follies, Harlem Tutorial, rugby) seemed to temper the work load. Columbia's campus atmosphere went a long way toward fostering a refreshing community spirit, far removed from New York's cold and calculating reputation.* »

A majority of the school's social life centers around student clubs, which have successfully created some semblance of community. The Black Business Students' Association organizes a casino night and charity auction. The Latin-American Business Association provides Colombian coffee breaks, and the Public and Nonprofit Management Association's "good government team" often indulges itself with trips to a luxurious Fire Island retreat. Perhaps the most active and highest-profile recreational club is Follies, consisting of some of the most creative students on campus. Boasting that Columbia is the "only business school on Broadway," Follies produces two shows a year. Scheduled just before exams, the shows are a hilarious combination of bathroom humor and bona fide talent. The dean, who bravely sits in the front row with Mrs. Feldberg, always takes the brunt of many fund-raising jokes. It is a time when the school laughs at its shortcomings in the hope that someday the toilets will flush, the ventilation system will work, the clocks will all read the same, and the computer center won't crash.

Aside from organized events, much of the daily social interaction takes place in three key areas. The Uris Deli, which *in no way* resembles a traditional New York deli, attracts a hodgepodge of students who like to eat, talk, and sometimes work at the same time. For sun worshipers, beautiful people, and smokers, the front steps of Uris Hall are the key place to be and be seen. And, of course, the shaking Watson Library, the second-largest business school library, built above the indoor running track, has been a mainstay for those who don't mind seismic or social interruptions while reading the *Financial Times* or material on reserve.

When not socializing at school or enjoying the activities around New York, you are likely to take refuge in your apartment. Most students live in Morningside Heights, the neighborhood that encompasses the few blocks surrounding the university. Bordered by the massive Cathedral of St. John the Divine and the Hudson River, it's one of many safe New York neighborhoods catering to the needs of budget-conscious students. The university owns dozens of buildings in the area and has in essence created an entire bureaucracy to fill them. Even though the apartments are subsidized, housing, like everything else in New York, is hardly cheap.

If you can't find what you are looking for near campus, it's not difficult to find an apartment in other sections of Manhattan. Since public transportation is so convenient, plenty of students live in other neighborhoods, such as Chelsea, the West Village, and SoHo. Some even commute from New Jersey. For first-time New Yorkers, the initiative to find an affordable and pleasant apartment must come from you. Be sure to consult a seasoned apartment hunter before embarking on your quest, and start early.

RECRUITING AND JOB SEARCH

UNDOUBTEDLY one of Columbia's greatest strengths is its consistent success in the job market. The Business School reports that more than three hundred companies conduct on-campus interviews, and 90 percent of its students have jobs within three months after graduation. While New York City is a favorable backdrop for both employers and students — the dean calls New York City "Columbia Business School's Campus" — the Career Services Department deserves high marks for steering Fortune 500 companies to Columbia and guiding students to make the best choices. The department is well equipped, with its own library, on-line information systems, a newsletter, computers, workshops, and an organized staff willing to provide personal attention to résumés, interview techniques, and cover letters. For those switching careers or unable to decide on one, students can speak with executives-in-residence or meet with alumni to discuss career options through the "take a student to lunch program."

At times the career search can be overwhelming. There are so many weekly activities that the quest for a job feels like an additional course. The school's weekly newspaper, the *Bottom Line*, keeps students informed of the important events, but many rely on Bill Bradford, the career librarian, who provides the most current information with a full dose of comic relief.

By the time students have suffered through the long, soul-tormenting process, 45 percent generally accept jobs in financial services. With Wall Street so close, it is not surprising that students easily fill openings in corporate finance, sales and trading, and investment research. Some choose intimate boutique houses, while others select empires with built-in skyscrapers. Major employers include a long list of familiar names, such as Goldman Sachs, First Boston, Lehman Brothers, Citicorp, and J. P. Morgan.

For nonfinancial types, there are several well-paid options. Consulting firms such as McKinsey & Co. and Booz, Allen & Hamilton pick about eight graduates a year, making competition for the $70,000-a-year jobs tougher than any. Top-brand management and advertising companies such as Procter & Gamble, Merck, Ogilvy & Mather, and Young & Rubicam are also popular choices. If you are not interested in working for a big-name company or do not want a training program, have no fear. Luckily, the Columbia name has an excellent reputation, and New York is packed with a large number of specialized companies. Finding a high-tech job in the Bay Area or landing a position in London is possible, but the independent job search requires a strong will and steadfast dedication.

« While impressed by the list of on-campus recruiters, I wanted a career in environmental management. The key to landing a job in this field successfully was the Columbia Business School alumni/ alumnae network. I had often heard that business school was a great place to make business contacts; however, I didn't realize till looking for a job that this also applied to the school's alumni. Having received several names from a helpful professor, I telephoned these graduates, who extended themselves on my behalf simply because we attended the same institution for two years. They provided advice and contacts that eventually contributed to a great position with a firm specializing in brand management. It is comforting to know that I can rely on this network throughout my career. »

The formal recruiting process begins the first day of classes. Almost every weeknight in the fall, students flock to corporate presentations to mark the beginning of the annual mating ritual. The slide shows usually last for forty-five minutes, after which students descend on a feast of chicken wings and pigs-in-a-blanket. The animalistic nature of your fellow students should not surprise you. With the tight job market, everyone knows the game is called survival of the fittest. Dressed in conservative blue suits and spit-shined shoes, students hope to make the best impression at every encounter. Some even hand out personalized business cards complete with the Business School Hermes logo, but most rely on a firm handshake and a warm smile to make the connection.

« I heard there were some students who videotaped themselves doing mock interviews. Others just pored through company documents to memorize sales figures and key elements of the mission statement. But none of these tactics would have prepared me for my McKinsey interview. The guy asked me to estimate the number of gas stations in the United States. Not having seen this answer on Jeopardy, I had to guesstimate, starting with the population. Under intense pressure to form coherent sentences, it was difficult to concentrate. I wanted the security of my HP-12C, and the silent moments seemed like eternity. Nevertheless, I remained confident, and plodded through the answer till I derived at between 70,000 and 100,000 stations. Although I never bothered to find out the correct answer, the interviewer must have followed my logic. As it turned out, I returned for another round of interviews and eventually was offered a job as an associate. »

For first-year students, the main goal is getting a respectable summer job. On-campus interviewing begins in February, but most students do not hear from employers until April or May. No one really cares about the average $1,000 salary per week. What counts is that an internship with one of the top investment banks or management consultancies can be crucial for a full-time offer. For career switchers, showing summer experience in a new field is even more important. As the economy continues to falter, employers have shown less willingness to take risks with career switchers. But almost everyone finds something respectable that he or she can glorify on the résumé or tout during an interview.

For second-year students the interview process begins in the fall. Interviews are either open or closed. Closed means that you have to receive a written invitation for an interview slot. Employers choose students after reviewing neatly bound résumé books (soon to be placed on computer disk) or, more likely, reading personalized cover letters. Most companies also offer "open" schedules, which means that students can use their computer bid points to sign up for an interview. The bidding process is so complex and confusing that Career Services requires students to attend an entire bidding workshop and provides students with detailed histories of past bids. Bidding the right number of points can be tricky. The dilemma faced by most job-seekers is whether to interview with many different companies or to save the previous points for the choice employers.

During the January vacation, on-campus recruiting begins. The corridors, usually filled with people in jeans and backpacks, is awkwardly packed with Hickey Freeman suits and leather briefcases. Students with sweaty palms pace nervously outside the interview rooms, waiting to hear their names called. After the initial pleasantries, the interview quickly moves into high gear. In only thirty pressure-cooker minutes, the students must impress their interviewers with a detailed knowledge of the industry, the company, and themselves. Call-backs for second interviews are sometimes given the same day, but most companies send a written response after touring other schools. Unless you are brilliant or overly sensitive, coping with rejection or "ding" letters becomes easier after a while. At the conclusion of the eight-week interview process, students shamelessly display their "ding" letters at happy hour, where they drink liquid courage and share interview war stories.

For every rejection, you also hear about fantastic job offers complete with signing bonus and four weeks of vacation. The Business School reports a wide range of starting salaries ($40,000 to $95,000), but the median for most industries is just over $55,000, exclusive of the year-end and signing bonuses. Despite the recession and a large number of job-seekers with MBAs, it's comforting to know that the Columbia Business School diploma continues to hold or increase in value. Students must share this credit with the placement office, which is always there to provide direction and extend a helping hand.

ON THE JOB — FIRST YEARS OUT

HAVING shaken the dean's hand and accepted your diploma, you immediately become a charter member of the MBA club. It is filled with the power elite of the business world who talk in a secret code of acronyms (LIFO, FIFO, EBIT). Dues are not mandatory, but gifts are regularly solicited and graciously accepted. To become a member, Columbia graduates, like those from the other top business schools, have had to crunch numbers, write research papers, and read hundreds of cases. After two years, students have been trained to think that they can think like CEOs of major companies. While they understand the fundamentals of running a business, they are excited and frightened by the prospect of testing all their newly acquired skills.

During their first few years on the job, most graduates do not have the opportunity to write a detailed marketing plan, perform a funds needs analysis, or determine pricing strategies. The days of raising your hand in class and suggesting how a floundering company should spend $4 million in new technology are a distant memory. The reality is that most graduates have to start at or near the bottom. Receiving real P&L responsibility may take years.

While graduates may use a few learned skills in marketing, finance, or operations research, most have to rely on the tools they acquired in management courses or outside the classroom. Developing teamwork and motivating people are some of the most useful skills for the newly minted graduate. Other soft issues, such as time management, negotiation, and presentation techniques, become increasingly important.

« *After graduating from Columbia with a degree in marketing and finance, I worked for an international brand management company specializing in food and beverages. My peers, who came from equally good schools, did not necessarily care where I studied, but rather how I contributed to the team. The MBA was simply entrée to the company. Whether people chose to soar with the eagles depended on their own initiative. In the team setting, I heavily relied on what Columbia taught me about group dynamics. It not only offered an entire course on the subject, but also the endless group meetings gave me the experience to help build consensus and move several projects forward at work.* »

While many graduates have the patience to wait for promotions and larger salaries, many discover after two or three years that better opportunities exist elsewhere. Columbia Business School graduates have great expectations for themselves. Since loyalty is not a corporate virtue, switching jobs is commonly accepted. Graduates are able to consult an international network of classmates and alumni or alumnae to facilitate a change. The school's ideal location also allows graduates to contact professors or conduct research on prospective local companies. The Business School's library is excellent, and many graduates do not hesitate to tap into this free and convenient resource.

The responsibility for achieving personal fulfillment and success ultimately lies with the individual. This is why values and skills learned in high school and college will most likely have a greater impact on your success than the two-year MBA. Business school simply accelerates a career, and the Columbia name provides instant credibility. But the honeymoon doesn't last very long. Others quickly measure you by hard work, perseverance, and ability to deal with others. While Columbia doesn't teach you these qualities, it will most likely give you more opportunities to succeed.

SUMMARY OVERVIEW

COLUMBIA is an exciting place to be right now. The impetus for change comes from Dean Meyer Feldberg, who said to the faculty when he arrived, "Unless you're prepared to change, unless you're prepared to support changes, then I'm not the right kind of person to lead the school." Well, the faculty, staff, and students embraced the change and together have instituted bold initiatives that have a direct impact on their lives. The most visible action is the introduction of the new curriculum, which has been geared to address the needs of business leaders operating in a new world order. "Quality," "ethics," "human resources," and "globalization" are the new buzzwords on the lips of every professor. Morale has dramatically improved as the dean has addressed basic quality-of-life issues. Clocks have been synchronized. Elevators go up and down. Safety has improved. Clubs have more money to spend on important programs. From mundane to urgent issues, the dean continues to empower students to find solutions. Upon speaking to him about an issue, you may find yourself running a task force to solve the problem. For all of these reasons, people like opening their wallets for him. The dean has already raised $65 million toward a $100 million campaign. This translates into the creation of new courses, more materials, and better professors.

With all of its problems, New York City is a vibrant place to be. Wall Street and the United Nations drive international business and politics. Opportunities abound for every student. Original research, jobs, and guests speakers are just the beginning. Students can venture into Chinatown or Little Italy. They can lunch at Sylvia's in Harlem or Le Cirque in midtown. Broadway shows, Lincoln Center, and MOMA are only a few subway stops away. There is no question that one of the greatest things about Columbia is New York.

The city attracts students from all over the world. Before entering Columbia Business School, many are already street-smart and cosmopolitan. They feel comfortable at Castel's in Paris or La Brea in Milan. Fifty percent of the student body speak a language other than English. Columbia's international student body enriches the school. Class discussions become more meaningful when students can relate their personal experiences in Japan, Israel, India, or Hungary. With so many diverse cultures coming together in a city such as New York, the Business School will never act like a close-knit fraternity. Instead, it is a wonderful mix of confident and competitive individuals.

They come to Columbia Business School because the program offers every student a solid understanding of the foundations of business. Finance continues to be one of the strongest departments; however, International Business and Management are both excellent, and many professors meld real-world and research experience. Students interested in marketing, operations, and nonprofit courses will also be well served. Getting into the hottest courses can be difficult, but the school tries to accommodate students by adding more sections or hiring more professors. Perseverance and luck are essential.

While the school thoughtfully responds to students' questions and concerns, Columbia is constrained by a facility that is too small for all the activity. There are days when Uris Hall feels more like Grand Central Station. With the hallways, rest rooms, deli, and computer center jammed with hyperactive students, it is difficult to find some peace of mind. Furthermore, the ventilation system is a mess. Uris Hall is either too hot or too cold. One statistics professor sarcastically jokes that "on average" Uris Hall maintains a comfortable temperature. Dean Feldberg has visions of building a new graduate facility; however, in the short term the Business School has been trying to deal with the space problem effectively. Rather than fight the crowds at the computer center, students can now plug into the system with their own Compaq notebook computers.

I have never met anyone who regretted spending his or her two years at Columbia Business School. Most graduates consider attending the school a privilege. There are few places where the environment can be so stimulating. Both inside and outside the classroom, every student is constantly challenged in new ways. Like riding a bicycle, there are some lessons that students can never forget. The benefits of a Columbia MBA are far-reaching and will certainly follow graduates throughout their careers and their lives.

Chapter 3

THE DARDEN SCHOOL
(UNIVERSITY OF VIRGINIA)*

THE PROGRAM

« *After I finished unloading the trailer, I decided to head over to the school to look around. Classes were not starting for another week, but I had wanted to get to Charlottesville early so I could finish the computerized accounting exercise that was assigned over the summer.*

The school appeared to be empty when I walked in. I sat in the lobby and reflected on my activities over the last year or so. Why was I here? I know what prompted me to go back to school; my oil and gas company back in Texas was heading south faster than oil prices themselves. But why The Darden School?

The thing that stuck out in my mind the most about the place was the feeling that I had after I visited the school the previous spring. I had spent the day sitting in on classes and talking with students and professors. Everybody had been friendly and supportive. But I was really surprised when the dean took twenty minutes out of his busy schedule to talk with me about my interests and to answer questions I had about Darden. Incredible. I wasn't even a student yet, and the dean thought it was important enough to meet with me. The familylike atmosphere at Darden that I had heard so much about was for real. I could not have chosen a better place to "live through hell" for the next two years. »

The Darden School was founded in 1954 by a Virginia statesman, Colgate W. Darden, Jr., for whom the school is named. Darden,

* BY FREDERICK STOW, JR., MBA

who was president of the University of Virginia at the time, enlisted some Virginia faculty and business leaders to help him with his cause. After the school was founded, a committee was formed to select a dean. This committee recommended Professor Charles Abbott, who left Harvard to come to Virginia and help start the new MBA program.

The core strategy of the Darden program has not changed since the school's beginning: ". . . to prepare men and women of high promise to act with determination, judgment, and integrity in increasingly responsible positions of leadership in the world of practical affairs." The school achieves this goal by using the case method of instruction. This learning process focuses on developing action-oriented decision-making skills. It requires students to spend the evening before class reading a twenty- to thirty-page real-life business scenario, putting the reader in the place of a manager confronted by several dilemmas. The case documentation ends precisely at the point where a decision needs to be made. Class time is spent the next day wrestling with the pros and cons of various alternatives that are impacted by quantitative and qualitative factors.

There are no "right answers" in a case. The objective is to perform a thorough analysis of the material, add a significant dose of common sense, discuss the situation with your study group the night before, and come to class prepared to state what your decision would be and how you would justify that decision. Students are human, and they tend to have different opinions. That, however, is the beauty of the case method. The discussion is directed by a faculty member, who explores all of the facets of each situation based on several individuals' analyses.

This mirrors the environment that managers will face in the real world: groups or teams of managers working together to solve the day-to-day problems of the business. An important realization is that each manager will look at the problem a different way, bringing his or her strengths to bear on the situation. Combining these strengths as a team can be more valuable than making decisions individually.

« I remember learning a valuable lesson from the group dynamics that took place in my first-year section. We had this fellow named Vince in our group, who was clearly a smart guy. His mind was like

a PC; he cranked out numbers in his head before I could even get the buttons pushed on my HP-12C.

Vince's problem, however, was that he wasn't very good at team building. In fact, this guy was brutal. He would intentionally seek out and destroy any weaker students in the class, simply to exhibit his own intelligence. I recall thinking what a shame it was that a guy so smart would probably spend his entire career in some back office crunching numbers, because no one would want him near any customers or coworkers for fear he would alienate them on the spot.

During the year, the group dynamics caused a strong bond to form among our section. Individuals like Vince were faced with the choice of toning down their competitive instincts and becoming a part of that group or remaining loners for the rest of the program. I think the real turning point came when Vince was involved in a car accident during our second year of school. Even though there had been many conflicts in the past, our classmates went out of their way to help Vince keep up with his work and to keep him psychologically tuned in.

By the end of the second year, Vince was still a little rough around the edges, but he had mellowed considerably and was able to work effectively in a group. The lesson I learned was clear. It doesn't matter how smart a person is; sooner or later they'd better learn how to get along and work well with other people if they're going to survive in the business world. If they don't, then they should be prepared to occupy the windowless office on the ground floor for a long time. Teamwork is critical at Darden. »

The first-year program at Darden is designed to promote support and team building among classmates. There are 240 students in each entering class. This group is divided into four sections of 60 people. Each section stays together for the entire fall semester. During the holiday break, the class is reshuffled, and four new sections are formed for the spring semester. This reshuffling gives everyone a chance to meet others in the class. Each section is assigned a room, and the group remains there as the faculty rotate through to teach each subject.

The section rooms resemble an ancient Greek amphitheater, complete with four tiers of seats rising gradually outward from an open space at the center. This space, or "pit," as it is fondly known at Darden, is the place from where the professor directs the discussion.

Every student in the first-year class takes the same nine courses: Quantitative Analysis, Business and the Political Economy, Accounting, Ethics, Marketing, Operations, Finance, Organizational Behavior, and Analysis and Communication. There are three classes on Monday, Tuesday, Thursday, and Friday, and two classes on Wednesday. Each class runs for about ninety minutes, and there is a coffee break between classes.

« *One of Darden's best-known traditions is the morning coffee break. Every weekday from 9:25 to 9:50 A.M. the entire school (students, faculty, administrators, staff, guests, et al.) descends to the lobby for coffee and doughnuts, just as they did during the first day of class in 1955. The topics of the informal discussions range from further clarification of the message derived from yesterday's case to last night's NBA scores.* »

The second-year program is designed to fine-tune the skills developed during the first year by mixing a required curriculum with a wide variety of electives. The only required courses are Strategic Management and Leadership and the Directed Study program. The Directed Study program provides students with the opportunity to work closely with a specific faculty member. Students may select courses from several options, including field or library research here and abroad, tutorial studies, or small-group research projects.

The rest of the second year is left for students to pick their own courses. There are three types of electives: capstone, foundation, and free electives. A capstone elective is a finishing course for a first-year subject such as accounting or quantitative analysis. A foundation elective explores the methodologies of a single subject, such as finance or marketing. The free electives are quite diverse and may be taken in any department in the business school. Given its emphasis on general management, the school encourages students to take a wide variety of electives and limits the number a student may take in any single functional area.

« *I cannot resist a suggestion which embodies all of my hopes for the school. It is that nothing will ever induce us to lay aside instruction in the ethical foundations of American business. Without a firm attachment to unimpeachable integrity, in our business as well as in our personal affairs, we build on shifting sands and there can be no future for any of us. (Colgate W. Darden, Jr.)* »

Mr. Darden's concerns are reflected in the prominence of business ethics in The Darden School's philosophy and curriculum. The Olsson Center for Applied Ethics, which has been part of The Darden School since 1966, sponsors research and serves as a critical resource for executives, scholars, students, and Darden alumni who are faced with the challenge of integrating ethical thinking into daily business decision making.

« *My sectionmates and I were a bit skeptical when we gathered for our first ethics class. What were these guys going to teach us that Mom, Dad, and the local preacher hadn't already tried to?*

The case study was written from the perspective of a restaurant owner who had just determined that one of her kitchen workers had AIDS. What followed was a fascinating discussion that included a wide spectrum of comments, from "Fire the perverted bastard!" to the expressed opinion that companies should put the well-being of their employees above that of customers, owners, and investors. It became clear that, as with most case studies, there was no "right" decision in this situation. The objective was to develop a methodology, a thought process, that would allow us to make the best decision we could, given these circumstances and our own moral predisposition.

After the course was over, I realized that no one had tried to tell me what was right or wrong. What I had gained was another tool to help me be a more effective manager. »

There is no typical student at The Darden School. And that's what makes the place unique. The admissions staff tries to put together as diverse a group of people as possible. This allows each student to learn as much from his or her classmates as from the academic program.

There are some characteristics, though, that all Darden students share. Each has some raw intellectual capabilities. Just as important, however, are good communication and interpersonal skills. And most, if not all Darden students, have at least two years of full-time work experience.

Probably the most important quality that a Darden student can possess is the willingness to support and work with his or her class-mates. There is no class rank at Darden, only a stringent minimum standard. This takes away the urge to back-stab and fosters team-work. By nature, everyone is still extremely competitive, yet the competitiveness is used in a very positive way.

A major factor in Darden's success has been the leadership the school has received from its dean, John W. Rosenblum. John pos-sesses the vision of what it will take to have a top business school in the twenty-first century. While not losing sight of the founder's original strategy, he understands the contribution the graduate busi-ness school can make to industry and how to position The Darden School in a leadership role. Major forces driving industry today include:

- the need for business leaders to maintain a general management perspective while at the same time having more depth in one or two functional disciplines;
- the globalization of the economy, including major international cultural differences;
- a drive toward better understanding of the ethical issues in man-agement;
- the value placed on the ability to deal with change, technolog-ical issues, and broad information management questions.

Rosenblum's leadership and vision places Darden on the leading edge of management education. As a result, the program provides each matriculant a damn good education at an extremely good price. Darden benefits from being part of the state university system of Virginia from both a cost and an academic perspective. Given the quality of each entering class and the placement statistics for each graduating class, Darden clearly ranks among the top ten business schools in America today.

GETTING IN

ABOUT 2,000 applicants compete for the 240 places in each year's first-year class. Getting admitted to The Darden School is a lengthy process that begins about a year before the fall semester starts.

The fun starts for the prospective student with the admissions application, which is more than thirty pages long. Besides the usual name, address, GPA, and GMAT scores, Darden requires four four-hundred-word essays. The essay topics include questions such as: "The Darden School seeks a diverse and unique entering class of future managers. How will your distinctiveness enrich our learning environment and enhance your prospects for success as a manager?" An optional essay asks for ". . . other information that would assist the [Admissions] Committee in evaluating your candidacy." The objective is to get as much information regarding each applicant as possible, so that the well-rounded candidate can be identified and accepted.

Another way to identify these individuals is via the interview process. Darden does not require each prospective student to come to Charlottesville for an interview, but it is highly recommended that you do so. This process is particularly advantageous to the candidate. Intellectual capabilities tend to be evident from the written application (GPA, GMAT scores, awards, languages spoken, and so forth). However, an interview allows the individual to exhibit his or her personality and the presentation skills that are highly valued by the Admissions Committee.

« I really enjoyed hosting prospective students during my first year. I got to meet some interesting people, and it was always fun to show off the school. I remember hosting a woman from Chicago who had the kind of qualities The Darden School looks for. She had received an undergraduate degree in engineering with a respectable GPA from a midwestern university, but more important, she had an interesting and varied background. She was an Illinois State Speech champion and had been a finalist in the Chicago Steinway Piano competition. After college, she had accumulated two years of solid work experience as a petroleum engineer and enjoyed a variety of outdoor activities. On top of all of that, she spoke fluent German, scored well on her GMAT, and had a great personality and interpersonal skills. She

clearly was the kind of individual who could contribute to the Darden community. »

If applicants can't travel to Charlottesville, they can take advantage of Darden's alumni/alumnae admissions network. This network consists of Darden graduates located in hundreds of cities around the world who are available to answer candidates' questions about the school, the program, Charlottesville, or any other topic. After one of these meetings or telephone conversations, the graduate is asked to complete a form that describes the encounter and the attributes of the candidate. The forms are sent to the admissions staff to be included in the prospective student's file when his or her application is received.

Now for the numbers. Again, out of approximately 2,000 applications (give or take a hundred), around 20 percent are accepted and 240 students are enrolled. A typical Darden class will have about 70 percent men and 30 percent women. The average age of entering students is 26 to 27, and 99 percent have had full-time work experience. Each class has roughly 10 percent minority students and 10 percent international students.

The average GMAT score is in the mid-600s, and the average undergraduate GPA is around 3.5. The usual breakdown of undergraduate fields is: humanities and social science, 50 percent; engineering and science, 25 percent; business, 20 percent; and other, 5 percent. Besides international students, who represent some eighteen different countries, Dardenites are divided as follows from four U.S. regions: South, 45 percent; Northeast, 30 percent; West, 10 percent; and Midwest, 5 percent.

There is no formula for admission to The Darden School. An applicant who has a 4.0 GPA and a 700 GMAT score, but the personality of a brick, will get denied acceptance just as fast as the candidate with deficient numbers. The well-rounded applicant is clearly the applicant of choice. Also important is a prospective student's background and experiences.

« *During one of the first days of Orientation we assembled for a presentation by the director of admissions. He ran through the usual laundry list of statistics about our class: where we came from, how many were women, and how many were married. The most interest-*

*ing part, however, was when he began describing some of my class-
mates' former jobs.*

*One guy had been a soldier in the Argentinian Army and had
fought in the Falkland Islands War (probably not hard to guess why
he thought it was a good time to quit and go back to school). Tom
Harrison had been on the PGA tour. Another had promoted rock
concerts in New York City, and our class patriarch, Don Webster,
who had been in the U.S. Navy for twenty years, was a submarine
commander when he took leave for his MBA. It was a scary thing to
think that some of these folks would be leading businesses into the
twenty-first century. »*

Unlike the other top business schools, going to Darden doesn't
require taking out a second mortgage on your life. This is because
the commonwealth of Virginia pays for part of the cost of your
education. In fact, contributions from the commonwealth and from
individuals and corporations make up more than 65 percent of The
Darden School's operating resources. As a result, the annual tuition
is currently $6,855 for Virginia residents, and $14,227 for residents
of other states and countries. Given the exceptional quality of the
education received at Darden, the competitive starting salaries, and
the corresponding costs at other top ten schools, pursuing an MBA
at Darden makes a lot of financial sense.

Personal expenses, including room and board, may vary considerably from student to student, but an unmarried student can real-
istically anticipate minimum annual costs of about $9,000. Darden
is determined to admit the most able candidates and believes that
lack of financial resources should not prevent qualified students
from attending the school. Approximately 70 percent of the students
currently enrolled receive financial aid, ranging from small loans to
full support. The school also offers fellowships and scholarships.
Because of the rigorous academic requirements of the MBA program, students should plan not to be employed during the first year
of the program.

*« From the foot-in-mouth department, I will relate a personal ex-
perience, in hopes of enabling other students to avoid my misfortune.
I had the bright idea that I would claim Virginia residency when I
arrived in Charlottesville, so that I could qualify for in-state tuition*

during the second year of the program. I did all of the things I could think of to declare myself a true Virginian, such as Virginia registration and license plates for the car, Virginia driver's license, Albemarle County voter registration. Unfortunately, the university had seen characters like me before and had passed legislation that would allow students to qualify for in-state tuition only if they could prove there was a good chance that they would stay in the commonwealth of Virginia and work after graduation. I was born in the state of Texas, raised and educated in the state of Texas, and worked the summer between my first and second years at Darden in the state of Texas. Needless to say, the University of Virginia committee that approved in-state tuition applications was not convinced that I was going to stick around after I graduated.

I overlooked one small thing, however: Virginia has a personal property tax. Since I registered my car in Virginia, not only did I not qualify for in-state tuition, but I also got to pay this tax for two years. What a deal! »

ACADEMIC ENVIRONMENT

I look to the diffusion of light and education as the resource most to be relied on for ameliorating the condition, promoting the virtue, and advancing the happiness of man.

Thomas Jefferson, 1782

Tucked away in the rolling hills of the Blue Ridge Mountains, the college town of Charlottesville (area population, 115,000) comes to life each fall as the 16,000 University of Virginia students return for another year of studies. I cannot think of another environment better suited for pursuing the goal of "enlightenment" that Mr. Jefferson so often spoke about.

The cornerstone of The Darden School's academic program is the case method of instruction. Of equal importance is Darden's focus on general management education as opposed to specific fields of expertise. A Darden MBA possesses the skills and abilities to perform as an effective manager in any job, in any industry.

Governed by a universitywide honor code almost 150 years old, the academic environment at The Darden School can best be described by the words "intense togetherness." I can honestly say that I have never worked harder in my life at any one task. Along the way I learned a great deal about business and about teamwork.

The grading system for both the first- and second-year programs is very simple. Fifty percent of a student's grade is based on class participation, and 50 percent is based on a final exam. The emphasis on classroom participation is one of the things that make Darden unique. It is imperative that a manager be able to present and justify his or her ideas in an effective manner. Therefore, Darden students are continually evaluated by each of the faculty not only on the quantity of participation but also, more important, the quality.

Exam day at Darden is very similar to a regular class day. The four-hour exams usually consist of reading a case and writing out the analysis and conclusion. A student is not graded on the solution given but on how he or she arrived at that answer and justified it. The analytical and problem-solving skills used on a test are supposedly acquired during the course of the semester and can't be learned the night before. Therefore, the most common preparation for a Darden exam is a good night's rest.

« *One of the greatest inventions ever to come out of the case method is what we at Darden refer to as the "chip shot." These are one-liners that students throw out from time to time hoping that they might get some class participation credit for a totally worthless comment.*

For example,

PROFESSOR JORDAN: *"Steve, what did we learn from Monday's case?"*
STEVE HANSON: *"I was wondering the same thing as I left class."*
If you didn't bring your clubs to class that day, another favorite pastime is section bingo. Before class, each student would receive a different bingo card that had randomly generated classmates' names in place of the usual numbers on the bingo card. During the case discussion, as each of the students added his or her comments to the analysis, if that person was on your bingo card, you would cross him or her off. The first person in the section to cross off all of the names on a card would then have to get called on by the professor, make a worthwhile comment regarding the case, and somehow work into his or her comment the "phrase for the day." Just think for a moment how

you might work the phrase "Toto, we're not in Kansas anymore" into a discussion about net present values and discount rates. »

All fun aside, case discussions are intense, educational, and extremely fast-paced. The Darden faculty expect each student to be well prepared for every case, regardless of other responsibilities. A very effective persuasion technique used by faculty is the "cold call" — the random selection of a student to open the case or to comment on a classmate's analysis.

« *I remember the first-year Toro Lawnmower case specifically. This case was a beast! It was a legend in its own time. This case was so infamous that on the morning it was taught, the second-year students drew a poster and placed it in the main lobby of the school depicting a Japanese plane flying over a U.S. Navy ship with the words "Toro! Toro! Toro!" painted in big red letters. Pages and pages of marketing case material that nobody could make heads or tails of had consumed the entire first-year study groups the night before.*

The tension in the section rooms that day was thick. Nobody wanted to open this case. We all felt as if we were playing Russian roulette. When the professor walked in, a hush fell over the group. Each student did whatever he or she could to avoid eye contact with the professor as she looked around the room for her victim. "Ms. Peters, would you please tell us what Christina Morgan should do about the Toro Lawnmower marketing plan." The wait was over. There was one terrified soul and fifty-nine others repenting their sins. »

The Darden School strictly requires a minimum level of academic performance from all of its MBA candidates. The school sets performance standards for the first-year program, each semester of the MBA program, and each course. For the purposes of cumulative academic standards, first- and second-year courses are worth either one or one-half of a course unit, depending on how many times the class meets during the year. An MBA candidate must ordinarily take the equivalent of 20 course units during the two-year program, receive below a B− in no more than 4.5 course units, and receive no grades of F. The majority of grades received are between a B+

and a B —. Given that there is no class rank at Darden, students' primary concern is that they meet the minimum requirements.

The work load at The Darden School is heavy, especially in the first year. It is not unusual to spend sixty to eighty hours a week preparing cases, participating in class discussions, taking exams, or writing papers. No prior graduate work credit is transferable to Darden and there are no part-time students.

A typical Darden day in the first-year program starts with the first class, from 8:00 to 9:25 A.M. There is a coffee break from 9:25 to 9:50, and the second class is from 9:50 to 11:15. A shorter, second coffee break takes place from 11:15 to 11:35, and the final class of the day runs from 11:35 to 1:00 P.M. From 1:00 to 2:00 everyone usually grabs a bite to eat, either at home or at Café North, a university-run restaurant that serves both The Darden School and the Law School. By 2:00 P.M. the case preparation for the next day has begun. Most students prepare the three cases for the following day's classes by themselves from 2:00 P.M. until 8:00 or 9:00 P.M., taking a short break for dinner or some exercise. From 9:00 to 11:00 or 12:00 midnight, study groups meet to discuss the cases. A student will tackle more than 600 cases during the two-year program.

The grueling schedule is thus designed for productive reasons; it is not simply an attempt to simulate army boot camp. In the real world of business, a manager is more than likely going to be faced with more tasks and responsibilities than he or she can intellectually, physically, or emotionally handle at one time. Therefore, that manager must set priorities based on importance and urgency. The Darden program forces students to begin learning that evaluation process while in school. There are clearly some times when all of the cases, papers, speeches, and group presentations can't be completed at the same time. Therefore, students learn to set priorities and rely on classmates for assistance in accomplishing as many of the tasks as possible.

Study groups are an essential part of the Darden experience. When a first-year student enters the program, he or she is assigned to a six-person study group. These groups meet every night to discuss the next day's cases and the analysis that has been done by each member. This is where the diversity of the student body really pays off. More than likely, each group will have six people who are each from a different background or industry. A typical study group would include an undergraduate liberal arts major, someone who has worked on Wall Street, a marketing expert, an engineer, a retired military person, and a CPA. Each individual is going to look at the case a little differently, so when they get together, members gain an insight as to alternate views of the business situation. And just because somebody is a history major doesn't mean he or she can't add value to a business case. Many times the CPAs have just as difficult a time with the "people" problems in a case as the history majors do with the income statements and balance sheets. Study group members grow to be lifelong friends, and few do well in the program without this teamwork. The study group becomes the basis of much needed academic and social support.

The attrition rate for each first-year class changes from year to year. My class had a fairly low rate — we lost six people after the first year, mostly for academic reasons. Other classes have lost ten or more. There are no predetermined attrition goals. The average rate seems to be 3 to 5 percent, which is down significantly from prior years.

Several programs have been initiated to try to keep the attrition rate as low as possible. One of the most effective has been the first-year Orientation program. Orientation is completely developed and coordinated by second-year students. Its main objective is to provide support during the early stages of the program so that as many first-year students as possible make a smooth transition from pre-Darden to Darden life. There are four major parts of the Orientation program: Big Brothers/Big Sisters, individual tutoring, section advisers, and study-group advisers. The Big Brother/Big Sister program attempts to match a first-year student with a second-year student based on common backgrounds, interests, and so on. A Big Brother or Big Sister is there to answer questions, give advice, lend psychological support, or do whatever else he or she can to help the first-year student. The individual tutoring offers help to first-year students who are having trouble in a particular subject by a second-year student who excels in that subject. These two programs tend to focus on the needs of the individual. Section advisers and study group advisers are there to lend assistance to the respective groups.

The strength of the Darden program stems in large part from its faculty. It takes a unique individual to teach a class of sixty students effectively using the case method. Not only does this person have to have a thorough knowledge and understanding of the topic, but he or she must also possess extraordinary talents for leading the case discussions so that each student grasps all of the lessons to be learned. Darden profs have developed and fine-tuned those traits by untold hours of case writing, teaching note preparation, and time in the classroom.

« MBAs from other schools would always ask me, "How do you guys at Darden teach accounting using the case method?" The answer is, "It isn't easy!"

Picture, if you will, a room full of first-year students, most of whom had never even seen an income statement or balance sheet before, let alone know how to read one. They are under the tutelage of Associate Professor Haskins, a young PhD from Penn State who also had prior work experience as a CPA with a large accounting firm and as a management consultant.

The assigned case was "Bear Balloon," a familiar story of an entrepreneur who owned a small company (in this case the business was selling rides in a hot-air balloon); he had entrusted his entire financial empire to an aged, green-eyeshaded accountant who had just checked out to that great Big Eight firm in the sky. The young entrepreneur (who had an extremely qualitative, liberal-arts education) was faced with the task of preparing several official documents, including a balance sheet, and income and cash flow statements. The twist was that he discovered his company's incomplete records had been kept by his "accountant" in a number of shoe boxes, absent anything closely resembling a filing system. Enter the young, aggressive MBA from The Darden School to help the entrepreneur avoid the wrath of the mighty tax god IRS.

The case began with the usual flurry of disjointed comments. From that point on, however, Professor Haskins seized the controls of the runaway train and guided the discussion through checkbook reconciliations, creating "T" accounts, accounts receivable analysis, and other procedures for organizing the data.

It was a grueling class for everyone, but the result was a complete set of financial statements and the building of a solid base for future accounting cases, all in ninety minutes' time! »

But the professors are not only academicians. Faculty members generally have close ties with the business community through consulting, serving on corporate boards, research, and teaching the school's programs for executives. Over half of the professors have lived and worked outside of the United States. The faculty (and the dean) have no formal office hours and are almost always available to students. There are approximately seventy faculty members at The Darden School. Fifty-three are full-time members and forty-six have doctorate degrees. There are no teaching assistants at Darden. The student-to-faculty ratio is approximately eight to one, and all faculty members teach first-year courses.

« *The Darden faculty truly are a remarkable group of men and women. As with any body of tenured academicians, there are a few that should already have headed to pasture, but on the whole this is as fine a gathering of pedagogical talent as you can find anywhere.*

One very delicate issue that relates to faculty development is that of a tenure candidate's division of time between teaching and research. Given the nature of the case method and the talents that each professor must possess to teach effectively, a balance must be struck that allows the candidate to excel in the classroom and establish a good relationship with the students, as well as to meet the minimum research requirements placed on him or her by the dean and the university. At times it appears to the students that a faculty member's commitments are out of balance because of the time it takes to satisfy the research requirements or because an excellent teacher is not granted tenure due to not satisfying those requirements.

Dean Rosenblum has stated that the primary focus of Darden's faculty development program will always be teaching. This position is wholeheartedly supported by the majority of the student body, faculty, and Darden administration. However, it always takes time to make changes in a large university system. »

The Darden School has exceptional academic facilities and resources, with plans for new, larger facilities under way. The school is located on the North Grounds of the university as part of a graduate/professional complex that also includes the School of Law. The school's building, completed in 1975, contains thirteen classrooms, many seminar and study rooms, computer facilities, and the Camp Library. The Darden School operates a network of nearly two hundred IBM personal computers, including twenty-four micros in the student Computer Lab. In addition, the school operates three digital VAX minicomputers. Students can access a variety of Darden, University of Virginia, and national information services.

The Camp Library of The Darden School houses extensive research collections in business and economics. The library's holdings include more than 80,000 volumes, subscriptions to 950 periodicals, and access to multiple computer reference services, including compact disc and on-line data bases. Darden students may also use the nearby Law School Library and all other university libraries, with combined holdings of more than 2.5 million volumes.

The highlight of the Darden academic experience, though, is that most blessed event — graduation! Darden graduation takes place in mid-May. After degrees are conferred during the universitywide event on the lawn, Darden holds a diploma ceremony back on the North Grounds. This ceremony is the culmination of a week's worth of revelry that includes the class dinner, Professor Sherwood Frey's famous "pig pickin'," numerous cocktail parties, and the dean's continental breakfast, held on graduation morning.

SOCIAL LIFE

YES, believe it or not, you can have a social life while attending The Darden School. It usually gets off the ground during and after the latter part of the first-year program. The work load does not get any lighter, but most students are beginning to "work smarter" by this time. A basic tenet of the Darden program is the need for a well-balanced approach to learning. Most Darden students, accordingly, take the opportunity to learn, have fun, and blow off some steam at the various academic, social, and athletic activities offered during the year.

Most of the social life at Darden is informal. It revolves around sections and study groups. Even after you have spent the better part of sixty hours or more each week with cases and classmates, you still look to the latter for your social life. Whether it is weeknight beers at a local watering hole or discussions about life over dinner on a Saturday night, your best friends are your fellow students.

This does not preclude organized activities (after all, Darden is a business school for aspiring organizational managers). The Social

Committee of the Darden Student Association plans and presents an array of occasions for fun, frolicking, and general craziness during the year for all students, both single and married.

The picnic at Birdwood Pavilion is a favorite fall activity. Birdwood is an antebellum estate that is now owned by the University of Virginia. It is home to the university's own championship golf course. Of similar caliber is the semiannual trip to the Foxfield Races. Students sip mint juleps and nibble hors d'oeuvres alongside the townsfolk of Charlottesville, who also turn out to watch the thoroughbreds compete. The fall semester is wrapped up with the annual Holiday Ball. Students dance the night away, in black ties and evening gowns, to the sounds of a live band.

The spring semester's activities begin with the Bahamas Party, complete with imported sand, rum punch, and limbo poles. This is followed by the annual Darden Talent Show, as well as second trips to both Birdwood and Foxfield. The school year is concluded with another gala event, the B Bar Ball. This is a celebration, of course, of the fact that everyone (well, almost everyone) received a B – or better in each of their courses.

A favorite event is the weekly Grad Happy Hour. On Friday afternoons, the University of Virginia Student Union honors its graduate students by throwing this soiree and giving them free admission and reduced prices on refreshments. Finally, several new traditions have been started in the last few years. The Darden Chili Cook-Off, for example, pits teams of chili cooks against one another, each with their own home-brewed concoctions, such as "Bambi's Revenge" (made with deer meat), "Drexel Burn'em," and the award-winning "New Jersey Waste."

Competition at The Darden School does not end in the classroom (or with chili). Fierce battles are fought in the context of athletic activities scheduled throughout the year. The most prestigious of these events is the Darden Cup. This yearlong competition matches the first-year class, the second-year class, and the faculty/administration teams against each other in such sports as golf, tennis, running, and basketball. Each of the teams gets points, not only for winning a particular event but also for members who attend just to cheer their teammates on to victory.

Another popular attraction is the university-owned North Grounds Recreation Center, located a few yards from The Darden

School, which contains facilities for weight training, aerobics, basketball, squash, racquetball, and much more. Lockers and showers are, of course, available.

Other university intramural sports that Darden students participate in include lacrosse, rugby, soccer, softball, football, and swimming. Darden even fielded a two-man team that competed in (and completed) the Boston Marathon.

« *The most famous Darden sports powerhouse is the Darden Old Guys, or the DOGS. The DOGS are a softball team consisting mainly of faculty members who compete in a university league comprising both students and professors. One of my classmates was asked to join the team soon after it was learned that he could finagle a corporate sponsorship for the DOGS from his previous employer, Ralston Purina. Ralston provided pin-striped shirts and red hats emblazoned with the familiar checkerboard squares. Unfortunately, the fancy equipment couldn't invigorate aging bones and tired muscles.* »

Organizational life abounds at Darden. Activities include the Darden Store, the *Darden News*, the Darden yearbook *(The 10K)*, industry-related clubs (finance club, marketing club, etc.), and Darden Outreach for communitywide volunteer projects. Students interested in general business issues can join the Business Forum, which is responsible for presenting government, industry, labor, and other types of speakers. Finally, students concerned about recruiting can work with the Placement Committee, composed of selected faculty, and the Career Services and Placement Office staff to address recruiting-related issues.

One of the most supportive groups at the school is the Darden Partners organization. This club is made up of the "significant others" of first- and second-year students. Their valuable projects include providing a helpful hints book to incoming students and their families, supplying the doughnuts for morning coffee, and treating all students to snacks and refreshments during the holiday season and exams. Most of all, it provides an opportunity for those who are sharing the same experience to get together and give each other support.

The nightlife in Charlottesville is better now than it has ever been, which isn't saying much. There are a handful of popular restaurants and bars that cater to both the graduate and undergraduate crowds. Most Darden students, however, prefer to throw their own shindigs at home or in their apartment complex party rooms. If Charlottesville doesn't satisfy the revelers in the crowd, Washington, D.C., is two hours away by car. Richmond, Virginia's capital, is an hour away.

The university provides some housing for both single and married graduate students. For single students, nearby accommodations are available in the Copley III apartment complex, and, after a year of study, the Ranges, in the original Jeffersonian quadrangle on the central university grounds. Accommodations for married students are available at University Gardens and Copley Hill, both within easy walking distance of The Darden School.

Since university housing is limited, the university also offers assistance in finding privately owned accommodations through its Off-Grounds Housing Office. Many modern apartment complexes are within walking distance or a short drive from the university. The most popular of these is Ivy Gardens (more commonly known as "Darden Gardens" because of its proximity to the school), which caters almost exclusively to Darden and Law School students. Some students also find houses or cottages to rent in and around Charlottesville.

RECRUITING AND JOB SEARCH

« *Let's face it. Most people return to graduate business school so they can gain what it takes to get a great job. Yes, all of the skills and techniques that are learned during the two-year experience are important. But those abilities won't do anyone much good unless he or she has an opportunity to use them. Therefore, recruiting at Darden is taken very seriously and is viewed as the first major step for a Darden MBA up the long career ladder.* »

Most of the recruiting activities at the school are coordinated by the Darden Career Services and Placement Office. This group goes far beyond simply arranging interviews and collecting corporate recruiting materials. Other services offered include seminars on résumé writing, interviewing techniques, and career development. Also, student exchanges with alumni/alumnae are arranged in selected cities during the holiday break so that students can get some first-hand exposure to a variety of jobs and environments.

Corporate recruiters begin to appear on the Darden School grounds during the middle of the fall semester. On-grounds interviews are not permitted until after Christmas. However, representatives want to advertise their companies' opportunities as early as possible. Several recruiters hold "company briefings" and social events during the fall. Students gather in one of the section rooms to hear several corporate representatives, many of them Darden graduates, extol the virtues of working for their firms. Company briefings are usually held during the lunch hour, and many companies sponsor a box lunch for those who attend. The briefings typically include a formal thirty- to forty-five-minute presentation followed by a question-and-answer period. Many companies will also host evenings of cocktails and hors d'oeuvres at a local hotel.

A service provided jointly by the Career Services and Placement Office and the Darden School's Camp Library is the maintenance of the Placement Library. Here a student can find a variety of printed material, including corporate annual reports, job descriptions, sample résumés, relevant books, and information on individual recruiters (names, titles, addresses, phone numbers, etc.). Also available is an updated list of all companies planning to recruit and the dates that they will be at the school. This information is particularly helpful when students begin to formulate their strategies for the interview bidding process.

« *During first-year recruiting we were each allocated 1,500 points for the competitive, computerized bidding process. Investment banking and consulting were hot, and I remember seeing several results sheets showing winning bids of 1,500 for a single interview slot. The name of the game, of course, was to leave as few points on the table as possible. Some students were winning one of the limited number of interview slots with those same companies for half the number of points. It looked as if the bidding skills learned in Quantitative Analysis class were being put to good use.* »

Each spring about two hundred companies from the United States and abroad conduct interviews with Darden School students for both summer internships and full-time positions. This results in one of the best company-to-student ratios in the country. First-year students average more than five interviews each, and second-year students average twelve each. Darden students can obtain on-grounds interviews by participating in the competitive bidding process or by receiving an invitation.

An invitation to interview can be given by a company for several reasons, such as prior work experience, demonstrated leadership qualities, involvement in extracurricular activities, or because of a positive experience during the company briefing or social event in the fall. Getting an invitation to interview does not subtract from the number of points a student is allotted. Therefore, invitations are the option preferred by students. If a company extends invitations, however, it must open a like number of interview slots to the bidding process.

On-grounds interviews begin in January and run through April. Most interviews are thirty minutes in length. Some companies, however, choose to conduct longer sessions. For full-time positions, the on-grounds interview is usually followed by a visit to the corporate location where the student would be working if he or she chooses to join that particular company.

For the most recent Darden graduating class, the average accepted salary was $58,840 with bonuses, and the median salary was $54,000. Ninety-five percent of all graduates found jobs within three months of graduation. The functional areas most students chose were: consulting and management services (22 percent), marketing and sales (19 percent), investments (17 percent), and finance (15 percent). Approximately 37 percent of these jobs were with manufacturing firms. Geographic areas included the South (26 percent), Northeast (excluding New York) (25 percent), New York (20 percent), Midwest (16 percent), West/Southwest (10 percent), and international (3 percent).

Since there are no summer-school classes at Darden, most students choose to work between their first and second years of the program. Many students view the summer as an opportunity to try something new. About one hundred students obtain summer internships from companies that come to Darden to recruit. Many others stay at Darden during the summer to work for individual faculty members or to work for Darden's executive programs. Still others find summer jobs on their own or return to the companies where they worked prior to going back to school. Summer salaries average about $3,000 per month.

« *The Annual Golden Bullet Awards are presented on April 1. A "bullet" refers to those gratifying letters students receive from a recruiter after the interview letting them know that there is not a snowball's chance in hell of their ever getting a job offer from that company.*

Students are asked to submit copies of funny, rude, or outrageous bullet letters that they received during the course of that year's recruiting process. Awards are given for the best letters in several categories.

Two of the most outstanding entries that received awards on a recent April Fool's Day were (1) a single letter sent by a consulting firm addressed jointly to two separate students (given the Keep the Cost of Recruiting Supplies Low award), and (2) a letter written by a Fortune 100 company to one of its own employees, who was attending Darden by way of the company's sponsorship program, informing that person that "given their prior experience, they didn't feel that there was a good match between the student and their company" (recipient of the Intracompany Communications award). »

ON THE JOB — FIRST YEARS OUT

A Darden MBA has two primary advantages in the marketplace after graduation. The first, and most important, advantage is the new skills and abilities that were acquired during the program. The second advantage is the respect that is given to those who obtain the degree.

The core strategy of the Darden program is to train individuals to be both leaders and effective managers. The true test to determine if the strategy is sound and well executed is to evaluate Darden graduates as managers in the business world. Even though The Darden School is relatively young compared to the other top business schools, many Darden graduates have risen to prominent positions within major corporations or started successful new ventures; for example, Thayer Bigelow, president and CEO, Time Warner cable programming; Steve Reinemund, president and CEO, Frito Lay; Patricia B. Robinson, president and general manager, Gilbert Paper; and entrepreneur Linwood Lacy, chairman and CEO of Micro D, Inc. As the number of Darden alumni and alumnae grows, no doubt many more individuals will join the ranks of these successful executives and entrepreneurs.

The Darden MBA degree also gives strong support to the manager whose career is just beginning. The newly hired Darden graduate is expected to be able to handle above-average levels of responsibility and challenge. As these expectations are met, further responsibilities and advancements are received quickly.

« I showed up for my first day at my new job on June 15. There were several others starting that day, too, and it was nice not having to run the Human Resources gauntlet alone.

After a few hours of filling out forms, reading about various policies and procedures, and repeating my life history at least twenty times, it was finally time to join my assigned department. My new boss was waiting for me with a cup of coffee and a comfortable chair. I needed both as he described my first assignment, which began with catching an airplane at 6:30 A.M. the next morning bound for an oil refinery in Montana. I was to join a team of five others who were already there and spend the next two months performing an analysis of the facility's operations.

I spent the next ten months leaving town every Sunday afternoon and returning home on Fridays. Each assignment involved working as a member of a team performing operational analyses on a variety of the company's plants.

From the very first day, I realized the value of the skills I had acquired at Darden. Each project was like another case study. I was able to dig through the mountains of data and extract the information that was the most relevant and had the most impact on the location's operations. I was also able to work effectively with the rest of the team. As at Darden, each team was composed of individuals who had strengths in particular, distinct areas, such as engineering, computers, and accounting. I felt very comfortable working with each person and was also able to stand back and see how each of the functions fit together in the overall business.

I enjoyed being able to add value to the organization from the *beginning. On one particular occasion I presented to a factory's management the application of linear programming to their production scheduling process, which enabled them to use their costly resources more efficiently.* »

Another source of tremendous support for the Darden graduate is the Darden School Alumni Association. The Alumni Association, located on the North Grounds, is the nucleus of a worldwide network that administers several programs on behalf of the alumni/alumnae community. These programs include organization of class secretaries (networking), class agents (fund-raising), and alumni/alumnae chapters located in major cities around the world. New programs being developed include an Alumni Continuing Education Program, which would bring Darden faculty and case studies to alumni/alumnae in various cities for seminars and executive programs.

The alumni/alumnae also support The Darden School by way of the Darden Annual Giving Campaign. Darden alumni/alumnae loyalty is shown by one of the highest participation rates of any graduate business school.

SUMMARY OVERVIEW

DURING the past thirty-five years The Darden School has had phenomenal success in rising to the ranks of the top ten business schools. The following are the key factors that contributed to that success and that will be the driving forces behind the continued success that Darden will no doubt have.

The program. A program based on the case method of instruction, a general management orientation, and a learning plan rather than just a series of individual courses.

The administration. An administration that truly takes a leadership role by promoting innovation and progressiveness.

The faculty. An extraordinary group of men and women who excel as teachers in the classroom and are always on the leading edge of new discoveries and technology.

The students. A combination of unique and diverse individuals whose strengths are teamwork, support, and an active student-run government.

The alumni/alumnae. A loyal and dedicated group who continue to support The Darden School through high levels of involvement in all of the school's activities.

As with any school, Darden has its areas of weakness, the primary one being a result of its youth. The Darden School has come so far in such a short time that it does not yet have the broad alumni/alumnae base that other institutions of its stature enjoy. This results in financial constraints that could potentially affect the school's growth. Given this challenge, The Darden School has launched a major capital-raising campaign that will benefit all of its constituents and provide a base for continued growth well into the future with new facilities.

Darden's other soft spot has also been a factor in its success. Without the support of the University of Virginia there is a good chance that The Darden School would not be alive and well today. As is typical of any large institution, however, certain policies, procedures, rules, and regulations of the university are not always in the best interest of, or consistent with, the core strategy of The Darden School. Examples most often mentioned are differences in opinion regarding tenure requirements, as well as the need for the university to give The Darden School more autonomy to realize its long-term goals and objectives. But considering the rich heritage that The Darden School does share with the rest of the university, the relationship continues to be generally attractive, beneficial, and desirable.

Was getting an MBA from The Darden School the right decision? Yes. The two-year Darden experience can, by far, be the most positive, significant factor in your educational and professional career. The program is not recommended to everyone. However, if a person possesses unique qualities and wishes to maximize those qualities as an effective general manager of the highest integrity, then I would highly recommend and enthusiastically promote The Darden School at the University of Virginia.

Chapter 4

HARVARD BUSINESS SCHOOL*

THE PROGRAM

« *The adrenaline shot through my system when the marketing professor called my name to open the Black & Decker case. Within seconds, I would present to the waiting class my action plan for integrating the GE Small Appliance Division into the Black & Decker Corporation. I shuffled through my notes, trying to recall the core points I had examined the night before. I felt a moment of panic as I realized that I had not calculated the break-even volume required to pay out my plans. I knew my classmates would discover the omission, but there was no more time. As I looked up from my notes, the room was quiet, and all eyes were focused on me. "I have a short- and long-term action plan," I began. The professor listed my objectives and core action steps on the blackboard as I spoke. My monologue ran fifteen minutes on the trade and consumer strategies Black & Decker should pursue, the cost and timing of the strategies, and a contingency plan for different competitive reactions.*

As I pulled the summary points together, I thanked my lucky stars that we had discussed this case at length in study group the night before. I was sure I had delivered a first-rate opening! Nevertheless, before my last word was spoken, fifty hands shot into the air, ready to pounce on my plan. It was the start of a typical day at the Business School. »

Nobody just passes through Harvard Business School. The experience is so all-encompassing that it profoundly impacts the lives of

---

* BY TOM LONG, MBA

those fortunate enough to attend. The B School practically owns your body and soul for two years as it pushes you to test the limits of intellectual strength and endurance, and then to expand them.

Nor is anything free or easy at the B School. Nobody goes part-time. The root of the educational philosophy is the case method, which forces class participation and requires students to think from the general manager's point of view. Students have to take the initiative in this class participation, form study groups on their own, and balance the enormous work load. To survive and succeed at HBS, a student must take an active role in his or her own learning. It is this participative Socratic philosophy that gives Harvard its competitive edge and prepares graduates for leadership positions in senior management. At Harvard, you don't just learn management, you learn how to think.

There are few right answers at Harvard. What counts is the thinking process that leads to a solution. Every case assignment involves a problem that must be analyzed, interpreted, and debated by the students. While the weak solutions are debated into oblivion, one hardly ever walks away from an HBS class feeling certain that a case has been completely solved.

In fact, the richest cases present several plausible courses of action for the general manager, and students often discuss the issues raised in a case long after class. It is the richness of the case method and the enormous energy it requires of student and professor that set Harvard apart as one of the premier business schools.

At HBS, there are no real lectures and few textbooks. Cases, again, based on real-world business situations, are the dominant teaching vehicle; after two years at HBS, each student will have completed more than eight hundred cases covering all of the major business disciplines. The success of the case method depends on class participation, which is related to the preparation that students put into each case. Harvard ensures student preparation by basing up to 50 percent of grades on the quality of class participation and by strong encouragement of the study group.

« *By the time I arrived at HBS, I had heard about the importance of forming a study group. The ideal study group would combine experience in marketing, finance, operations, accounting, and human resource management, resulting in the most well-rounded anal-*

ysis of the cases. The moment section assignments were made, I began trying to find or create a study group that combined the perfect features. After forming a study group and working together for a few days, it became clear that the most important elements in our group's success were our commitment to help one another and a shared desire to make HBS lots of fun. To that end, we supported each other in class at every opportunity. Most of the time our group discussion provided excellent practice for the next day's classroom experience, and a friendly environment that helped us endure the pressure of the class. Were it not for a friend's late-night coaching and encouragement, I would never have made it through Managerial Economics. Before long, our study group was transformed from an academic survival tactic to a welcome forum on the issues of the day as well as on our academic work. By the end of the first semester, we were best of friends. As the academic pressure subsided, and we got better at the case method, the case-related portion of our discussions was dispatched straightaway in order to allow for the inevitable breeze-shooting sessions that evolved on sports, travel, career, and various other topics. We met nearly every night that first year, and studied for exams together our second year. »

Another distinguishing feature of HBS is the section. The entire class is divided into sections of eighty to ninety students for the first year. If you have ever seen *Paper Chase*, then you have a good idea of the layout of an HBS classroom. Sections are assigned to a single room, and all classes for that section take place in the same room for the entire year.

Every semester at Harvard has its own character, but it's undoubtedly the first that is particularly memorable. The first semester at HBS is intimidating. The case method is unfamiliar, the work load onerous, and the pressure intense. Moreover, all courses are required in the first and second semesters, so you can't postpone difficult ones to make your schedule easier. In the first few weeks, even those destined to graduate with distinction are unnerved — and work all the harder as a result. At midterm exams, anxiety peaks, even for the top students.

« The day before the first midterm exam, I took a break to play tennis with Jim. He knew the material cold and was a fine tennis player,

but he was so nervous about that first exam that he could hardly hold on to the racquet. Discussing the exam between points, we both worried that there weren't ten people in the class who deserved to fail this exam, because everyone knew the material. It was going to be a real dogfight to determine who would receive "loops" (low passes), the bottom 10 percent of the grades. We could only hope it wouldn't be us. Sufficiently paranoid by now, we both went back to studying for the rest of the afternoon and night. I later learned that Jim scored in the top 1 percent of our section on the exam. »

For most students, getting through the first semester brings a sigh of relief and a confidence that the rest of HBS will be downhill sledding. The universal feeling of inadequacy that exists in the first few months gives way to a sense of achievement and optimism. By the second semester, most students are buried in work but are certain they can make it through.

The second year at HBS is completely different from the first. Students may choose all of their courses except one, so there is high interest from participants. Classes are smaller, too. Rather than the eighty-nine classmates you stay with all year in the first year, classes in the second year usually have forty to seventy members. Cold calling by professors isn't ubiquitous, and preparation time for cases hovers around the two-hour mark or less (still amounting to about six hours per day). This is not because the cases are easier in the second year. In fact, cases are usually longer and more difficult, but students are much better at finding the heart of a case and analyzing its core elements after the first four hundred or so tries in the first year.

Also a major focus in the second year is recruiting. This is probably the only part of HBS that every single student is excited about managing! And manage it they do. With over two thousand companies contacting the school, and over five thousand interviews given per year, students have a once-in-a-lifetime opportunity to assess career options carefully. Thankfully, Friday classes are suspended in February for second-year students so that they may take full advantage of Harvard's placement power.

The second year at HBS is also an opportunity to challenge yourself with courses taught by the world's foremost authorities. In my second year, I took classes from two Pulitzer Prize winners and a former Bush administration assistant secretary of the Treasury. But even the less-known profs have a talent for teaching. They use the case method to challenge students and make them think. While this method sometimes can be frustrating and even infuriating, on the whole it is an exceptional way to learn. The process works because the B School attracts top professors and students.

There are approximately sixteen hundred full-time students at HBS. Harvard's philosophy is that B School is a way of life, not to be confused with other priorities; therefore there are no part-time programs. The average age of B School students is twenty-six, and the work experiences and backgrounds are widely varied, though the Ivy League is abundantly represented. The geographic composition is diverse, but slightly skewed to the Northeast. Approximately 25 percent of the class are international students.

« *When I learned that one of my classmates had worked with a dance company, I looked forward to talking to her about the arts, but I wasn't sure how she would contribute to our business discussions. As it turned out, not only was she an excellent student, but she contributed enormously to our understanding of managing creativity! And the international diversity was a blessing, too. With sixteen countries represented in our section, we were a mini-United Nations, with each individual offering the insight and perspective of his or her own culture. Our many discussions on Japanese business practice would not have been the same without the point-counterpoint provided by Jiro and Kanoko. Jiro would brilliantly contribute to our understanding of Just In Time (JIT) manufacturing, the Japanese distribution system, and lifetime employment practices from the viewpoint of an empowered man who had worked for an international Japanese firm. At the end of his comments, he'd have the class eating out of his hand, only to be countered by Kanoko, a Japanese woman who clearly saw the advantages of the American system of market-based movement of labor and capital. By the end of the class, we'd all gained invaluable insight into the pluses and minuses of Japanese culture and business techniques.* »

Regardless of the students' backgrounds, all are bright and talented. A casual conversation with B School students generally reveals something unique about each individual. As a rule, HBS students are energetic, articulate self-starters and have a wide range of interests.

The B School campus and the city of Boston are well equipped to accommodate this demanding group. The Harvard Business School overlooks the south side of the Charles River directly across from Harvard Square, the epicenter of the Harvard University community. The B School campus is self-contained in a rough rectangle of ivy-covered buildings. Baker Library, which houses the largest collection of business literature in the world, is at the center of the campus. The campus grounds are immaculate, especially when the Boston weather cooperates. Falling leaves seem to be collected in the fall before they hit the ground.

Harvard has a reputation for being arrogant, intensely competitive, and all-consuming. That representation is fair. But at the same time, Harvard pushes students to achievements beyond their expectations. As a result, almost no one who has graduated from HBS regrets the experience.

GETTING IN

COMPETITION for admittance to Harvard is fierce. More than six thousand applications from all over the world are received for the eight hundred available spots. There are no quotas at Harvard. Typically, though, women have made up approximately 30 percent of the entering class, minorities 15 percent, and international students 25 percent.

The Harvard admissions brochure says that "excellent top management potential [is] the only absolute admissions criterion." However, three primary factors are considered by the Admissions Committee: intellectual ability, leadership and management potential, and personal characteristics.

HBS changed its evaluation process recently. It no longer requires, or even considers, GMAT scores in making decisions. The change in criteria was explained as an effort to diversify the student body and to identify more accurately other factors leading to postgraduate success. Evaluation is made on the basis of the application, references from former professors and business associates, and, increasingly, on the interview. But the core of the process remains the written application for admission.

Of all the business schools' applications, Harvard's is one of the longest and most difficult. It gives the aspiring student the opportunity to express himself or herself on a variety of topics, including evidence of ability to perform academically at HBS, the handling of an ethical issue, demonstration of creative thinking, rationale for pursuing graduate education in business, and a strength-and-weakness assessment. A basic axiom for success in completing the application is that you must find a way to differentiate yourself from and position yourself in the crowd. It might be said that those who enter HBS should be exempted from Marketing, since they have already successfully demonstrated positioning and differentiation skills on the application.

Another important factor in getting into HBS is the quality of references. Harvard is interested in knowing what others think about the quality and character of your academic and professional work. The number of required references has grown over the last few years, indicating their rising importance in the admissions decision. References are required from business associates and from former professors. Central to the references are an assessment of the applicant's leadership ability, ethical behavior, and intellectual capacity.

The interview has recently been added as an assessment tool at HBS. With more than six thousand applications every year, accepting petitions for and even encouraging interviews was a major decision for the school. Formerly, an interview was nearly impossible to obtain.

« *Almost everyone who applies to the B School has excellent academic credentials, good references, and superior potential for success in business. What I found exceptional about my classmates at HBS was their versatility. Almost every individual was exceptional in fields outside academics and business. The fields of music, athletics, public service, drama, religion, philanthropy, and the military were well represented. The better I got to know my classmates, the more appreciation I had for this. Casual conversation turned up the most unusual facts. In my section alone, we had a nuclear submarine commander, an Olympic skier, a rodeo champion, a professional dancer, a NATO captain, and several published authors. The cocktail chatter at the B School is superb, because everyone has a fascinating story to tell.* »

ACADEMIC ENVIRONMENT

HARVARD'S academic objective is to train general managers. The first-year curriculum at Harvard is the same for all students because the school wants to ensure that graduates are well rounded in the basics of general management. While students may specialize in certain areas in the second year, there are no majors at HBS. The school believes that its graduates must be capable of managing a broad variety of functions in different environments. To that end, the cases in the areas such as marketing, sales, finance, etc., generally have cross-references to issues of interest to the general manager.

The first-semester schedule consists of the following courses, plus a two-week introduction to the principles of accounting: Marketing, Managerial Economics, Organizational Behavior, Management Communications, Production Operations Management, and a required nine-session ethics module.

Marketing is generally perceived as a training course for the case method. The HBS philosophy of marketing is that you must identify and focus on the needs of the buyer, or, as described in HBS jargon, the "decision-making unit." Only after the true buyers are identified and analyzed can an effective marketing plan be assembled. Cold-call openings are particularly tough in this class and often last twenty to thirty minutes. If you get the opportunity to open, you will get the added pleasure of having eighty-nine bright students defend or attack your position. The only defense against a cold call in Marketing is thorough preparation. The cases in Marketing cover the basics of consumer, as well as industrial, marketing. After first-year Marketing, the five P's (price, place, promotion, product, packages) and four C's (channel, consumer, competition, cost) will be indelibly burned into your brain.

Managerial Economics (ME) deals with quantitative methods of decision making that will be particularly important to the general manager. The concepts of time value of money, net present value, and internal rate of return are introduced in the context of business cases in which quantitative analysis is the key to a good business decision. Decision trees, risk preference assessment, regression analysis, forecasting, and linear programming are the tools learned in ME. The less quantitatively oriented students often find this the most difficult course at HBS, particularly if their prior education or job experience has not touched on the topics. Selling your ideas is a critical skill at HBS, but you won't find much opportunity to sell in ME, since it is one of the few courses where there are right and wrong answers.

Organizational Behavior (OB) deals with the dynamics of interpersonal relationships in business and focuses attention on techniques for managing individuals and small groups. Situation analysis gives students practice in separating emotional issues from substantive business issues and dealing with each appropriately. While many students think OB is too "touchy-feely," visiting lecturers, recruiters, and former HBS students frequently say OB is the most valuable course at HBS, since it provides training in dealing with the human side of general management. One particular case drove home the point that real people were behind the cases we discussed.

« *Gene Harms, CEO of Henry Manufacturing, has decided to fire a key employee. The class is discussing the merits of the decision, and I get a chance at some quality "airtime." In the middle of my vituperative attack on the decision, into the classroom walks Gene Harms himself. With a cold stare he walks directly over to me and says, "Suppose you tell me just exactly what you would have done?" The class roars with laughter as I apologize for my response but then continue to let him have it with both barrels!* »

Management Communications (MC) is the "weekend buster" at HBS. Short papers are assigned nearly every weekend in the first semester for MC. Aside from ruining beautiful fall weekends in New England, this course is designed to improve students' communication skills and provide practice in writing on sensitive issues such as plant closings, firings, questionable ethical practices by employees, and consumer lawsuits.

Production Operations Management (POM) begins as a highly quantitative exploration of production systems and the ways to measure efficiencies and the quality of a production process. Students analyze steel-mill processes as well as McDonald's and Benihana's food production processes. After giving students a firm grounding in the basics of the production process, POM turns to the larger issues of operations strategy, such as plant location, make-versus-buy decisions, and the effects of innovative human resource management techniques in the operations arena. Some background in operations is especially helpful in the first few weeks of POM, and it becomes immediately obvious which students have this. In one brief comment, the "POM gods" (those students already proficient in operations) can unleash a withering array of terms that will send the uninitiated running for an operations glossary.

« *When I arrived at HBS, I didn't know throughput from cycle time. Neither did a number of my classmates. The first step in POM was to understand the various types of production: job shop, batch, assembly line, stall build, etc. The professor used a simple example to distinguish assembly line production from a job shop. Two teams of four were chosen. Each team was to take plain sheets of paper, fold them in thirds, place in envelopes, seal and stamp them. One team formed an assembly line, the other formed a job shop, where each individual performed all four operations on his or her own. After ten minutes, the assembly line team had produced 30 percent more work than the job shop. I was beginning to understand POM, I thought. To my amazement, the assignment that night was to analyze the production system of Texas Instruments' digital watch factory and find the bottleneck, calculate throughput, cycle time, and inventory tied up in buffer stock. Even the operations experts were baffled by the case. Such is the nature of academics at HBS. There is no introduction. You dive right in.* »

There are other required courses at HBS, including Finance, Human Resource Management, Management Policy and Practice, Control, and Management Information Systems. These can be tough courses, too, but because they fall in the second semester or the first semester of the second year, students are better prepared — having survived the first semester.

Stories abound about the cutthroat nature of competition at Harvard. Competition is certainly built into the grading system and into the case method, but the competitive element is hardly more pronounced than in the business world itself. The quality of a student's HBS experience will be determined by how well the individual deals with the pressure that does exist.

HBS students spend thirteen to eighteen hours a day in class or in preparation during the first year — a heavy work load. Classes begin at 8:30 in the morning and go until 2:20 in the afternoon three days a week, and until noon two days a week.

The grading process generates the majority of the hype regarding the competition at the Business School, primarily because it operates under the forced curve principle. Grading is by category: I, II, III, IIII. No pejoratives or accolades are specifically attached to the grades, but students know the marks in the vernacular. The highest grade (I) is considered excellent, called an "E." II is satisfactory, a "Sat"; III is a low pass, universally known as the "Loop"; and IIII is unsatisfactory.

I is given to the top 10 to 15 percent in each course. The middle 70 to 80 percent of students get II's, or Sat's, and the lowest 10 to 15 percent receive III's. The IIII is a rarity, as it implies behavior clearly disruptive to the learning process of other students. Generally, class participation counts for 30 to 50 percent of the course grade, with the rest based on exams and projects.

The quest for First Year Honors enhances the competition at HBS. Many of the top 10 to 15 percent of students are pushing toward this goal, for it not only represents worthwhile achievement in its own right, it also draws the attention of most of the highest-paying summer job recruiters, especially consulting firms. The letters start pouring in to Honors students from McKinsey, Booz Allen Hamilton, Bain, Boston Consulting Group, and others. Everyone else has a chance at these jobs as well, of course, but the Honors students are particularly sought after.

« *Students at HBS are terribly concerned about grades. While it is always mathematically possible to flunk out, about 97 percent don't. In my section a couple of students "hit the screen" (i.e., had to appear before an academic review committee), but only one had to leave school. I remember a sectionmate who looped two courses in the first semester, only to finish one point shy of First Year Honors. For those out of the Honors race, the oft-repeated phrase "Sat is where it's at" sums up the quest for grades.* »

For those having trouble in any first-year course, tutors are available, and, if you have the discipline to prepare your work every night, you can get through Harvard without much fear of failing. An easy way to make certain that you are keeping up with your work is to join a study group early in the first semester. A study group will usually meet the night or morning before classes. It provides an excellent opportunity to check your understanding of a case's vital points (before exposing your ideas to eighty or so people in class), or to get clarification on a thorny issue. Besides, study groups are a great way to make friends.

SOCIAL LIFE

HBS students play as hard as they work. And there is plenty of opportunity for fun both on and off campus. The abundant gala social events, New England sojourns, bar bashes, sun basking on Baker Beach (as the lawn outside the library is called), and intramural athletics put the classroom back into perspective and are essential to a high-quality HBS experience. Much of the value of a degree from Harvard is in the friendships and contacts you make, so anyone pursuing graduate education at Harvard should tackle its extracurricular aspects with academic fervor.

The best of the social events sponsored by the various school clubs are imaginative affairs reflective of the high energy of their creators. The granddaddy of them all is the Booze Cruise, sponsored by the European Club. This late-September formal affair is a blessing to the first-years, who will need a break after a month of the worst HBS has to offer, and an opportunity for second-years to relish the excesses that lasting friendships and second-year status afford.

« *During the first few weeks at HBS, you can cut the tension with a knife. By late September, everyone needs the Booze Cruise, a four-hour cruise into the Atlantic during which everyone lets their hair down. Thirty minutes into the cruise, I looked over to the bar and saw a guy who had come from Salomon Brothers, whom I had thought to be a real stuffed shirt, challenging all comers to a beer chug. Half the crowd took him up on it! I met two of my best friends from the B School chugging that night. By the time the ship returned to harbor, the decks were a fantastic wasteland of boozed-up, danced-out bodies. Thankfully, there were buses waiting to take us back to campus.* »

The Ibero-American Club sponsors the annual Halloween costume party, guaranteed to produce outfits that must be seen to be believed. I particularly remember three blind mice, Conan the Barbarian, and a six-person Chinese dragon. Learning to mambo is de rigueur if you can shake your costume long enough to dance to the steel band.

The Australasian Club produces one of the best and biggest parties of the year, with the support of Australian-backed companies such as Swan Lager and Qantas Airways. Dress for the evening is strictly formal unless you have proper Aussie "bush" attire or the odd koala or kangaroo outfit about the house. Dancing is the thing to do at the Holidazzle.

The Newport Ball graduation celebration takes place in one of Newport, Rhode Island's, poshest testaments to the rewards of capitalism. The Great Gatsby–like setting, dinner and dancing under the stars, and the prospect of graduation conspire to make this the only suitable close to the HBS experience.

Back out of the black tie, intramural athletics are alive and well at HBS. Almost every section fields more than one women's and men's team in basketball, touch football, soccer, softball, volleyball, and more. Intramural basketball was one of the best ways to meet students from other sections. We had three men's teams from our section alone and pickup games at the Cage (part of the athletic facility) on Saturdays or after class. Though the Section C teams were of varying skill levels, everyone had a good time and could be counted on to give 100 percent.

Running is a major pastime at HBS, and the banks of the Charles are packed with devotees even in the worst weather. Aerobics, dance, film, and gourmet-cooking classes are other popular distractions and are taught by students at the B School. Fortunately, working out is better than ever at HBS thanks to the new health and sports facility just completed. I'm told that this facility rivals any club in the country.

Burning the candle at both ends is an art form at HBS, and the many diversions available in Greater Boston test this skill to the max. Boston is a fascinating cornucopia of neighborhoods with varying personalities. Whether your taste is Bohemian or Fifth Avenue, you will find a district catering to your dining, shopping, or strolling pleasure. Public transportation extends to the Business School campus, so getting around Boston is easy by train or bus. However, the best way to experience Boston is on foot. Start with the Freedom Trail, which meanders past the most notable sites of Boston's colonial and revolutionary history; or try Faneuil Hall, a bustling food and shopping emporium in the heart of old Boston.

Cambridge is a ten-minute walk across the Charles to Harvard Square, a standby for HBS students. Cambridge offers endless opportunities for eclectic shopping, eating, and drinking. A highly revered skill at the Business School is to unearth a restaurant or pub unknown to fellow students. Because every nook and cranny in Cambridge is packed with some commercial or academic enterprise, learning the landscape is a fascinating education in itself.

Boston is also blessed with splendid proximity to ocean and mountains. For the HBS student, this means spring visits to historic Marblehead, Cape Cod, Nantucket, and Maine. Winter skiing is only a few hours away at Stratton, Bromley, Killington, and other resorts.

« Nearly every year, each HBS section will rent a place on the slopes so that the entire section may ski at will. Mike Roos negotiated a great condominium for us at Stratton, just a couple of hours from the B School, where we could jump off the slopes into the sauna. During these excursions away from school, my section friends and I discussed our career goals and plans for the future. A couple of small businesses and investment partnerships were created during these trips. So much for smoke-filled rooms! »

Beyond the spectacle of the gala parties, road trips, and sporting events are the more frequent gatherings at the Pub, HBS's on-campus watering hole now housed in the new athletic facility. Even the heartiest of drinkers have been felled by the drinking games played there. But the Pub is a fine place to hang out on campus whether or not you imbibe. It is the launch pad for excursions to anywhere for any reason, but especially for the impromptu jaunt to Cambridge.

Between all the studying, classes, skiing, touring, interviewing, exercising, and partying, many HBS students contribute to the community in some fashion. The HBS faculty is especially supportive of these activities, so if you have a charitable bent, you will be encouraged at HBS. Regular projects include Project Outreach, Red Cross blood drives, Heart Fund and American Cancer Society walkathons, and even a summer bicycle trip across America to raise funds for the March of Dimes.

More students are single than married at Harvard, but the Partners Club (for spouses and significant others) makes up in enthusiasm what it lacks in numbers. The Partners Club holds regular section and neighborhood cookouts, dances, wine tastings, New England excursions, and other events. It strives to provide members with the opportunity to share the HBS experience as fully as possible. The Partners Club is probably the best way to meet other couples, hence most spouses and significant others are members. Because so many school activities necessarily exclude partners, and the school can be so engrossing, the Partners Club fills an important need at HBS. Almost without exception, the spouses of HBS students are exceptional. One particularly memorable Thanksgiving Day dinner was hosted by a Louisiana couple that my wife and I met through Partners. Burt and Jody worked for days on an incredible Thanksgiving dinner that included a Cajun recipe known as turducken. This was a large turkey, stuffed with roasted, boneless duck, which was in turn stuffed with chicken and an oyster dressing. At an Easter party hosted by a Partners couple, the guests had to decipher a code and hunt for clues all over campus in order to find their specially hidden Easter egg. All the while sporting hand-sewn rabbit ears! Such was the creativity and positive energy of the Partners Club.

Affordable housing near HBS is difficult to find, so most single students spend at least the first year in the HBS dorms. These on-campus cracker boxes command Manhattan rates, but it's hard to beat the convenience and social life they provide.

In addition to the dorms, there are a number of Harvard-owned freestanding and multiunit apartment buildings on campus and nearby. It takes time to find a place, so if you choose to live off campus, start the search early. The best place to start looking is at the Harvard Housing Office, which is a clearinghouse of sorts for housing in the Cambridge area. They have listings of apartment vacancies and houses for sale. Most units are listed by individuals or brokers, but Harvard University does own over 2,300 apartments in Cambridge. About 1,600 of these are reserved for students and faculty, and the others are open to everyone. It's particularly difficult, if not impossible, to get the "open" apartments for which there is a long waiting list because they are rent-controlled, thus offering the very best values in town. To give you a sense of the housing challenge, approximately 40,000 people visit the housing office in any given year seeking the 1,600 reserved Harvard housing units.

Despite the seemingly difficult odds, it is not impossible to find a place near HBS. If you can afford the rents, the Soldiers Field Park complex is a popular B School property. It's a one-minute walk from Aldrich Hall (home of all first-year classes), and offers modern conveniences, secured parking, and some excellent views of the campus. Monthly rents start at about $900 for a one-bedroom and top out at about $1,500 for the three-bedroom units.

Across the Charles River in Cambridge are a number of popular addresses. Peabody Terrace is a fifteen-minute walk from class, less expensive than Soldiers Field Park, and relatively close to Harvard Square. The two-story brick residences on Shaler Lane are a quiet, competitively priced alternative to the apartment buildings. Shaler Lane apartments are a fifteen-minute walk from HBS and offer great fireplaces, perfect for the long Boston winter!

« *Thankfully, having fun in Boston doesn't require a car. Because Boston and Cambridge are so densely populated, it is likely that you can find housing within a short walk or bus ride away from the Business School. Parking is incredibly scarce and expensive in the Boston area, so a car can be as much a hassle as a blessing. Most students are happy to do car pooling for those occasions when the "T" (bus and subway) or walking won't do.* »

RECRUITING AND JOB SEARCH

IF job hunting were a religion, HBS would be a cathedral. No place attracts more companies or commands more attention than HBS during recruiting season.

Beginning in February of the first year, the investment banks, consulting firms, and multinational corporations descend on HBS in a flurry. The limos and shrimp dinners provided by the recruiters come fast and furious, and testify to the value of the HBS experience in the marketplace. But this is only the warm-up to the main event in second year!

The first few hectic weekends spent interviewing first year produce summer opportunities for a select few and an education in interviewing skills for everyone else. In a word, the process is competitive, and everyone gets "dinged" (HBS vernacular for being turned down) from a company or three.

The most lucrative and sought-after summer jobs are typically in consulting, investment banking, venture capital, brand management, and real estate. While these are also popular full-time career choices, they are particularly attractive as summer jobs, as quite a few students want this opportunity to experiment in these fields.

Companies will usually interview at least ten students for every summer job, and the investment banks and consulting firms probably interview twice that number. Getting an interview may require an invitation from the company, in which case you will need to write a note to the recruiting personnel extolling your virtues. Other times, companies will have open schedules, which means you can simply sign up for an interview in the Career Resource Center. The first round of interviews generally takes place on campus or in one of the nearby hotels. Interviews range all over the map in terms of their intensity and duration.

« *Investment banking and consulting interviews are known to be the toughest. They often severely test composure, analytical skills, and industry knowledge. A friend was in the final round of interviews for summer positions at a well-known investment bank in New York. A particularly feisty interviewer asked him one question, interrupted on his third word, and then gave him the silent treatment for two or three minutes. Having been exposed to this unnerving tactic once before, my friend simply stared back at the interviewer, waiting for his next move. Finally, the interviewer cracked a joke about how tough you had to be in sales and trading, stood up, and extended his hand to end the interview. Having interviewed with this company three times already, my friend was not going to let the interview end like that. It was only when he confronted the interviewer with a last-minute pitch on why his company should hire him that the conversation began in earnest. Two weeks later, the company offered my friend a job. Later that summer the interviewer told my friend that he had been asked to test his nerve in the interview. There are hundreds of similar stories about bizarre interviews at HBS.* »

Happily, almost everyone who wants a summer job gets one. The summer is especially fruitful, since pay scales for summer work are generally the same as those for full-time jobs. Most of the companies help students find housing.

The full-time job search for second-years officially begins in January. Starting in February, classes are not held on Fridays to allow students to interview and do job research at will. The job search, though, is a focal point of the entire second year. The average student's food bill drops dramatically as the shrimp wars at the Charles Hotel, a favored interviewing site, begin.

Where HBS students ultimately land employment is largely determined by market conditions. Consulting is the profession of choice for 24 percent of HBS graduates. This is due primarily to the high starting salaries of $70,000 to $80,000. In the postcrash, post-Boesky era (after October 1987), the number of HBS students entering investment banking jobs has declined dramatically, particularly in sales and trading. Still, approximately 15 percent of graduates flock to Wall Street at base salaries starting above $50,000 for sales and trading (where commissions and bonus can triple base salary) to $80,000 or more for mergers and acquisitions. Venture capital, brand management, commercial banking, and manufacturing round out the largest categories. Change may be in the wind, however. Small business, waste management, and arts and entertainment are garnering a surprising number of students.

The Career Resources Center offers the HBS student every opportunity to find the perfect job. It contains files on more than two thousand companies, industry packets on different fields, and core data about industries. A valuable tool is the career advisory service, a list of more than twenty-six thousand alumni/alumnae who have volunteered to discuss industry and company issues with students. In addition, Baker Library has a broad array of statistics on most cities, describing the cost of living, housing availability, major industry, cultural variety, and so forth.

« Making an intelligent choice of an industry and a few companies to focus on is a difficult process for many students. It certainly was for me. After spending the summer on Wall Street, I was certain that there were a number of industries I wanted to work in at some point. Which one to start in was the tough question. I interviewed

with so many companies and flew so many miles that the Harbus
News *listed my frequent-flier account as a contingent liability for
Delta Airlines!* »

In the end, most students land four or five solid offers. Negotiating
and weighing the offers are tough. Generally, the money is good;
often it's incredible. Because most students coming out of school
have sizable debt, immediate cash flow looms large in the decision-
making process. Job responsibility, geography, and quality of life
probably follow in the hierarchy.

There is always a trade-off. Many jobs for those just out of HBS
require seventy- to eighty-hour weeks and heavy travel. On the
whole, however, the Harvard B School degree provides access to
better jobs, at higher salaries, than other schools' degrees.

ON THE JOB — FIRST YEARS OUT

ADDING value in the marketplace is the name of the game in business, and there is no question that HBS gives students the tools to
add value in almost any company. Essentially, the schooling at
Harvard packs several years of high-level business experience into
two. But, more important, it provides the student with broad exposure to the functional areas of business and with a set of tools and the
framework to help structure decision making. Of particular long-
term importance is Harvard's recognized ability to produce especially capable general managers. And due to their understanding of
the structure of a variety of industries throughout the world and how
they fit into the global economy, HBS students are well prepared to
adapt to change.

If the HBS tools are applied properly, the degree is an enormous
advantage on the job. The work habits developed at Harvard are a
real asset, and the self-confidence that comes with the degree is also
important. But HBS graduates, like everyone else, have to earn their
stripes.

The new MBA can expect to be under sizable pressure in the first
year or two out. Companies generally expect you to hang the moon
while you're learning the business and paying your dues. It can be
a tough assignment.

Some employers complain that Harvard graduates want to "run the company before they learn the business." There is probably an element of truth in that, since HBS graduates have just spent two years being trained to run companies. And the recruiters have done nothing to dispel the myth that you will be given wide responsibility immediately on their way to hiring you. For this reason, there can be a mismatch between expectations and reality once on the job. This is the root of the universal criticism that MBAs switch jobs too often. Another reason Harvard MBAs switch jobs is because they can. Graduates are highly marketable. Money is not the primary reason B School grads switch jobs, but it is a contributing factor. In a survey of a recent class, students ranked salary below job content, responsibility, and opportunity for advancement as the primary criteria for choosing a job.

Harvard graduates are a demanding lot. When they don't see what they expected or were promised, they don't let much grass grow underfoot. Consequently, the real world can be a letdown if the new graduate has not managed expectations carefully, or if the company became overzealous in the recruiting process.

Still, most HBS graduates believe that they have an advantage over non-MBAs in the first years out. First of all, the salaries are definitely higher. More important, the vast majority of business concepts likely to be encountered are at least familiar to HBS grads, and the primary skills of risk analysis, financial analysis, and strategy development are highly developed. The ability to make data "talk" seems to be a skill especially valued by employers. Whenever there are data that need to be turned into useful information and actionable steps, MBAs tend to get the task. Being aware of this beforehand, Harvard MBAs tend to drift toward jobs requiring strong analytical skills and industries undergoing rapid change, where creativity is at a premium.

Since HBS is one of the largest and oldest business schools, its alumni/alumnae are widely dispersed into almost every major U.S. corporation. There is a special bond among HBS graduates that transcends generations and makes the network very powerful.

« *A friend who graduated a couple of years ago experienced the value of this network firsthand. As she said: "They always talk about the HBS network. When you think about it, it is probably one of the most powerful organizations around, based on the accomplishments of its members. But I never really believed in the system until I called on it for help. I developed a plan to start my own business and needed capital to get it off the ground. The banks wouldn't touch my plan, so I sent some of my HBS friends a prospectus on the business in the hope that they would invest. Well, one phone call led to another, and within a couple of months, all of the capital was raised."* »

SUMMARY OVERVIEW

THE Harvard University Graduate School of Business Administration sets the standards by which all other business schools are judged. It has developed the school's reputation by producing more business leaders than any other business school. In fact, 19 percent of the top three officers in the Fortune 500 companies are HBS graduates. Harvard strives to produce graduates prepared to lead companies as general managers.

The case method is the engine that drives the learning process at HBS. The process depends upon extensive daily preparation of case material and the students' willingness to take a position on the issues in the case and defend them aloud in class. This process develops exceptional oral presentation skills, good work habits, and strong analytical skills. HBS graduates are trained to think carefully, decide quickly, and then act. They also become particularly well suited for entrepreneurial endeavors, since unconventional thinking is encouraged.

HBS is both highly competitive and supportive at the same time. The case method fosters competition by design, since students must defend their points of view in class. The grading system at HBS contributes to the competitive atmosphere, too, because the forced curve mandates that 10 percent of the students in each course receive less than satisfactory grades. Fewer than 3 percent of students are actually forced to leave school because of low grades, and students and faculty are readily available for tutoring. Study groups are an important support mechanism that is strongly encouraged by the faculty. Because you live HBS every waking moment while you're there, classmates become the closest of friends, many for life.

Nothing at the Business School is halfhearted, especially not social life. The school provides a full calendar of social activities throughout the year. There are more than twenty-five active clubs at the B School and dozens of intramural athletic teams. In addition, Boston, Cambridge, and the New England area offer an unending variety of worthwhile diversions from studying.

The HBS degree is highly valued by employers. Over five hundred companies actively recruit at Harvard, and graduates can expect significantly higher salaries as a result of obtaining the degree. The average graduate chooses outstanding career opportunities from among five or more offers.

There are, however, some drawbacks to the program. The work load is onerous, with twelve to sixteen hours a day for the first year. A great deal of stamina is required to complete the program, since preparation is required every day and the pace is relentless.

Harvard is often accused of being too pressure-packed. Some students, in fact, do not learn as well in this high-pressure environment. The pressure of HBS is both self-generated by students' desire to achieve and inherent in some structural elements of the program, especially the case method and the grading system. Nevertheless, by the second year, you almost never hear this complaint from students.

Another criticism concerns the curriculum's being primarily based on individual rather than group activities. Graduates often point out that group process skills are just as important as individual skills in the marketplace, and that Harvard would do well to build more group work into the program. Harvard has been struggling to address this issue over the past few years.

Finally, people interested in specialization during business school should not choose HBS, since Harvard's general management emphasis may not allow for the optimal amount of depth on any particular subject. Quite frankly, Harvard does not train functional specialists or technicians.

Still, all in all, HBS is in a class by itself. It is an all-consuming experience unique among graduate schools of business. The vast majority of graduates believe that the experience is definitely worth the effort it took to get it. From an educational, social, and certainly from a financial perspective, the Harvard MBA provides far greater rewards than the two years spent earning the degree.

Chapter 5

KELLOGG GRADUATE SCHOOL OF MANAGEMENT (NORTHWESTERN UNIVERSITY)*

THE PROGRAM

« *Each of the top business schools has, rightly or wrongly, a reputation that seems inextricably wound around one particular field of study or method of teaching. And each school will argue that, reputation aside, its program is strong in a variety of areas. So there I was at the Business School Olympics (an annual event at which students from seven top business schools gather for a weekend of primarily social frivolity and networking that tries to masquerade as a serious conference by presenting a dinner speaker of some import and prestige); everyone was trying as hard as they could to dispel their own program's stereotyped image. At a party on the last night, a group from Wharton entertained us with an impromptu staging of a skit from their Follies. The skit was based on Star Trek and found the crew of the Enterprise racing to the far corners of the galaxy to investigate abnormal beta variances on the planet Arbitraggia. It was a finhead's dream. What made the skit funnier for the Kellogg students was that we were finishing up rehearsals for the Special K Revue, and our show included a Star Trek skit as well. But instead of having a financial twist, ours focused on giving the crew of the Enterprise a workable mission statement — defining a successful niche instead of simply boldly going where no man . . . It was a skit*

* BY SANDY ZUSMANN, MBA, AND JULIE SELL, MBA

based on barriers to entry and competitive advantage. It was, in short, a marketing approach with a dash of management policy thrown in for good measure. In addition, our ship went to the far reaches of the galaxy reflective of Kellogg's international bent. Naturally, we thought our skit was far funnier than the finance version, but we realized that, all talking aside, our way of thinking had been shaped by our environment, and at Kellogg that environment was marketing-driven. »

Unless you've been avoiding the business press assiduously for the past several years, you know that both the *Wall Street Journal* and *Business Week* have separately bestowed upon the J. L. Kellogg Graduate School of Management the distinction of being the best business school in the country. The news immediately gave rise to a booming cottage T-shirt industry in Kellogg's hometown of Evanston, Illinois, proving once again that students at Kellogg know a good marketing opportunity when they see one. Although schools on both coasts decried the surveys' methodology and results, make no mistake about it, Kellogg has earned the right to be considered one of the top business schools in America.

So what is it that has put Kellogg in a league with the nation's traditional business school powerhouses? How has this affected getting into Kellogg? How has this affected getting out of Kellogg and into the job of your dreams?

Things at Kellogg may have changed more in the past several years, since the school first attained a top ranking, than in the past. The spotlight is on Kellogg, and a conscious effort is being made to keep improving. Alumni or alumnae who graduated just a few years ago might find some things fairly different about today's school than the one they attended. For instance, Kellogg is still best known for its marketing program, but its growing reputation in other fields means that more current students are aspiring consultants or financial wizards than aspiring brand managers. The increasing emphasis on being "international" is evident in the variety of accents and languages heard in Leverone Hall. The huge increase in applications makes gaining admission much more competitive than it used to be. There has been some tinkering with the grading policy. And even the physical space is changing: Kellogg has outgrown its current home and is planning a major expansion over the next few years.

Something that hasn't changed about Kellogg — and this still differentiates it from the competition — is the emphasis on teamwork. The school has been lauded for producing managers who are team players. At Kellogg everything, it seems, is done in groups.

The team concept arises even before orientation formally begins. Incoming students have the option of going on preorientation trips, known as Outdoor Adventures, that involve activities ranging from backpacking to canoeing to bicycle touring. The trips, designed to emphasize the teamwork philosophy, take groups of ten to fourteen students to destinations such as Alaska, Mexico, Wyoming, and the Upper Peninsula of Michigan.

For those who don't do preorientation, first exposure to group activity comes immediately at the outset of the orientation program, Conceptual Issues in Management (referred to by everyone as CIM Week), which is designed primarily to establish the teamwork dynamic that is so fundamental to the Kellogg experience. During CIM Week, the entering class of approximately five hundred students is divided into sections of about sixty people and then subdivided into groups of five to seven.

Like most other orientation programs, CIM Week is littered with department heads appearing, in what often seems like an endless procession, to extol the virtues of their various disciplines. The deans all say a few words, the most chilling of which is the reminder that even though "you are the strongest class ever to enter Kellogg," half of you will be in the bottom of your class. Students often find it gets harder to stay awake during these morning presentations as CIM Week goes on, since there is also plenty of socializing at night. After all, this is the week to meet as many classmates as possible before the real work begins.

A series of high-profile speakers from business and the nonprofit sector add a "real world" perspective to CIM week. Executive speakers in the past couple of years have addressed issues ranging from quality to managing diversity. In addition, each section has the opportunity to interact in smaller groups with one or two members of Kellogg's Advisory Board. The board members, who represent a cross section of industries, spend a morning discussing management issues with students.

One of the highlights of CIM Week is the CIM Game, a computer simulation in which teams of three to five students (the group thing again) try to dominate a hypothetical industry across several hypothetical markets. The game starts innocently enough and proceeds at the rate of one strategic decision per day. By day three, the competition begins to accelerate. As with all aspects of the School of Management, some people take the game more seriously than others, but the game generally ranks as one of the week's favorite activities.

Students are assigned to sections at the outset of the program, and the sections stay together through the fall quarter, taking the first four core classes together. After the fall quarter, students pick and choose the order in which they take the remaining core classes, and the sections disintegrate, to be reunited (voluntarily) only for "reunion" parties, intramural teams, and competitions with the University of Chicago Graduate School of Business.

There are advantages and disadvantages to this initial section format. On the plus side, you become very well acquainted with this group of people. And the sections are anything but homogeneous.

« *I figured that my classmates would be people like myself, with two or three years of experience in a bank training program or a brand training program. But on the first day of CIM Week, they had each of us in the section stand up and tell where we had gone to school, the degree we had received, and what we had done for a living for the past year. Instead of a room full of econ majors and brokerage house escapees, our section included a former philosophy major who had spent ten years in the army, including a stint as a company commander in Korea; a woman from Taiwan with public relations experience; our Hispanic-American group member was a former bank examiner; and a Japanese man was sent to Kellogg by his employer, a major truck manufacturer. Needless to say, we all brought very different perspectives to the case discussions.* »

On the downside, you have each of the fall quarter classes with the same group of people, and that often translates into having the same study group for more than one class. If the dynamics of a study group go bad, the impact may ripple out and affect more than one of your classes. Also on the downside, the section system forces you to make an effort if you want to meet people in other sections during the fall quarter. There is little mixing of sections until the winter quarter.

Kellogg offers both a two-year, six-quarter program and a one-year, four-quarter program. Students accepted into the four-quarter program have worked for several years and are proficient enough in Marketing and Finance to exempt those core courses. Kellogg has also introduced a Master of Management in Manufacturing program, which involves a mixture of management and engineering courses. The MMM program has been very well received by industry and has gained recognition among corporate recruiters.

Given their abbreviated time at Kellogg, four-quarter students are required to take only four core courses in lieu of the usual nine. They begin in the summer and spend their first quarter taking courses in Economic Analysis, Management of Processing Systems, Management Policy, and Decision Sciences.

In contrast, six-quarter students are required to take introductory core courses in Organizational Behavior, Marketing, Finance, Management Policy, Financial Accounting, Managerial Economics, Operations, and two courses in Decision Sciences. There can be some variation in these core courses, depending upon student experience.

Kellogg offers intensive introductory courses in some disciplines, which cover two quarters' worth of material in one quarter. The work load in the intensive introductory finance course, known to students as Turbo-Fin, is almost legendary. This course is generally taught by the most highly regarded members of the Finance Department. Courses in Ethics and Diversity also are offered, and the school includes chaired professors in those fields among its forty-two chaired faculty members.

One interesting note about the core classes: both four- and six-quarter students are required to take a course in Management Policy. Other B schools reserve this course for the second year as a capstone to their programs. At Kellogg, Management Policy is required during the first quarter as an introduction to the methods and thought processes that will be needed over the course of your two business school years.

From a financial standpoint, a clear advantage of the four-quarter program is that it virtually halves the cost of getting your degree. But the savings are not without some sacrifices. With only three quarters available for electives, four-quarter students don't have as much opportunity to explore all disciplines as their six-quarter counterparts do. This is not a big problem if you know exactly what you want to do once you graduate, but it can be constricting if you lack a very specific focus. On the other hand, Kellogg looks for individuals with a specific career goal for the four-quarter program, so this mitigates the problem somewhat.

Very focused training is available at Kellogg. Students have the option of majoring in a functional area such as Marketing, Operations, Management Policy, or Managerial Economics, or in a specific industry such as Transportation, Real Estate, or Hospital and Health Services. Kellogg also offers a major in Public and Nonprofit Management, with course work covering a variety of functional disciplines viewed in light of the specific requirements and concerns of public and nonprofit entities.

The core classes tend to be among the largest you will have at Kellogg and are filled with your entire section of fifty to sixty-five people. Some of the more popular electives — Advertising Policies and Management, Real Estate Finance and Investment, Power and Politics in the Organization, and Managerial Leadership — are as large as or larger than the core classes, but these are exceptions to the rule. Most electives are taught to classes of thirty to forty-five people; in disciplines such as Organizational Behavior and Operations, the classes are often half that size.

There is intense competition for slots in the more prized electives. In the past couple of years these have included Marketing Channels; Negotiations; several of the Finance offerings; and the Communications Workshop. Kellogg has solved the problem of who gets into what course through the use of a computerized bidding system. Students are given one hundred points each quarter. The points are to be allocated among the classes each student wants to take. The student enters his or her own bids into a computer system in strictest confidence, giving fuel to a rumor network that reaches a crescendo about two breaths short of panic. Once the bids are closed, all students' bids on each class are arranged in order, from high to low. The computer scans the list and, when a class is full, cuts off everyone who bid below the clearing price. Class waiting lists are compiled based on points bid, and it is often possible to get into a class if you're near the top of the waiting list. Computerized bidding is the free market operating at its most efficient and most brutal. Most students get at least three of the courses they bid on (four courses per quarter is the standard load), but inevitably some people are less fortunate. All points bid unsuccessfully are returned to students, who then have a shot at classes with openings remaining. There are, of course, stories about the hugely popular Marketing Channels closing in the high nineties, but many classes close between the twenties and forties, and many don't close at all.

One of the most dramatic changes at Kellogg over the past few years has been the increasing focus on international business. The changes have permeated virtually every aspect of Kellogg life, from composition of the student body (the number of international students has more than doubled in the past three years) to the curriculum. In addition to offering a major in International Business, Kellogg now offers a series of country-specific international business classes. These classes are designed by teams of students who, in conjunction with a faculty sponsor, arrange the syllabus, assume responsibility for guest speakers, determine research topics, and identify key issues facing industries in the country of focus. Course work is done in the winter quarter, and students travel to the selected country for ten days to two weeks over spring break to perform group consulting projects. In the spring quarter, students complete analyses of their chosen companies/industries, and present their findings to Kellogg faculty and company representatives. Countries studied and visited in a recent year included Japan, Thailand, Chile, Argentina, Russia, Germany, Spain, and Czechoslovakia. At least ten such trips are planned for next year, with more than three hundred students expected to participate.

Independent study courses like these, as well as study groups and other student organizations, meet on Wednesdays, when no regular classes are scheduled. Rather than being a "day off," Wednesday is the busiest day of the week for many students. The midweek break seems to be much more conducive to work than the Fridays off that other business schools schedule. Of course, inevitably a few students take the opportunity to play some golf on Wednesday mornings when the weather turns warmer.

« Wednesdays seem to be the day that everyone schedules everything they can't fit in during the rest of the week. I'm often away from home from 8:00 A.M. until 11 at night, running from study group meetings to career placement workshops to job interviews. I can't remember

having a Wednesday "free" since the first week of school. But thank goodness they exist; otherwise, I don't think I could juggle it all. »

Classes at Kellogg are taught by a combination of both the case method and straight lecture. The courses in Management Policy tend to be the most case-driven, and the quantitative courses, whether in Decision Sciences, Accounting, or Marketing, generally make the least use of the case method. There's nothing unusual about that. But you will also find courses in Organizational Behavior and Marketing that use cases sparingly and courses in Finance that use them a great deal. It's a wonderfully flexible approach that allows the use of whichever teaching method gets the particular subject across better.

Some of the most interestingly structured courses are taught by the Organizational Behavior Department. The much-sought-after Negotiation class uses role-playing almost exclusively and relies heavily on cases. Organizational Structure and Design is perhaps the most punishing course on campus. Its heavy work load requires maximum group effort, but the burden is mitigated by a professor who makes it a point to attend every meeting of every study group, changing a small class into an even smaller series of seminars. Power and Politics in the Organization has featured a film festival as part of its course work and demands that each study group get involved in the community by working with a politically powerless group.

Kellogg's academic reputation was initially built on the strength of its Marketing Department. And while the overall results of the various ranking surveys may be disputed by other business schools, no one disputes the preeminence of Kellogg's Marketing Department. Students flock to the Marketing Department for both the strong academic training and the stepping-stone the major provides into brand management and advertising jobs.

The faculty boasts a number of superstars in the field, including Phillip Kotler, who literally wrote the book on marketing — and updates it just in time to destroy the resale value of your copy. The department is well respected for its research, and the school has, for a long time, climbed on the strength of that respect.

But, interestingly enough, the students have espoused a broader view of Kellogg's strengths in recent years. Each year, the students select the outstanding teacher in the school. Over the past several years, that award has been given to a Finance professor, two Organizational Behavior professors, and a member of the Management Policy Department. What the students are suggesting is not that the Marketing Department has lost its luster, but rather that other departments are gaining in stature. Also, much of the Marketing Department's strength lies in the school's Organizational Behavior Department, which is gaining in stature, as are the programs in Transportation Management and Hospital and Health Services Management. Kellogg is also known as a research leader in Game Theory, and even publishes a journal in this field. The three highest-paid faculty members are two members of the Finance Department and a professor of Accounting. Underlining the point that Kellogg is not just a marketing school is the fact that more than three quarters of recent graduates went into fields other than product management.

Like other schools, Kellogg acknowledges the concern its students have expressed over teaching quality. The school has taken several steps to ensure excellence in the classroom. Kellogg now provides a mentor program for new faculty, through which experienced faculty work closely with them on teaching skills. Every faculty member is also videotaped while teaching and provided with professional assistance to improve classroom performance. Peer reviews have been started to give faculty direct feedback from colleagues who occasionally sit in on their classes. Finally, teaching quality has become an integral component of the tenure-decision process.

So we find a Kellogg with a split personality. It has a long-standing reputation for research excellence in one field, strong teaching in several others, and a burgeoning reputation in still others. But there's one more ingredient to add to the stew: Kellogg's reputation among recruiters and corporations. While a recent *Business Week* survey reported that recruiters ranked Kellogg tops in marketing and very strong in general management, a *Wall Street Journal* survey touched on another of the program's strengths: the ability of Kellogg graduates to work in and manage groups. Kellogg appears to have recognized years ago that, while learning is traditionally a solitary task, real-world work is more often than not a group effort. The school reflects that realization in the almost obsessive attitude toward groups mentioned earlier. And obsessive or not, the attitude has paid off for Kellogg and its graduates.

GETTING IN

IT should come as no surprise that applications to Kellogg have risen dramatically in number, up almost 50 percent in the past five years. A large part of the growth is fueled, no doubt, by the surveys mentioned earlier. Growth of this magnitude would put a strain on any admissions department, but the burden is more heavily felt at Kellogg than it might be at other institutions. Why? Because Kellogg interviews every applicant. Interviews are conducted both in Evanston and by alumni/alumnae in cities around the country.

« *I was impressed to learn that Kellogg interviews all applicants. They're really interested in students as people, not just grade point averages and GMAT scores. They're looking for people who can communicate their ideas and aspirations. The interview also underlines the school's interest in team players. That's a quality that doesn't always come through on a résumé. For example, I have a friend who went through a tough physics program as an undergrad and didn't have a very high GPA. That fact alone would have knocked her out of competition at some schools. The Kellogg interview gave her a chance to demonstrate her "people" skills, which she honed while teaching science to high-school kids in Kenya. Kellogg obviously made the right choice. She really shines in class discussions and has been a leader in building team-oriented activities.* »

There is no such thing, administrators are fond of saying, as the "average" Kellogg student. It is a claim that is not unique to Kellogg. Still, there are some common characteristics in recent entering classes: GMAT scores tend to be high, as do undergraduate grades; almost everyone has previous full-time work experience (the most recent figures suggest an average of four years). Beyond those commonalities there seems to be only one varying characteristic even faintly suggestive of a quota system: undergraduate major. The most recent entering class is split almost evenly among students who majored in social sciences and humanities, business, engineering and natural sciences, and economics.

Kellogg, like virtually every other top-notch business school, is looking for exceptional individuals without regard to their gender (27 percent women in the most recent entering class), race (16 percent minority), marital status (76 percent single), or nationality (22 percent foreign). The *New York Times* recently reported that Kellogg is making a special effort to attract female applicants, and the composition of the student body has assumed an increasingly broad international flavor in the past couple of years.

Contrary to some people's perceptions, Kellogg is not just a school for Midwesterners. In fact, 52 percent of current students come from either the Northeast or the West, while only 16 percent are from the Midwest. Of the students entering in the most recent class, 94 graduated from Ivy League colleges, 36 graduated from Big 10 schools, and 209 different undergraduate institutions were represented.

The resulting mix of students is as diverse as you will find at any major business school, but a common thread unites many of them: marketing. Ask Kellogg students or graduates about the factors that lead them to select the program and a majority of them will mention the school's reputation in marketing — this despite data in *Business Week* that ranked Kellogg third among business schools for the quality of their finance graduates. Some perceptions are hard to overcome.

It's a function of Kellogg's reputation that perpetuates the reputation itself; students interested in marketing head to Kellogg because of its reputation. Subsequently, the school graduates large numbers of capable, effective, successful marketing students, who go out into the marketplace and feed the reputation of Kellogg among corporations as the place to go for marketing graduates.

Kellogg now offers applicants the opportunity to complete and submit their applications electronically. This option is being provided exclusively for the convenience of Kellogg's applicant pool, and it represents a first among top business schools.

As for the application itself, it's a pretty straightforward document — until you get to the essay questions. There are three. The first focuses on your career goals and the role Kellogg will play in achieving them. It's a question designed to probe your commitment to business school, your motive for coming, and the degree of thought you've given to both those issues. The second question asks you to talk about your most challenging work-related problem. Pretty standard stuff and a forerunner of the dreaded "What is your greatest weakness?" job-interview question.

The last question, unlike the two straightforward inquiries that preceded it, is a nebulous question sprung straight from the mind of the demon interviewer from hell: "Respond to a question of your choice." It's like asking "Why is there air?" or simply "Why?" This is the make-or-break question. You've got to figure that everyone can handle the first two pretty well. They're gimmes. But this one is like trying to nail Jell-O to a wall. It is the question that more than any other will present a clear picture of you to the application reader. And for that very reason, you're on your own. No inside dope on this question. The inside info on this one has to come from you.

And then Kellogg puts a final spin on the whole package in the form of the Admissions Committee. After you fill out your application and send it in, your efforts are read and evaluated not solely by an administrator, but also by current Kellogg students. The Admissions Committee numbers about seventy-five members, approximately two thirds of whom are students. At least two students read each application, and their comments and recommendations are factors in the final decision. "The students don't make recommendations," one Kellogg administrator said, "they make decisions." What it all means to you is that your application is going to be read by people who went through the application process recently themselves, by your peers.

One more thing about this peer evaluation. Kellogg is not the only business school to have student readers. But Kellogg may be the only one in which the readers are not hired to do so. Membership on the Admissions Committee is sought after by the students and done on a voluntary basis.

ACADEMIC ENVIRONMENT

« *Typically business schools are thought of as highly competitive environments with remote, research-oriented faculty, which befits the professional nature of business training. Kellogg professors, on the other hand, really seem to care about their students. They're generally very accessible. Less emphasis is put on grades and competition than on participation and learning. Kellogg seems a lot less cutthroat than some other schools, and students don't hesitate to get on the case of a classmate who's being overly aggressive. The academic reputation of any program starts with the faculty. As one Kellogg graduate explained: "Students respond to people who have written the texts, who sit on corporate boards, who consult. You knew when you were sitting in front of Kotler or Lew Stern that you were sitting in front of eminence, and you hoped it would rub off on you."* »

Of course, reputation can only take a course, a department, or a program so far. What makes the classroom program work is that professors enhance case discussions with current business-world examples — often culled from their consulting work. This recurring topical anecdotal approach lends a stronger sense of applied practicality to cases that were written years earlier and have been used by several successive classes. And because the students thrive on this approach and respond to it strongly, the professors thrive. It's a classic feedback loop.

Kellogg's preeminence in marketing and its burgeoning reputation in other fields enhance the school's ability to tap into corporate resources and speakers. It is the ability to attract an executive like Quaker Oats chairman William Smithburg for a CIM Week conversation with fifty-five students that adds prestige and excitement to Kellogg's academic environment.

« *United Air Lines had become Allegis and was under some fire from investors, unions, and the financial markets, but there was Richard Ferris (CEO at the time) in front of a Leadership class. "I looked at my calendar this morning and saw that I had to come to Kellogg to speak," he said. "And I thought, oh, great, they're going to grill me about their frequent-flier accounts." What followed, however, was a discussion about the airline industry and corporate management that was open, very frank, honest, and more riveting than any lecture I had ever had.* »

Once you're accepted to Kellogg and actually enroll, you're going to graduate — barring a gross moral indiscretion or total neglect of classes. The question is simply how well you will perform the work, not whether you will complete it. To that end, it seems as if the gentleman's C of undergrad days has been replaced with the gentleman's B at Kellogg. It is possible to receive a lower grade, but you really have to earn it. Still, there are occasions when people fail classes. In these instances, the student retakes the class (though not for credit) and must pass.

Classroom competition seems to occur less among students than against whatever internal standards of excellence drive each individual. Horror stories of cutthroat business students removing required assignments from the reserved section of the library are just that at Kellogg: stories. A major reason for this cooperation is the group mentality that pervades everything at Kellogg, both the social scene and academic work.

Academic life at Kellogg is built around groups. There are four- to five-person study groups charged with developing sales campaigns in Advertising. Three-person study groups work on weekly computer projects in Introductory Finance. Four- to six-person project teams are charged with developing a business plan in Entrepreneurship. Five-person study groups analyze industries in Mergers and Acquisitions. (The only course work that doesn't seem to lend itself to the group approach is Operations.)

« I happened to run across my Month-at-a-Glance planner from my second year the other day. I opened it up and got exhausted just looking at what went on one week. There were three Strategy group meetings in three days, plus a Strategy class session — all in preparation for the paper due Thursday; three Advertising meetings, two of them open-ended, to work on the group paper; two Channels of Distribution group meetings; plus other classes. The only thing I did alone that week, besides sleep, was a job interview downtown — and I know people who would have liked to go on that with me, too. »

Study groups are never more visible at Kellogg than near the end of the quarter, when the computer labs are filled with clusters of three, four, or more students gathered around each terminal, hashing out the final versions of their group projects. These end-of-quarter crunches are the few times that students have difficulty getting on Kellogg computers. There are well-equipped labs situated both in the basement of Leverone Hall and in the Kellogg student apartment complex, commonly known as McManus.

Speaking of computers, many Kellogg students are proficient at what needs to be done on the computer, and nothing more. Computers are used when necessary for classwork (particularly Decision Science and Finance) and frequently for interview letters and PC golf. That doesn't mean that Kellogg students suffer acute anxiety attacks at the sight of hardware, and the school's reputation for attracting nonquantitative, non-computer-oriented people is exaggerated.

Classroom discussions are by and large fairly freewheeling. Some professors are better at guiding the flow of case discussions than others, but everybody gets a chance to get their two cents in. Fall quarter of first year, everyone is somewhat hesitant to speak up initially. This lasts two weeks. Maybe. After that initial period of uncertainty has passed, the pace of discussion and interaction picks up noticeably and continues unabated until graduation.

« *At the end of CIM Week, one of the teams in our section unveiled a weekly award honoring the prime comment of the week (technically, I think the award honored "impudence above and beyond the call of duty"). The idea was that the award would be bestowed on the deserving student at the end of Friday's Policy class. It was a fun way to retain a modicum of sanity amid first-quarter doubts, and the professor made it a point to save a few minutes of class time at the end of the week for the presentation ceremony. Well, one week our Policy prof had gotten caught up in the midst of a heated discussion about clothing from Scandinavia and the advantages of vertical integration and inadvertently raised the issue of "shearing cattle." An understandable slip, but one worthy of that week's award. He actually seemed quite pleased at having won.* »

Kellogg students rarely complain that there are not enough good courses being offered. Rather, they tend to complain that there are too many attractive courses offered at once. And they do mean at once. For reasons known only to the trolls in charge of class scheduling, several prime classes are almost always offered during the same period. It seems to happen every quarter. This confounds the bidding process somewhat, and the students quite a bit.

As has already been mentioned, there are courses that are always in demand, no matter when they are taught (and it is a mark of Kellogg's general excellence that these "hot" courses span most departments): Negotiations; Marketing Channels; Advertising; Investment Banking; Portfolio Management; Power and Politics in the

Organization; Management and Its Environment; Managerial Leadership; and the Communications Workshop. There are other strong courses, and courses that are good in general but excellent with specific professors, but those listed are the most popular.

Discussion of Kellogg's academic environment should include mention of the physical environment. It is abundantly clear to anyone trying to navigate the stairs at Leverone Hall between classes that Kellogg has outgrown its home. There aren't even enough lockers for all the students. But the school has big plans to address this problem. Kellogg is expanding its facilities by renovating and moving into Anderson Hall, which now stands adjacent to Leverone. In addition, the Allen Center (Kellogg's top-notch executive education facility) is being expanded by 50 percent to accommodate growing demand for executive training, and the downtown Chicago building that houses Kellogg's evening classes is renovated.

SOCIAL LIFE

As one would expect from a business school, Kellogg has an abundance of planned social activities. There are almost two dozen student organizations at Kellogg, and all of them, whether primarily academic in nature or not, plan social activities throughout the year. The largest activities are usually sponsored by the Graduate Management Association (GMA), the student government. In addition to the fairly standard array of Halloween parties, cookouts, and Cubs games, the GMA sponsors a formal dance in the spring that is always fairly well attended and that sets new standards in creative formal wear each year.

But the fact that the GMA is the largest and best-financed organization does not mean it holds a monopoly on popular social events. The Marketing Club's Brand Challenge Night offers students the chance to conduct their own blind taste tests and, at the same time, avoid another night of microwave cooking. Another organization, Joint Ventures, plans a full year of activities for Kellogg spouses and children and really works overtime to make Kellogg a special experience for the whole family.

While most Kellogg students live in apartments around Evanston and toward downtown Chicago, approximately three hundred live in the Living Learning Center, university-run apartments three blocks from the school. Group meetings, *Special K* planning meetings and rehearsals, barbecues, late-night computer sessions, and more are all held at the "Living Learning Loving" center, as the students have dubbed it. It is a center of Kellogg activity and, because it is occupied only by Kellogg students, the building takes on a life of its own. There are few civilian friends around to break the tension or provide a fresh perspective, and occasionally life in the apartments gets a little manic. Social privacy is almost nonexistent as well, which may play a major role in the paucity of romantic activity among students.

Friday afternoon happy hours, known as TGs (short for TGIF), are popular events held in the student lounge. TGs are almost always crowded and usually include at least cameo appearances from a few faculty members and a dean or two. Friday night plans are frequently hatched at TGs. Another popular place to drink is Tommy Nevin's, an Irish pub in Evanston where students and local residents mix. A Kellogg contingent can usually be found at Nevin's on Tuesday nights, since there are no regular classes on Wednesdays.

The International Business Club sponsors an International Beerfest that is hugely popular each year. Students set up booths featuring imported beers from around the world. Taste of Kellogg, featuring foods from around the world, is also a popular IBC event.

Evanston's proximity to Chicago provides Kellogg students with a plethora of social options, although some take more advantage of the city than others do. The trip to the Loop and Michigan Avenue from campus takes about forty-five minutes by El and thirty minutes by car (avoiding rush-hour traffic). But many popular nightspots are on the city's North Side, which makes them easier to reach from Evanston. The only things limiting student access to the bars, theaters, restaurants, and comedy clubs of Greater Chicago are time and money, both of which can be in very short supply at certain times of the year.

Kellogg students are active in Northwestern's intramural athletics program, fielding multiple teams in volleyball, softball, indoor soccer, and football. But the king of Kellogg sports is broomball, a sort of childproof, coed version of ice hockey in which players run around and fall down a lot and are occasionally fooled into hitting a plastic ball into a net. Kellogg's devotion to the sport is the stuff legends, and oligopolies, are made of: during one recent year, eighteen of the twenty-four teams in the broomball league were Kellogg teams.

One of the biggest clubs at Kellogg is Business with a Heart, which focuses on philanthropic endeavors throughout the Chicago community. In addition to providing student support for everything from soup kitchens to literacy programs, BWAH raised more than $40,000 for the Evanston Shelter for Battered Women and Children.

No discussion of nonacademic life at Kellogg would be complete without a few words about the *Special K Revue*. This student-produced, student-directed, student-everythinged show has become a Kellogg tradition by skewering everything that is wrong and right with business school life. The show started modestly and has grown over the course of almost a decade to three nights of multiple performances, sold-out shows, and a New York performance on the strength of skits such as the aforementioned *Star Trek* saga, a rhyming interview with Hallmark, and dinner with Phil Kotler and Wrestlemania — a refereed interview between the Kellogg Call-Back Kid and Dr. Ding.

« *Profits lagging? Sales down? Or just looking for someone to do your thinking for you? Introducing the new Ronco Consult-O-Matic. Why pay premium prices for advice from an overtraveled, overworked, overpaid, and overrated consultant, when the new Ronco Consult-O-Matic is at your disposal? Just toss in your favorite annual reports, 10-Ks, stock prices, payroll stubs, and unshredded confidential memos, and the Consult-O-Matic will compute, refute, dispute, and convolute. That's right. The Consult-O-Matic can slice, dice, and give advice. And boy, can it catch fish. And unlike those fly-by-night consultants you've heard about, the Consult-O-Matic is warranted for a full fifty years. How much would you pay for this revolutionary capitalist tool? (from "Speedbumps on the Fast Track," the* Special K Revue). »

RECRUITING AND JOB SEARCH

THE approach at Kellogg is a generalist one, in keeping with the growing prominence of the Management Policy Department. Students are encouraged to take more than one major, broadening both their base of knowledge and, subsequently, the opportunities and options that will be available to them when they graduate. Students who choose to major in an industrial specialization such as Real Estate or Public and Nonprofit Management are trained in a variety of functions within the industry. Conversely, students who choose a functional specialization are encouraged to understand how the function applies across a wide range of industries. Consequently, as the interview season begins (though it never really seems to end when you're in business school), Kellogg students find themselves in a position to explore a variety of different options without straying from their major area of interest.

And there are a variety of options available, because Kellogg is one of the recruiting hot spots on the business school circuit. The latest survey results have only added fuel to the fire. More than 350 companies interview students on campus for full-time positions, and almost 150 come to Kellogg to interview first-year students for summer internships. More than 100 other firms send information to the placement office about full-time positions or internships that are available within their organizations. These are posted on a correspondent opportunities board jokingly referred to as "opportunities at companies too cheap to come out and interview like everyone else."

Jesting aside, the present appears to be a time in which everyone is happy. Corporate recruiters rank Kellogg as their top choice for recruiting managers for consumer products firms and one of their top five choices for recruiting top-flight individuals to work in basic manufacturing industries and in the financial world. Recent Kellogg graduates polled regarding their attitudes about recruiting reported a higher level of satisfaction with both the caliber and the quantity of firms recruiting on campus and the help they received from Kellogg in finding the ideal job than graduates of the other major business schools reported vis-à-vis their alma maters.

One other source of job-search support comes from some of the extracurricular groups on campus. Groups with an industry or functional specialization — real estate, transportation, marketing, communications, health, and health-related services — assemble (for a fee) résumé books, which are then sent to corporations in the appropriate fields.

Virtually all Kellogg students work as paid interns between the first and second years of a program. In several instances, interns are offered full-time positions early in the second year, taking some of the heat off the most grueling and brutal event of your business school life: the full-time job search.

But before we get to that, let's explain the rules of the interview game. If you thought the class bidding system sounded like fun, you're going to love this. Students are given a fixed number of points, traditionally 800, to last the entire recruiting season. Interviews are divided into bid periods, and the bidding for all interviews during one period is completed before the next period comes on the market. So far, so good. Now the devilish part. All bids are entered confidentially and then tallied and tabulated, just as is done for classes. But once the clearing price is set, each student who bid above the clearing price for a given interview is awarded a slot on the schedule (but you have to get up early and get in line to sign up for which slot), and any excess points bid are returned for use during the next bid period. Students who did not bid above the clearing price get all their points back. This gives rise to some very bizarre scenarios.

« *Scenario 1: Everybody you want to interview with is coming during the same bid period. Do you suicide on the most important ones and let the others go? Do you try to get them all, running the risk of getting none if they're all sought-after slots? What if only some companies are hot this year? Which ones? Respond to the question of your choice.*

Scenario 2: You want to speak to only one firm, but you want to speak to their recruiter in the worst way. But how many other people feel the same way? You want to bid a lot of points, but you don't want to look like a fool if you're the only one who bids, and it closes at 600 points. Who can you get to bid 1 point as a fail-safe to lower the closing price? Who's your buddy? Who's your pal?

Scenario 3: The last bid period. Only a handful of companies coming. Everyone who has not yet landed a job is nervous and wants that interview. And they're not getting any points back this time because it's the end of the season. It's use-them-or-lose-them time. It's a company with twenty-four interview slots closing at 435 points. For a job in International Falls, Minnesota. »

Of course, there are alternatives to the bidding system. Several companies come to recruit using both open and closed schedules. The open schedules are for the hearty who survive "The Price Is Right." The closed list is by invitation only. In some instances students are invited out of the blue by companies who have attacked the résumé book with the enthusiasm of a starving piranha. In most cases, students are asked to contact the firm if they are interested in *applying* for a spot on the closed list, which will entitle them to apply yet again for the job in question. It's a form of double jeopardy or triple indemnity or some such thing. The placement office, though, has instituted a rule designed to ease the pressure slightly: any company which wishes to recruit via closed interview schedules must make an open schedule available through the normal bid process as well.

Now that you know the rules, take them and stretch them out to cover a recruiting period that lasts from September to June and perhaps beyond for second-years and from January to June for first-years. As the interview season drags on and the spirit is ground down little by little, a funny thing happens to group meetings. A smaller percentage of the meeting time is devoted to the case or project at hand, and a growing share of the time is devoted to "peer-group support functions" and the latest job-hunting rumors and innuendos. The fact that this all comes to a head during the second quarter of the second year makes February in Chicago just a great time to be alive.

But there's more to the job search than bidding and interviewing. There's the corporate presentation, business school's answer to the rising cost of groceries. At Kellogg, corporate presentations are generally held in one of two places: the Orrington Hotel, which is conveniently located across the street from McManus and specializes in large shrimp and abundant fruit and cheese; and the Allen Center, a Kellogg-constructed, Kellogg-run facility built on campus to house the school's growing Executive Management Program.

« *Some of the corporate presentations are incredibly elaborate. McKinsey invited dozens of students to a formal dinner at one of Chicago's poshest restaurants and flew in partners from around the world to chat with the students in small groups around the dinner table. That kind of treatment doesn't happen all the time, but a lot of very prestigious firms are trying to woo Kellogg students. The consulting and finance firms in particular go to great lengths to win recruits. For instance, when Lehman Brothers flew one of my friends and his wife out to New York for an interview, the firm reserved them a room at a small luxury hotel for several days, arranged for limo service around the city, got them tickets to a sold-out Broadway show on just a couple of hours' notice, and picked up the tab at several outrageously expensive restaurants. And to top it off, all of that was just for a summer job.* »

Despite Kellogg's excellent reputation for marketing, more graduates from a recent class accepted positions in finance and consulting (each accounted for 25 percent of acceptances) than product management (21 percent of acceptances). The firms that hired the most Kellogg graduates in a recent year were Coopers & Lybrand, McKinsey & Co., Deloitte & Touche, Procter & Gamble, A. T. Kearney, Inc., and Northwest Airlines.

More than three quarters of recent Kellogg graduates accepted jobs in the Midwest or the East, including the 28 percent of graduates who stayed in Chicago. Ten percent headed for the West, and 11 percent took international positions. Students seeking jobs in places other than the Midwest and New York have found they often need to work harder on their own outside searches to find the right fit.

As Kellogg has admitted more foreign students and Americans with international interests, there have been calls for better placement services for overseas positions. The school is trying to build its reputation and alumni/alumnae network overseas, and those efforts should help future students find positions abroad.

ON THE JOB — FIRST YEARS OUT

« *What did I come away from Kellogg with? Some very good friends that I still keep in touch with two years later. And a depth of understanding and a breadth of knowledge about the academic side of business that I didn't have before and that I went to Kellogg to get. I really came away with the fundamental tools. I find myself using things we learned in accounting almost every day, and I'm not in an accounting job. I use things I learned in finance and marketing all the time. And I'm in a job that I love that I didn't even know existed when I got to Kellogg.* »

The criticism heard from recent Kellogg graduates centers on the jobs they have gone into and not the school. The Kellogg program receives high marks in retrospect, with a number of graduates lamenting only their failure to take more elective courses outside their major field or fields. And it's a legitimate complaint. There is a danger at Kellogg, just as at other schools, of focusing too narrowly on one specialty, though the program makes a serious effort to produce talented general managers.

But most of the criticism centers on the jobs chosen after school. Graduates are beginning to question the grind and its demands, and the impact of those demands on quality of life.

More often than not, students say that the job was almost what they expected, only more so. The Kellogg program gives you the skills to handle almost any task an employer will throw your way, but the pacing of the work world, particularly in the fields of consulting and investment banking, seems to be catching some people by surprise.

« *We were discussing employee attitudes and expectations in a Human Resources class, and the professor commented that the average Kellogg graduate has changed jobs eighteen months after graduation. Not simply different jobs within the same firm, but different firms. We were all quite surprised and, at the time, somewhat doubting. But now I find myself two years out of Kellogg, and when I look at my circle of closest friends I see four still with the same firm, one recently laid off as part of a corporate restructuring, one leaving in the next few months, one already gone from her first employer, one laid off because of bankruptcy, and one on his fourth city and second company in eighteen months. I guess we're an average Kellogg bunch.* »

More and more recent graduates seem to be itching to get away from the large corporate environment and into a smaller setting. This is probably a reflection of the Kellogg approach and the school's changing reputation. In keeping with the growing ascendancy of the Management Policy and Organizational Behavior departments and the growing popularity of courses such as Entrepreneurship and Small Business Management (in which students form small consulting groups and work with Chicago-area businesses), more Kellogg students are seeking an environment in which they can practice more general management skills and have a bigger impact more quickly. Some might call this impatience, but it is more likely a by-product of the skills Kellogg works hard to give each student, and the students' desire to use them immediately.

Kellogg graduates are well paid. Recent figures suggest an average starting salary of more than $55,000. Other schools may have higher averages, but this may be partly explained by the 20 percent of Kellogg students who are concentrating in fields other than business management, such as public and nonprofit management and health services management.

As Kellogg has grabbed more of the limelight, the respect accorded the Kellogg degree has risen. The school's name is popping up much more frequently in the press, including overseas: when the *International Herald Tribune* ran a special report on international management education last spring, the Paris-based newspaper's lead interview was with Dean Donald P. Jacobs of Kellogg. Graduates are finding that they can answer questions about their background by mentioning Kellogg and omitting the parenthetical phrase "Northwestern's business school."

SUMMARY OVERVIEW

In the beginning was the word. And at Kellogg, the word was "marketing." But recently, word has gotten out that there's much more to Kellogg than an outstanding Marketing Department. Organizational Behavior, Finance, Management Strategy, Health-Care Policy, and Real Estate Management are among the departments that are gaining in stature. They make Kellogg an excellent place to get a well-rounded management education.

I recommend Kellogg to everyone who asks, but not just because of the school's excellence in a variety of disciplines. I recommend it because of the atmosphere. The attitude at Kellogg is definitely less stressful than what I've heard about in other programs (except, of course, at the height of interviewing season). Kellogg students work hard, but they also know how to keep school in perspective. A conscious effort is made by students and faculty to maintain some balance between school life and "real" life, even at the most trying times. The result is an environment that is rigorous and challenging, but not debilitating in its frenzy.

Some of the professors at Kellogg will probably rank as the best you will ever have in your academic career. There are a few at Kellogg whom some students find to be lacking in ability, and their shortcomings are magnified by the excellence of the rest of the faculty, making a tough situation sometimes appear worse than it objectively is.

Kellogg is not a haven for the digitheads of the world. In fact, some Kellogg students are happy to spend as little time as possible grappling with statistical packages and mainframes. But the school's reputation for being nonquantitative is exaggerated. There are Kellogg students who will go head-to-head with any "quant jock." The school could be more rigorous in its required quantitative course work, but there are challenging numbers courses for those who want them.

If there is any other weakness in the Kellogg program, it stems from the school's location. Don't get me wrong. Chicago is a thriving city with as much cultural diversity and entertainment as you could ask for (and not a stockyard in sight!). Many a New Yorker has arrived at Kellogg with doubts about Chicagoland, only to become a true fan of the area (comments like "The city is so clean!" and "People are so nice!" come to mind). The problem for some students arises during interviewing season: The volume of companies from the coasts that come to interview, particularly from the West Coast, is not as great as some students would like. On the other hand, no program can match the offering of midwestern job opportunities that come through the Kellogg placement office. Twenty-eight percent of recent graduates accepted jobs in Chicago, 27 percent went to the East, 24 percent went elsewhere in the Midwest, 11 percent took international jobs, and 10 percent ended up in the West.

Still, all in all, Kellogg offers a uniformly excellent program. Writing recently in Kellogg's alumni/alumnae magazine, Dean Donald P. Jacobs commented on the pressures for continued excellence. "I am often asked," he wrote, "shouldn't we open a special center for ethics studies? Or one for international business? Should there be a separate focus on Europe? Or Asia? Or the new capital markets? Or the communist turn to capitalism? As the list grows, our challenge is to continue to teach the core principles that will serve the manager and his or her organization best, over time, against a background of change."

That balance, that focus, lies at the core of Kellogg. The school, like most other business programs, is trying with general success to achieve excellence in all fields. But it is what Kellogg does with the excellence that makes the program so worthwhile. Rather than produce narrowly trained specialists, the school pushes hard to translate Jacobs's vision to reality, to produce general managers who can understand the ramifications of a new policy or project in the context of the big picture rather than simply in terms of immediate consequences — and who then consider and understand the human factor when analyzing the implications of bottom-line policies.

Chapter 6

THE MIT SLOAN SCHOOL OF MANAGEMENT*

THE PROGRAM

THE MBA program at the MIT Sloan School of Management is unique in many respects. From its strong quantitative reputation and excellent teaching to its international flavor and charming Cambridge, Massachusetts, location, MIT manages to differentiate itself effectively, not just from the other Cambridge business school but also from other top ten schools. MIT is particularly special in that it is a mecca for top faculty talent, as the current roster illustrates.

Walk through the halls on any day, and you may hear Nobel Prize winner Robert Solow preaching the benefits of high technological growth rates, catch zero-sum theoretician Lester Thurow (now dean of the school) lecturing on international competitiveness, and see long-running economics textbook monopolist Paul Samuelson scribbling late revisions to the fifty-fourth edition of his evergreen introduction to the joys of "macro" and "micro." The students taught by this faculty team are an extremely eclectic bunch, with more than 35 percent holding foreign passports. Many come from Japan and other Asian countries; others are on two-year sabbaticals from companies in Europe eager to prepare their top employees for the rigors of post-1992 competition in the Common Market. And despite diverse backgrounds, most students here have an important characteristic in common — the ability to share their experiences

* BY JOHN KRAFCIK, MS IN MANAGEMENT, AND ANTONY SHERIFF, MS IN MANAGEMENT

and contribute effectively to the many "team" assignments ubiquitous in the school's curriculum.

Part of MIT's strategy to continue luring its share of top faculty, students, and recruiters is reflected in a recent name change — from the Sloan School of Management to the MIT Sloan School of Management. The switch had nothing to do with a dislike of former GM chairman and big-time MIT benefactor Alfred P. Sloan (the master of decentralized management) but rather reflects a concern that the cachet that comes with the three magic initials MIT was being underutilized through reliance on the Sloan moniker.

« *The first few days at MIT are spent in Orientation activities. After meeting many fellow Sloanies in a large lecture hall (soon to be your home for many Sloan core classes, including the infamous first-semester Microeconomics course) and listening to esteemed faculty give diatribes on the importance of the next two years in our lives, we were shuffled off into groups of ten students for our first taste of teamwork.*

After introductions, during which I learned I was the only one who fit the typical "Sloan profile" (an engineering undergraduate with three years of work experience), our diverse group found itself facing a daunting problem constructed by the clever Human Resource Management faculty at Sloan. Our plane had crashed, we had only a modicum of provisions, and together we had to work out a survival strategy. We tussled with the issues for thirty minutes, trying to decide between an aggressive strategy of striking out in search of help or waiting for a rescue team to find us. As you might expect from a group of fresh business school recruits, we ultimately decided on the aggressive strategy.

All the groups met back in the lecture hall for a debriefing session and a spiel on group dynamics from John Van Maanen, our wild and wonderful Organization Studies prof. It turned out the passive strategy was the optimal one, for a whole slew of what were in retrospect pretty obvious reasons. For example, it turned out that our emergency kits contained everything we needed to survive in the desert for a few days. Most groups had gone with the aggressive strategy, but, of course, in the end it really didn't matter. We had all made a group of new acquaintances, many of whom would soon become close friends and study partners, and most of us got the point Van Maanen was trying to make with the group exercise — the best strategy isn't always the boldest — very useful advice for aspiring masters of the universe. »

The Sloan core requirements are currently the source of some debate within the school. Some say the core is too broad and too long and does not allow enough time for investigating more appropriate elective courses. Others claim the core teaches a set of analytical tools and conceptual frameworks that are essential for every manager, while beneficially keeping new students on the same track for most of the first year. Currently, the core consists of thirteen classes, about half of which are full-semester classes that meet twice a week (marked *), the others being half-semester classes that meet three times a week. The quantitative side of the core includes Applied Economics I (Micro)* and Applied Economics II (Macro), * Accounting and Finance I (Financial Accounting), * Accounting and Finance II (Financial Management), Decision Support Systems I (Information Systems), Decision Support Systems II (Statistics), * Decision Support Systems III (Decision Models), * and Introduction to Operations Management. The other side of the core includes Communication for Managers, Managerial Behavior in Organizations, * Industrial Relations and Human Resource Management, Strategic Management, and Introduction to Marketing. All in all, the core courses seem solid preparation for life in the business world. There is a good mix between quantitative and qualitative, rigorous and laid-back classes, and lectures and case presentations.

« Despite the best efforts of most Sloan professors, some of the core classes seem impossibly boring, especially at 9:00 A.M. on Monday morning. Sloan students, being the resourceful lot that they are, often devised novel means to alleviate the boredom. One particular class featured a trio of students who unwittingly relieved the ennui for the rest of the class. One student could be counted on to fall asleep, his slumber signaled by a hearty clunk of his head on the desk; another would incessantly scribble on his Styrofoam coffee cup once its contents were consumed; and a third would always respond incorrectly to a question and suffer a rebuff from the lecturer. After a few weeks of watching these events unfold with uncanny regularity, a group of students in the rear of the class began to hold a lottery,

with the object of predicting as accurately as possible the exact time of the head clunk, the cup scribble, and the rebuff. No great sums were wagered, but the stunt served its purpose of keeping otherwise groggy students remarkably conscious. »

If you have the background, it makes sense to waive as many of the core requirement classes as possible. You can find out about waiver possibilities after you are accepted, at which point you should choose your targets and start preparing immediately. The core classes are generally very good and well taught, but the real fun at Sloan is found in the elective courses, which you can fine-tune into a program that suits your own idea of an MBA to a tee. In fact, with the help of a few waivers and a couple of six- or seven-course-per-semester course loads, it is possible to graduate a semester early, thus saving substantial tuition and getting a jump on the job market. The downside is that you miss the standard February–March recruiting season at Sloan and the luxury of completing the thesis requirement while taking on an otherwise relatively light course load spring semester.

Unlike another local business school (a school at which you, as a Sloanie, will learn to poke fun at the slightest provocation), Sloan does not slip into the folly of presenting everything in case form. The Micro and Macro courses, for example, are taught as lecture courses, with application and discussion coming from interaction within study groups and during TA sessions, just as God intended. TA sessions are not required but are highly recommended; in fact, many had even higher attendance than the course itself. Most of the nonquantitative courses and quantitative courses such as Accounting and Operations Management are taught with a healthy mix of case and lecture. In general, this mixed approach seems to be an enlightened one — the professor has ample leeway to decide on the most appropriate method to present the course material. In those classes where cases are deemed most appropriate, students often dictate the pace of discussion. Most Sloan professors prefer to rely on voluntary student participation, which is a real plus when you just did not have time to finish reading the case. (But be aware that too much of this type of shirking will get you into trouble in the long run!)

A heavy emphasis at Sloan, especially prevalent in courses such as Finance, Operations Management, and the Decision Support Systems trio, is on the proper application of analytical tools to the solution of sketchily defined problems. This is a real strength of the program, for it approximates what one sees in the real world: a need to effect change, to complete a deal, to improve performance — without a clear road map on how to get it done. One learns to spend a lot of time defining the problem, using the skills and experience of teammates, and making the appropriate assumptions before finally applying a well-selected tool from a rapidly expanding analytical tool kit.

Sloan's image is that of a finance/economics powerhouse, with a heavy emphasis on quantitative training. Office doors in Building E-52 with names like Samuelson, Modigliani, Solow, Thurow, Pindyck, Myers, etc., ad nauseam, confirm that this image is largely reality, with the caveat that other "concentration" areas at Sloan are also very strong. Corporate Strategy and International Management have received a lot of the school's attention over the past few years and now boast impressive programs with strong research and teaching faculty and plenty of interesting courses. The Organizational Studies and Industrial Relations area is also very strong. Management Information Systems, a real MIT-style concentration, is highly regarded as well.

One strategic move under way now at Sloan is an increased emphasis on the importance of manufacturing. While this in no way endangers the strong finance area or other Sloan strengths, it certainly marks a policy shift for the school in keeping with MIT's motto, "Minds and hands." MIT recently published a book called *Made in America* (written in part by Lester Thurow and Robert Solow), outlining the reasons behind this country's relative decline as an economic superpower. One major finding was that American incompetence in manufacturing (or "making things," as we often say) is a significant driving force behind the decline. Much of this incompetence, it is argued, springs from a short-term financial outlook taught at certain business schools (but not Sloan!), and a lack of interest in the mechanics of mass production. The MIT School of Engineering and Sloan have teamed up and, with the help of a huge endowment from several Fortune 100 companies, have launched a program called Leaders in Manufacturing — a rigorous program with full stipends for forty extremely motivated and soon-to-be-sleep-deprived students who will receive master's degrees in

Management and Engineering after twenty-four months of continuous study. For the right students, this program is certain to be a spectacular educational experience. The rest of the Sloan class is also likely to benefit, not only from the added expertise and resources of the program but also from the fact that the Leaders in Manufacturing students will be so tired that everyone else will look sharper in case discussions.

Teamwork is a way of life at Sloan. You learn to work with a team from the start of your Sloan experience (the survival game), and often work with some of the same folks over the next two years in study groups. Some students rely heavily on study groups to discuss cases ahead of time and complete tricky problem sets. Others find study groups a luxury because of time constraints, particularly married students or those living far from Sloan. Whether or not you use study groups is, of course, totally up to you.

On the other hand, some classes require group participation for certain assignments. The core IR/HRM class, for example, has as its main attraction a model labor/management bargaining session that requires teamwork. One of the marketing core classes uses a computer simulation of competitive product marketing that requires four people to work very closely together for eight weeks. This particular exercise ended up being one of the most enjoyable experiences of my Sloan education.

« *Markstrat is a computer simulation game used in a core Marketing class. Each four-person team starts with two products, some funds to be allocated for marketing and R&D activities, and a set of rules guiding play. Then the fun begins. Over the course of a half-semester class, each Markstrat team battles the others for profits and market share in an imaginary consumer electronics product segment. My team members were a product planner from Mazda, a former product planner from Chrysler, and a manager from a large Japanese trading company. As you might imagine from the composition of this group, our strategy stressed innovation through heavy R&D spending (a strategy that served us well). But what a time sink the project became. We all enjoyed the interaction and realism so much that we spent far more time than we should have on the project. Mind you, it wasn't all work. For example, under the pretense of a "business dinner," we would often meet at a local sushi bar for Kirin and sashimi, where we ended up discussing in great detail the pros and cons of adding wasabe to soy sauce in the dipping bowl and the reason for the success of "dry" beer in Japan.* »

Like most business schools these days, Sloan has made computers an integral part of the master's program. IBM PCs and Apple Macintoshes (there are enough of either so that you can take your pick, although some course work requires the use of Lotus 1-2-3 on the PC — urgh!) are scattered about the Sloan building in clusters, while heavy-duty mainframe computing power awaits in the basement of E-52 should you ever need it. If you are not computer literate before you come to Sloan, fear not. Introductory classes are available at Orientation time, and there are always lots of people around to help you master an Excel macro, a Word shortcut, or the silly little intricacies of PC-DOS.

Before graduating from Sloan, you are required to name an area of concentration. This is rarely a problem, as the requirements for a concentration are not so rigorous — often just two or three elective courses. I managed three concentrations in areas of interest to me: Finance and Applied Economics, International Management, and Corporate Strategy. Others have completed as many as seven concentrations, a strategy that in the opinion of some tends to defeat the whole purpose of a "concentration." Multiple concentrations do have several advantages, though. For example, if you are not sure just what field you want to go into upon graduation, you can fine-tune your résumé with concentrations best suited to the companies you are talking to. (The concentrations are "official," but they do not show up on your diploma.)

Last of the hurdles for most Sloan students before graduation is the controversial thesis requirement. Unlike most MBA programs, Sloan requires a scholarly thesis to be completed before the vaunted sheepskin can be awarded. This keeps Sloan in line with every other graduate program at MIT; all require theses of their graduates. It is also one reason why at Sloan you receive the Master of Science in Management rather than the somewhat more pedestrian Master of Business Administration. But is the thesis a good thing? Well, I would certainly vouch for it. The Sloan thesis allows students to go into great depth on a subject that interests them. In terms of course units, the thesis requirement is equal to about three full-semester

courses, so it is clearly a serious commitment. Thesis work is su-
pervised by a faculty adviser (sometimes closely, sometimes not so
closely, depending on how busy your adviser is), but otherwise you
have relatively free rein over the intellectual content of your very
own magnum opus. Most of the completed theses are more than a
hundred pages long and look terrific suitably bound and promi-
nently displayed on a bookshelf in your office.

*« The thesis allows you to escape from the confines of the Sloan
classroom in any one of several directions. I decided to align myself
with a research project called the International Motor Vehicle Program at the MIT Center for Technology, Policy, and Industrial Development, right across the street from Sloan. The IMVP was so
taken with my background that they not only sponsored much of my
thesis fieldwork but also paid a couple of semesters' worth of tuition.
I ended up visiting automotive assembly plants in several countries,
comparing their productivity levels in search of the Holy Grail of the
auto industry — how much more productive are Japanese vis-à-vis
American companies, and why are they better? For my efforts (aided
greatly by the good fortune of finding a sponsor like the IMVP), I was
rewarded with numerous citations in the business press, a few published articles, an appearance on an ABC documentary (for all of
fifteen seconds!), and best of all, a rather relaxed recruiting season
(although after several attractive overtures from consulting companies, I decided to start my own business). »*

The moral of the story is that the Sloan thesis, like most of the Sloan
program, is what you make of it. The opportunities at Sloan, and at
MIT in general, are vast and perhaps a bit overwhelming at first.
Those students who seek out the opportunities, and embrace them
for all they are worth, receive a management education experience
without parallel.

GETTING IN

SLOAN admissions officers spend a lot of time looking for the ideal
candidate, although all of them will deny there is such a thing as an

ideal candidate. However, a composite portrait of successful applicants would probably look something like this:

(1) people who have succeeded in the things they have attempted to do;
(2) good problem-solvers (as evidenced by employment success; good quant course performance in undergraduate school is a plus but is not essential);
(3) people with an international experience base (either by education, personal life, or employment);
(4) team players (tough to document, but should come through in the written part of their application).

If you have most of these attributes and you don't mind winters in Massachusetts, then the Sloan School could have a place for you. And I'll repeat the parenthetical reference in point number 2 above (for those of you who have not been listening): MIT is clearly trying to attract a broad group of applicants; therefore, C's in math courses and A's in Comparative Literature from a good university could give you an advantage over a more conventional, "techy" MIT undergrad applying to Sloan.

The statistical profile of a typical recent Sloan class reveals more about what the admissions staff is looking for. An average Sloanie has a 650 GMAT score, a 4.5/5.0 GPA, and has four years of full-time work experience. Average age at admission is twenty-seven, with only 8 percent of the class under twenty-three and 17 percent of the class twenty-nine or over. These statistics translate very simply to the following: substantial work experience is looked upon very positively, as are good GMATs and GPAs, but a deficit in one area can be compensated for by strength in another (remember, these are averages, and there *is* a wide spread across all these variables).

That Sloan is not simply interested in grooming 240 quant jocks each year is illustrated by the distribution of undergraduate majors, which in recent years has been split evenly among engineering, humanities/social sciences, and physical sciences/preprofessional. An average class will be chock-full of students with varied backgrounds — including quite a few quant jocks, about half a dozen auto industry refugees, a few liberal social-scientist-turned-budding-capitalist entrepreneurs, several heirs to European business empires, and perhaps even a Russian émigré turned management consultant.

About 25 percent of the typical Sloan class are women. And, geographically speaking, about 30 percent come from New England, 30 percent from foreign lands, 10 percent from the Far West, and 30 percent from the Midwest, South, or Mid-Atlantic states.

The application process for Sloan is similar to that for many other business schools. Included are lots of personal information, cover letter, résumé, references, GMATs, grades, and a personal essay. Mercifully missing from the application catalog, though, are the dreaded "long essay" questions. But do spend plenty of time polishing the short essay and personal essay sections — they are your best shot to convince the admissions team that you really are deserving of a spot in the program.

Each year, about 1,750 people apply for the 240 or so spots in the Sloan master's program. As noted, a good portion of the applicants, and 35 percent of those who come to Sloan, come from foreign countries. Because of MIT's strong overseas image, Sloan is a top choice for striving young Asians and Europeans working in global companies. Our class had twelve Japanese students from some of the largest companies in Japan — all but one of whom were on a company-funded two-year American boondoggle. They drank a lot of beer, played a lot of golf (much cheaper in Massachusetts than in Japan), learned about the Capital Asset Pricing Model (among lots of other things), and returned to Japan with a new global perspective. They also enriched the program for everyone by offering a Japanese perspective in class discussions, in study groups, and at the weekly Consumption Function.

My advice to both international and American students applying to Sloan is simple — to have a good chance at acceptance your "attribute portfolio" should include an international outlook, some interesting real-world experience, decent grades in college, above-average GMAT scores (over 600 is best but not essential), and good written communication skills (to complete the ever-important essay section). The importance of real-world experience, both for the admissions process and for the business school experience itself, cannot be stressed enough. You really do get more out of business school if you have some experiences to relate your education to.

ACADEMIC ENVIRONMENT

THE academic environment at MIT is a happy conundrum — too many good courses and professors and not nearly enough time to take all the interesting ones. The variety of functional areas taught well at Sloan is impressive — from established strengths such as Finance and MIS to rising stars such as Corporate Strategy and Marketing. One indicator of the popularity of classes at Sloan is the number of non-MIT MBA students enrolled in some of the "open" (to non-MBAs) classes. (This is generally a plus, unless you tend to arrive late and the class is really overcrowded, in which case you often end up sitting on the floor.) Frustrated Harvard B School finance aficionados are frequent enrollees in Sloan finance classes*; MIT Technology and Policy students complete some of their core requirements in Sloan economics classes. The overall mix resulting from this influx of students from outside the MIT MBA program, along with the great diversity within the class, creates an atmosphere in which class discussions are often a primary mode of learning. All in all, it makes for an exciting academic environment.

« *One particular class that built on a lot of Sloan strengths was Japanese Technology Management, taught by Michael Cusumano. This twenty-student class met twice each week for ninety minutes, and was quite popular with second-year students. Cusumano structured the class around a series of cases describing some of the innovative methods Japanese companies use to manage technology. The class discussions were extremely stimulating, based as they were on some of Cusumano's own cutting-edge research in the Japanese automotive and computer industries and the experiences of various well-traveled Sloanies. Discussions were far-ranging and insightful, and there was rarely any feeling that people were participating just to impress the prof. The class culminated in a series of final student projects. We all picked an area of Japanese industry, did some original research, and shared the results with the rest of the class in a thirty-minute pre-*

---

* MIT students longing for an insider's look at fishbowl classrooms filled with ninety high-strung students can sample such an academic environment, should they wish, by taking a class at Harvard — it's easily done through a transfer credit scheme endorsed by both Charles River schools.

sentation. When the semester ended, the entire class gave the prof a well-deserved standing ovation. He had provided consistently interesting material over the course of the semester and had challenged us to apply original research to actual business problem solving, all in a remarkably international context. As learning experiences go, they don't get much better than this. »

Grading at Sloan reflects the reality that if you're good enough to get in, then you're good enough to get at least B's in most classes. Maintaining a B average at MIT is not a difficult task. If you want A's across the board, though, you will have to put your nose to the grindstone.

Following the universitywide format, the grading system at Sloan is on a 5.0 to 1.0 scale (A = 5.0 and F = 1.0). Professors have no set grading standards to adhere to, and so allocate A's, B's, and C's as they desire. In general, a strong effort will bring an A or a B, little effort a C, while D's and F's seem to require a level of performance so wretched as to be beyond human comprehension. (I did not know of any D's or F's in my time at Sloan.) Grades are based on exams, classroom participation, or projects, depending on the class, with the relative weight being determined by the professor.

The Sloan grading system more accurately reflects the real world than the Harvard bell-curve, 10-percent-of-you-will-fail system. Even in the real world, it generally takes a pretty monumental screwup to get fired, and at Sloan likewise; it would take a concerted lack of effort on your part to be asked to leave. Our business culture tends to reward high performance and tolerate all the rest. Sloan professors seem to take the view that since most Sloan students clearly will not fail in the business world, there is little reason to fail them in graduate school classes.

The major arena of competition at Sloan is among teams, not individuals. Team competition, in the classroom or on the playing field in the popular intramural sports program, is the healthy, Sloan-approved way to vent business school frustrations. On the other hand, grade competition in most classes is socially frowned on as antisocial behavior by all but the most competitive students (often those without work experience who zoomed in straight from undergraduate school). Some courses, though, like those in the finance core, are by nature highly competitive, since they are populated by the most analytical of Sloan students striving for the most lucrative of positions after graduation.

« *One of the best things about Sloan is the cosmopolitan nature of the class. I spent a lot of time hanging out with the Japanese students, partially because of my experience working for NUMMI, the GM-Toyota joint venture. Ironically, the Japanese students were among the least competitive groups in the school. They didn't care too much about grades (perhaps because their sponsoring companies didn't care so much either) but did strive to maximize "cultural learning." I am sure they learned a lot about U.S. business culture while they were at MIT, and those who cared to certainly learned a lot about Japan and things Japanese from them.* »

The team spirit at Sloan is fostered by classes that are generally quite intimate. Most second-year classes, and most of the nonquantitative core, range in size from fifteen to thirty-five students. The quantitative core classes can get large — Micro and Macro generally pack the one-hundred-seat main lecture hall.

Sloan does award prizes at the end of the second year for accomplishments in various areas: thesis excellence, overall performance and potential, and performance/potential in various functional areas. These awards are very low-key — most students don't give them a second thought, and fewer still make any conscious effort to attain them.

SOCIAL LIFE

DESPITE Sloan's relatively small size, there are a multitude of opportunities for an interesting and varied social life. An interesting social life starts with interesting people, and Sloan's student body has a fantastically rich assortment of backgrounds and cultures. However, it's no use having an interesting group of classmates if it's difficult to meet them. Sloan's emphasis on group learning gives you a great opportunity to meet much of the class quickly.

The layout of Sloan encourages a great deal of daily contact and exposure to fellow students. At about noon, most students grab a sandwich at the cafeteria and congregate around the lobby or on the school steps overlooking Memorial Drive for lunch before going back to class. Others pop upstairs to the faculty club, where you can get the same cafeteria food served to you at twice the price, but with a better view. The more adventurous trek to local restaurants. The complete renovation and revitalization of the Kendall Square area has brought with it a range of gastronomic options hitherto unknown to the Sloan student. Everything from health food to Indian food to sandwiches to the best pizza this side of Tuscany is available within a short walk. Many memorable Sloan hours are spent discussing the importance of focused product strategies for major corporations over a pizza abruzzese at Florentina.

One of the major contributors to the entertaining nature of Sloan social life is the tremendous variety of international students at Sloan. While most business schools have a modest representation of students who aren't from New York, L.A., or Chicago, at Sloan you are almost as likely to find yourself in class sitting next to someone who is from Osaka, Rome, Paris, or Bombay as you are a New Yorker or a Bostonian.

« *The international flavor of Sloan was perhaps best manifested toward the end of second year by the internationalization of the Consumption Function. The Consumption Function is a well-attended Thursday afternoon event at which a goodly portion of the Sloan student body and faculty congregate to celebrate the beginning of the weekend (despite the fact that some still have classes on Friday morning) over beer, wine, chips, and pretzels.*

One week, the Mexican contingent of Sloan thought it would be a good idea to throw a Consumption Function with a Mexican theme. It was. Friday morning classes became irrelevant as Dos Equis and tequila flowed, while trays of burritos and chili rellenos came waltzing through the Sloan lobby, serenaded by a Mariachi band. In the time-honored tradition of a quick response to a competitive challenge, the Japanese students arranged a Consumption Function on an emperor-sized scale. Cases of Kirin were hauled in (courtesy of a popular student who worked for them) joined, just in time, by gallons of sake and mounds of yakitori, sushi, and gyoza. In the meantime, much of the Sloan student body was seen engaging in a play-at-home version of a popular Japanese game show, while several previously respected Japanese students belted out a karaoke version of "Take Me Home, Country Roads."

Next to respond was the usually neutral Swedish contingent. If the platters of köttbullar (Swedish meatballs) and cauldrons of glögg were not enough to attract a large turnout, the parade of young Swedish women dressed in white robes holding candles and singing "Santa Lucia" (as is traditional at Christmastime in Sweden) captured everyone's attention. Needless to say, the international experience that Sloan provides takes several forms. »

The organizing body behind the Consumption Functions is actually a student-elected team of professional party throwers/students who are responsible for most Sloan-sponsored (and Sloan-funded) social events. The Sloan administration allocates a fair amount of money for these events. In addition to the weekly Consumption Function, the GMS sponsors beach parties, booze cruises, barbecues, Christmas parties, and pub crawls. These events form the core, but by no means the whole, of the Sloan-based social life. There are quite a large number of organized sports such as softball, soccer, sailing, and ultimate frisbee teams that compete on an intramural basis. The various clubs at Sloan also provide a forum to get to know other Sloanies, while Sloan ski houses and weekend trips always seemed to be available.

Despite these relatively structured events, the social life at Sloan is really quite informal. The Sloan social scene, much like the Sloan student, is not big on image and flash. It strives for old-fashioned content. Tuxedos at Sloan are best used for wiping the beer off your chin. Parties vary in size from small, impromptu dinner parties to large, invite-everyone-you-know bashes. Most parties take place at students' houses rather than campus buildings and contain an equal mix of Sloanies and non-Sloanies. This stems from the housing situation at Sloan. The MIT housing is quite close to Sloan (one building reserved for married students is right next door), and some campus apartments offer spectacular views of the Charles River. But because of limited space most students choose to find their own housing. One might think that a business school where everyone commutes would have no intraschool social life whatsoever. In fact, it breeds an almost ideal environment for socializing. Many people share apartments with non-Sloan friends or find roommates through the MIT housing office. Thus many non-Sloanies become involved in the Sloan social life.

« *I opted for sharing an apartment with an old college friend who was working in Boston. This setup worked perfectly for me. I never felt any detachment from the Sloan social life, but when I wanted to escape, I could. It is actually quite similar to the real world, where you spend much of the day at work (or, in this case, school) and then go home. Those who choose to extend their Sloan social life to after-hours have ample opportunity to do so, while those who need time away from Sloan life are able to find it. I never felt the claustrophobia that small schools tend to breed in return for their relative intimacy.* »

In spite of the decentralized housing structure, Sloanies like to do things together. While the class did seem to segment into distinct cliques, the cliques all tended to hang out together, fostering a very open and relaxed social scene. During the week, Sloanies often go out for dinner after a work session, and postclass (and sometimes preclass) sessions at the Muddy Charles pub are not uncommon. On weekends there are usually a variety of Sloan parties, and there always seems to be a group of people going somewhere to do something, whether it's whale watching or Sox watching (a dangerous experience for me, as my blood runs Yankee blue). There seems to be little difference in the social life for single and married students, since the social experience is very open and inviting.

Boston is a tremendous place to spend two years. It is probably the only remaining U.S. city that still has Old World charm. It has a wealth of museums, concerts, restaurants, and shopping areas along with a full complement of sports teams. Its proximity to northern New England gives Sloanies the opportunity to sample New Hampshire fall foliage, Vermont winter skiing, and Maine spring clambakes with regularity. The contrasts among the colonial feeling of Cambridge, the bustle of Chinatown, where you brunch on dim sum and then wander past butchers selling live chickens, and the Italian flavor of the North End, where you can sit in a café at midnight sipping a cappuccino after dining on a *risotto con frutti di mare*, provide Boston life with a great deal of interest and variety.

RECRUITING AND JOB SEARCH

IT might be said that the job search in business school begins the moment you set foot in the door, and the scene at Sloan is no exception. Most people coming to Sloan will not go back to the company they left, and so much time and discussion, formal and informal, are spent talking about future options. Because of the diverse background of the student body, there is an equally diverse group of employers eager to get their hands on them, leaving a wide range of options open to the student. Many major and not-so-major corporations in industries ranging from automotive to software to chocolate recruit heavily at Sloan, joined by a wide variety of consulting firms, commercial banks, and investment banks.

To help provide a road map through this maze of companies and to help the student interested in employment outside of the group of companies that recruit at Sloan, the placement office provides information on a great number of job sources. Job description letters from companies that have been unable to come to campus, along with information on all recruiters who have come to Sloan over the past several years, are kept in the placement office library. Also, the placement office produces a bound résumé book that is distributed to potential employers.

The search for jobs at those companies that recruit Sloan is organized by the placement office. Those students who choose to do something more out of the mainstream must go through different channels. One of these channels is the alumni/alumnae network. Although it is not as large as the networks of other, larger, business schools, its size can be a distinct advantage to students. Because it is relatively small, almost all the alumni and alumnae are especially eager to help out and, if possible, arrange interviews. At the very least, their accessibility is enormously helpful in providing information about jobs, companies, or industries. The placement office provides convenient access to the names and jobs of this ever-growing network of Sloanies worldwide.

A second alternative source of jobs comes from the MIT community itself. Because the university has such close ties to industry, there are numerous interesting and entrepreneurial opportunities to be explored. The advantage of being so close to industry is that it allows you to keep somewhat in contact with the real world while you are immersed in intellectual pursuits.

Firms are not allowed to commence interviewing until January for both full-time and summer jobs, keeping the first semester somewhat less stressful than it otherwise would be. Firms are, however, allowed to give presentations during the first semester. These get-togethers provide a useful source of information for those people who want to find out more about an industry, those who want to know what a consultant actually does, and those who want to inhale massive quantities of the shrimp and bacon-wrapped scallops that are de rigueur at these events. By the end of this presentation season, many people have sent out the résumés and cover letters that are required for getting on a company's interview list; they then go away on winter vacation. Those who do not find anything that interests them through Sloan's standard offerings spend some of the break, as well as MIT's optional January term, seeking alternative solutions. Those who are satisfied with their roster of interview choices spend the month of January preparing for them on sunny beaches or sunny (but slightly chillier) ski slopes.

The beginning of summer job interviews can be a bit of an uncomfortable situation. While Sloan is busy breeding a group of supportive people who work best while working together, interviewing puts these same people into head-to-head competition with each other. The first few days are filled with people trying to get the inside scoop on what questions are being asked. Soon people are wondering whether company X has come back with call-backs. This situation is especially difficult with the summer jobs because these intern positions are necessarily limited. Those who have difficulty securing a summer job through these channels often go back to their pre-Sloan employer for the summer with a new outlook or take on research work at MIT.

Upon return to Sloan in the fall, there is much excitement as stories and rumors abound about people's summer experiences. Some people have gained a much clearer idea of what they want to do when they graduate. Some have even accepted full-time positions with their summer employers. Most people, however, haven't a clue as to what they want to do. As the month of October rolls around and companies make their appearance on campus once again, blue suits come into full bloom. This time, though, it's for real, and people are somewhat more serious about the process. The companies are also more serious. Whereas first-year pre-interview recruiting is accompanied by presentations only, most companies recruiting for full-time positions throw dinner parties as well as giving presentations. These dinners can be a great deal of fun, but the invitee list often bears little resemblance to a company's eventual acceptance list.

As the end of first semester arrives, most people have assembled a list of companies they are interested in. Generally speaking, the list comprises an assortment of companies that recruit at Sloan and companies that students are pursuing on their own initiative. Even the most hard-core consulting and I-bank prospects are contemplating "doing something a bit different" at this stage. As with the summer job process, letters go out in the hope of securing an interview spot on a company's closed-interview list. Companies that have a closed list interview by invitation only. However, those companies that recruit at Sloan are required to leave some spots open for "lottery" candidates. Each student is allocated a certain number of points that he or she can use to bid for remaining spots in closed schedules. In reality, though, I cannot recall anyone who was not able to secure an interview spot, so it becomes a moot point.

The second-year interviewing process starts in mid-January and is at once more serious and more relaxed than the summer process. Because they are nearing the end of the road, people get somewhat more anxious about the whole process. Nevertheless, most people by this time have at least a couple of interviews under their belt (from the summer process) and are somewhat more confident. People spend the free weeks leading up to interview season in several ways. Some go long distances to get away from everything or to interview with out-of-town prospects. Others stay in Boston to take advantage of the interview seminars and mock interviews that the placement office offers or to do further research on potential employers.

« *I actually straightened out my thoughts on my job search quite a bit in the days before interviewing. I came back to Cambridge a week early to get prepared and spent an hour a day running with a group of friends. During these runs we would discuss interviewing tactics and our respective story lines on what we really wanted to do in life and what made us different from the typical job candidate. The pros and cons of consulting versus corporate life were tossed about and potential new cities to live in were evaluated. During these runs, we rarely came to any definitive conclusions, but we inevitably managed to agree on finishing off the run with a few cold ones in the muddy Charles. »*

For all the buildup toward interviewing, the actual process passes surprisingly quickly. Within a couple of weeks most firms have been through their first two rounds of interviews, and a somewhat diminished pool of candidates is preparing for the final round of interviews at the company's site. This time has the potential to be brutal because for every hopeful third-rounder stopping by class with a garment bag and a suit on the way to catch the four-o'clock shuttle to New York, there are four or five people who have received the dreaded "ding" letter from that same company. Nevertheless, Sloanies remain tremendously supportive of each other, and sniping and jealousy are kept to a minimum.

« Those who are doing well in the interview process are wise to keep their success to themselves because, as Professor Yogi says, "It ain't over till it's over." One friend who was sailing through the interview process was getting mentally into the mode of deciding which of four or five companies would be lucky enough to get him. In the final round, though, he "hit the screen" on all but one company. »

By the end of May, most students have happily accepted offers at a wide variety of companies at very comfortable salaries. There are those, though, who have either not received an offer or decided not to accept their outstanding offers. By the end of fall, these students have usually found a very attractive position somewhere and, months down the road, can be happier than those who found jobs much sooner. Three quarters of Sloan grads accept positions in management consulting, sales and marketing, and finance (in roughly equal proportions). From an industry perspective, consulting is most popular, followed by the electronics industry and I-banking.

The Sloan education is by no means cheap, both in purely monetary terms and in terms of the uprooting cost that most Sloanies have to go through when they leave their relatively settled work lives for a two-year detour *not* climbing the corporate ladder. But in terms of the respect which potential employers have for a Sloan education, this detour is well worth the trip.

ON THE JOB — FIRST YEARS OUT

« *Being a manager in the 1990s requires much more than being a manager in the 1980s did. The 1990s manager must have an increasingly global and broad strategic perspective while at the same time being able to understand increasingly complex business situations that require a detailed, operational understanding of the problem at hand. The 1990s manager must be able to operate as effectively in Milan, Abu Dhabi, Melbourne, and Pusan as in New York or L.A. Does Sloan make you into such a supermanager? . . . Probably not. Does Sloan give you a good head start? . . . Absolutely.* »

Sloan graduates reenter the job world with a formidable set of tools to get them on the way to being a supermanager. First and foremost, the absolute quality, breadth, and depth of the education received provide a Sloanie with as sound a foundation as one could want. Not once during my first few months at work did I feel outclassed by my peers from other business schools in any particular area. Sloanies learn to hypothesize, generalize, and synthesize as well as the best of them, while being able to add and subtract better than most of them. The combination of cases and lectures at Sloan ensures that the Sloanie has an action-oriented approach toward solving problems as well as the tools actually to solve them and implement solutions.

One problem most business school graduates face upon entering the corporate world is that of credibility. After all, in the eyes of most outsiders, MBAs are far overpaid and far underexperienced. In this respect, the MIT brand name comes in really handy. Unaided recall is extremely high all over the world and carries with it a great deal of respect and a perception of the high quality that is usually associated with top universities, along with a pragmatism that usually isn't. Especially in foreign countries, MIT's reputation gives a Sloanie a certain unique credibility that can be extremely useful initially.

Gaining a global perspective on problems and learning to deal with different cultures on business, rather than casual, terms is not particularly easy when you're in Boston, New York, Chicago, or San Francisco. At Sloan, though, it's certainly easier than at a lot of other places. The fantastic assortment of different nationalities and cultures at Sloan at any one time along with the emphasis on group problem solving virtually ensure that you will work with quite a large international contingent over the course of two years. Any one student may work with Japanese, French, Italians, Spaniards, British, Germans, Ecuadorians, *and* Chinese, among others. You will find this of particular use and value in the real world.

« For my first major project with a consulting firm I was packed off abroad to work with a major multinational company. I soon found myself dealing on a day-to-day basis with top-level executives from just about every European country. It can be difficult enough to try to adjust to working with one different culture, but learning to be equally effective with the theoretical French, the creative Italians, and the analytical Germans can be a real challenge. Nevertheless, I feel that my Sloan background was a major contribution in making that first project a success. »

As attractive, well-paid, and fascinating as most first jobs are, the average business school graduate is more likely than not to switch jobs after a few years. Although at this stage your recent on-the-job experience is far more relevant than what you learned at business school, the Sloan degree remains a valuable credential to have and is likely to make your first and future job experiences extremely fruitful.

SUMMARY OVERVIEW

SLOAN is a great place to spend two years going to business school. It exposes you to a smorgasbord of different cultures and backgrounds while surrounding you with interesting and ambitious people. The faculty is top-flight in both stature (i.e., "name brand" recognition) and in teaching ability. The structure of the program ensures that a Sloan student is exposed to everything, yet a very relaxed collegiate and social atmosphere is maintained.

Clearly the most unexpected aspect of Sloan is the variety of different people with whom you will have the opportunity to work. While there are several stereotypes of what one might picture as a typical Sloan student (engineers, Easterners, MIT graduates), you are just as likely to find a French philosopher, a Japanese entrepreneur, an Italian banker, or an English management consultant. All of these people share a large amount of creativity, a healthy dose of ambition, and demonstrated problem-solving ability.

If learning with these students is a great experience, learning from the Sloan faculty is a pleasure. The professors are adept at maintaining a fine balance between case and lecture, depending on the subject material. This mix allows the faculty to draw more easily on their specific expertise than if they were tied to a rigid case approach. In most cases, they are "the expert," whether it is Lester Thurow holding forth on economics or Mike Cusumano explaining the historical development of Japanese companies.

Finally, the structure of the Sloan program helps to bring the whole student body together. There is a group of "core" courses that every student must take (or waive) that primarily creates a solid base of knowledge for everyone. A secondary but still very important program goal is to foster a strong sense of teamwork among Sloan students. Most of the core classes require team projects, and in those that do not, study groups often emerge. Because the Sloan class is relatively small, you get to know a huge portion of your class. This relaxed, team-spirited approach also carries over to the Sloan social life, which generally embraces everyone. However, the mostly off-campus housing situation at Sloan and the tremendous opportunities that exist in Boston give everyone a chance to get away from the Sloan scene every now and then for a bit of a break.

As with most things, there are areas where Sloan could be better. While the placement office does an excellent job of handling those companies that come to recruit and providing leads on those who do not, there are still a number of firms who find it hard to justify sending recruiters to a relatively small school when there is a very real chance they might come home empty-handed.

Another problem that comes with the small size is limited course offerings. While Sloan does have a remarkable array of courses, they are often given at conflicting times and may not all be offered every year. Thus, in many cases, a course is offered only once during your stay at Sloan. You sometimes have to make sacrifices when that course is offered at the same time as another that you want or are required to take. This, however, is a problem of too many choices rather than too few.

In summary, Sloan is a particularly special place to spend two years. The diversity and talent of the student body, the quality of the faculty, and the overall congeniality of Sloan make it a wonderful place to get a management degree. For a top ten business school that is no small feat.

Chapter 7

THE UNIVERSITY OF MICHIGAN BUSINESS SCHOOL*

THE PROGRAM

MICHIGAN is probably the most innovative business school in the country. Over the past two years, spearheaded by a new dean, some exciting developments have freed faculty as well as students from the bounds of tradition. Grades are no longer at the forefront of everyone's mind — students come to Michigan to get an education and field experience that can make them productive leaders and trendsetters for business in the future. The number of classes available has nearly doubled with a change in the semester schedule. Experience in dealing with numerous types of people and problems has become the priority, with on-site field projects now required for all entering students. Above all, students and faculty can pursue the latest trends in business by developing new classes and even traveling throughout the world to get the latest information firsthand. Dean B. Joseph White has made it a priority to emphasize the quality of teaching and the ability to offer a variety and depth of courses that best serve the school's customers — the students and faculty in addition to business.

Like most other leading business schools, it is impossible to get through Michigan's program without learning the basic key phrases and meanings of core competence, corporate culture, diversity, flexibility, and globalism. Michigan sets itself apart, however, in the

* BY DAVID ARDIS, MBA

manner in which these ideas are expressed. Within the first week of Orientation, students have been introduced to their fellow students via team projects and have personally met numerous business executives. For a recent entering class, this meant visits by the chairmen of Merck and Whirlpool corporations during Orientation week, with a follow-up session by the executive vice president of the Commonwealth Fund and representatives of more than twenty Fortune 500 companies. Throughout the year, students will have had access to workshops with trendsetters such as Stephen Covey, who has led workshops at Michigan on leadership skills based on his best-selling books and leadership center. With such close interaction between members of the Michigan academic community and corporate America, an agenda is set for the ensuing two years: school is meant to be a hands-on learning experience, and not just memorization and exposure to leading textbooks and journals. Where else can you be one of over 420 students to wake up in the morning the first day of Orientation with a sinking feeling in your stomach that says, "What have I gotten myself into? I had a job. I had a nice apartment. I had friends. Did I jump off the deep end?"

Although all students probably have these feelings at one time or another in their preliminary search for an MBA, the University of Michigan offers yet another advantage: your fellow students. Diversity is a fact, not an often-talked-about goal or lofty promise. Students come from all over the United States as well as the world to Michigan. While there's a good chance that the person seated next to you in class is an engineer, there's an even better chance that he or she has a liberal arts degree in economics or one in business administration. Almost half are proficient in a language other than English, and more than 95 percent have worked a minimum of one year, the vast majority with over three years of full-time experience. Whatever their degree, you can be assured that your fellow students are aggressive, goal-oriented, and have something unique in background and in personality to contribute to the program. And because it's located in Michigan, there is a definite sense of midwestern hospitality and no-nonsense work ethic.

Your two-year experience at Michigan starts out with the inevitable bureaucracy of Orientation: paperwork, handbooks, and welcoming addresses. But at Michigan there is one additional twist, which comes in the form of acid rivers, electric fences, and traffic jams. Is it a jail break? No! It's groups of MBAs participating in team-building exercises as part of the Global Citizenship Program, which sensitizes students to the needs of society as well as erasing a stigma of insularity often associated with graduate-level business education. In a two-day program, incoming students are divided into groups of ten. Each team has a faculty member and/or corporate executive, and a second-year MBA team leader. Led through team-building exercises, the groups then travel throughout the state of Michigan to do civic projects ranging from rehabilitating homes in depressed areas to neighborhood cleanups and painting projects. Often these projects evolve into a continuing commitment over the course of students' education at the Business School.

« *When I first heard that I was part of an Orientation group of students going to downtown Detroit, I was skeptical, to say the least. But what I found, along with a group of fifty other students and faculty members, was a true renaissance spirit. Sure, the Motor City has serious crime and other social problems that are broadcast on the news every day. What city doesn't? But those stories all miss the most important aspect: the people. We met individuals from the Ravendale community who had a fantastic attitude and were actually cleaning their community from within — renovating homes and ridding their neighborhood of abandoned homes and drug dealers.*

They gave us a new point of view, a perspective that the majority of us had never seen before. These people were extremely proud of their community and their efforts. They didn't want any handouts. Rather, they wanted a helping hand from business so they could learn how to do things on their own and establish a sense of pride and personal spirit. We learned that working together as a group brings results that are much greater than the sum of individual accomplishments.

But the learning was also a two-way street. While we were helping the community complete its own master business development plan, which involved developing marketing budgets along with seemingly simple but significant help in literally picking up trash off the streets, members of the community also began to realize that maybe business was beginning to realize the importance of community involvement to its own successful operations. Students made a significant step toward erasing the image that students at the Michigan Business

School have no understanding of the types of problems that face inner city residents. »

The point is simple: no longer can businesses separate themselves from the communities in which they are located. As public funds become more scarce, local communities are turning toward private funding and corporations to make up the difference. If companies want to be able to hire fully qualified employees, it is in their best interest to have school systems that turn out students who can read and write at appropriate levels. For employees to be most productive, certain community services and resources must be made available; this can be translated to mean social, cultural, or recreational facilities, which cost money. Businesses have a vital interest in the communities, both in the present and in the future.

And what does this have to do with your MBA? The University of Michigan, and the Michigan Business School in particular, sees itself as a progressive institution in training future leaders who can clear the path for this more socially and environmentally progressive future. The school provides eye-opening experiences to students who learn to work in teams, and what was initially just a group of individuals thrown together by fate is transformed into a well-honed team able and willing to tackle any problem.

After a rigorous week of Orientation in which meeting your fellow classmates and gaining a sense of class identity is a major goal, students are ready to hit the books running. But a managerial writing proficiency test and placement exams come first. All entering students are required to take the writing assessment, which presents a specific management situation that requires a persuasive written response. Students' responses are evaluated on a number of different criteria: clarity of thought, organization, development of ideas, audience awareness, persuasive appeal, and English usage. While the majority of students pass the test, those who demonstrate weaknesses are required to take a managerial writing course before graduating.

Placement tests are also available for nine of the ten required core courses at Michigan. Tests are offered at the beginning of both first and second terms. By passing a placement examination prior to being in the required course, the student may waive that course and substitute an elective in its place. Placement exams can be taken only once, and credit hours are not awarded for showing proficiency. As your time at Michigan is limited and the number of electives you will want to choose far exceeds the available time, it is strongly recommended that you study in advance for those areas in which you have experience and gain the freedom for electives. A new program also being implemented allows waivers based on previous educational and/or work experience without taking the traditional placement tests.

With Orientation and placement exams under their belt, entering classes are divided into six sections of approximately seventy students each. Students spend their first year of classes with these students, moving from class to class. What started out as a large, impersonal mass of bodies soon evolves into a cohesive team made up of new friends.

The Business School is on a modified semester (or "term") schedule in which students take fifteen credit hours (typical full-term courses are three credits) during each fourteen-week-long term. Not one to follow the rest of the pack, the Business School is changing its entire curriculum and modifying this traditional schedule. The new modular system breaks the traditional fourteen-week term into two seven-week segments, thus allowing traditional fourteen-week classes in addition to numerous seven-week classes. The reasoning behind this change has to do with flexibility. In an effort to make the MBA degree as meaningful as possible to students who are entering the program with varied backgrounds and purposes, more and more classes are being created. It is now possible to pass out of the first and/or second seven-week segment of most core classes. For professors, it means that they can teach shorter modules with leading-edge materials and still maintain outside consulting ventures. It also means they can create classes around specific areas of expertise that can be fully covered in the shorter amount of time. For students, it means the opportunity to take twice as many courses from that many more professors. Students are able to define their program of study to include dimensions never before possible.

Perhaps the biggest change to the academic program at the Michigan Business School is a new curriculum designed to give students more hands-on learning and practical experience. Probably named by some academician who feels that acronyms make anything sound more important and professional, the MAP (Multidisciplinary Action Project) program takes first-year students away from campus, resulting in a unique and truly innovative academic environment. For students in the classroom phase of the program, classes are held for four days each week, with a Friday "free" day that is quickly filled with tests and group meetings. Students in the MAP portion of their education (the last seven-week segment of their second term) spend time away from campus in a corporate setting, often working with upper-level management. In MAP, emphasis is placed on integrating the functional areas, working with fellow students, and working with "real world" problems in business situations. It is a consulting project giving valuable access to company records and personnel, with the bonus of having the professors at the Business School as backup resources and tools for guidance. Most important, it is a way to put concepts learned from the core courses into practice, a very valuable experience to add to your résumé.

« I can't tell you how nervous we were to present our findings to our MAP corporate sponsor, a Fortune 500 company with offices nearby. The CEO and three vice presidents were scheduled to attend. Our presentation combined the latest in audio and visual technology, using multimedia facilities at the university. Using ideas that we had learned in our Operations Management and Statistics classes, we came up with a revised method to streamline the Customer Service hot-line program. Whereas the average time for problem resolution used to take up to fifteen weeks, the new system avoided unnecessary duplication and bottlenecks and cut the time in half — and reduced time meant money both to the bottom line as well as an increase in customer satisfaction and repeat orders.

Not only were we able to impress them with our presentation, but also we were able to recommend a profitable solution that no one to date had been able to propose. Our project was definitely not "make work" — it might even get us one of those elusive jobs! MAP was definitely the culmination of a fantastic first year. »

As much as you think you have learned after the first year at Michigan, the second year is when you really earn your MBA. Taking the last core class in Corporate Strategy, the rest of your courses will be electives. By this time, you will probably have a much better idea of what classes will best serve you in the future, and since Michigan does not recognize fields of concentration or "majors," you are free to customize your MBA in countless ways, with courses in the Business School as well as from the university as a whole — up to ten credit hours of graduate courses in other units of the University of Michigan at Ann Arbor can be taken for degree credit. The possibilities are endless, since some of the most respected schools in the United States are in Ann Arbor, including the Michigan Law and Medical schools.

Other possibilities exist outside the traditional university setting as well during your second year. The Michigan Business School is a member of the Program in International Management (PIM), a highly regarded international organization composed of members of leading graduate schools of management throughout the world. There are international exchange programs with ten schools of business from Austria to Singapore, with varying degrees of fluency in the native tongue required. More than fifteen joint degree programs with other units on the University of Michigan campus are available, from Architecture to Southeast Asian Studies. Additionally, the past two years have had classes structured around emerging business opportunities in the former Soviet Union, as well as in the European Community. These two classes were suggested and initially organized by students, with the focus on a corporate-sponsored trip by the entire class to Europe over the spring break. Rumor has it that future classes will be organized around business opportunities in Australia and other places. The nice thing about Michigan is that if students want a class taught on a specific topic not now available, and if they find a professor willing to teach and sponsor the class, the dean has bent over backward in cooperating and providing funds to organize one of these "one time only" classes. It's also a very important sign of how customer-focused the administration at Michigan is.

Other resources available to Michigan MBAs include the Executive Education Program, recently recognized as the best of its kind in the world, as rated by attending executives in a *Business Week* poll. While contact with executives can be limited, certain professors are known to make announcements in their classes when groups of executives have requested a meeting with current students for help in using the research facilities available at the Business School, or just for socializing . . . and the name of the game is contacts!

The Michigan Business School was also the recipient of one of the largest donations ever made to a business school, resulting in the William Davidson Institute, dedicated to helping countries make the transition from a command to a free market economy primarily through instruction, student and faculty development, and research. The goal of the institute is to become the world's leading center on market economics and to have a significant role in influencing world economic development. What this means to Michigan Business School students is an opportunity to participate in leading-edge research, as well as instructional and fellowship programs.

So with all these facilities available within the Michigan Business School itself as well as the University of Michigan as a whole, probably everyone's question becomes, what kind of school is Michigan? Perhaps a better way of putting it is, "The answer is yes. Now, what's the question?" Michigan is a lot of things. It is a marketing school as well as a finance school. It is an organizational behavior school as well as an international business school. The administration's feeling is that a well-balanced school of management education is best. While the majority of students probably emphasize marketing or finance, it is feasible and quite common that a person who considers himself or herself a marketing major might take as many classes in finance or accounting as in marketing. The critical element is that you can decide what classes you need most to fulfill your own MBA and future management needs.

The Michigan Business School has facilities that are the envy of most schools. The physical plant is outstanding, having been almost entirely renovated in the past ten years. There are two fully equipped computer labs with over 150 computers, with plans for additional facilities to be added in the next year. In addition to all academic buildings being connected to avoid the unpredictable Michigan winters, a large student lounge serves snacks and light foods for the greater part of the day into the wee hours. Lecture rooms are outfitted for computer graphic displays as well as videotape and overhead projection systems. The Business School is also embarking on its own part of the larger University of Michigan 175th anniversary development campaign, with a $100 million goal earmarked for Business School student, faculty, and educational/research support. These new funds will be targeted toward the human capital at Michigan — the talent and the people who *are* the Michigan Business School.

GETTING IN

As with most competitive business schools, there is no one secret to getting accepted at the Michigan Business School. There are the basic educational requirements, including successful completion of a college-level course covering integral and differential calculus, as well as the required GMAT. Proficiency with microcomputers and basic applications is expected. Other than these general requirements, the rest is up to the individual. The school is looking for management potential and distinguishing characteristics that set you apart from the other roughly four thousand applicants. They want to know why you would be a better candidate than someone else, what traits you have developed that demonstrate your potential to become a manager.

Probably most critical to your application is the written portion, in which you are asked to answer several questions. Four essays are required, with a fifth being optional: (1) Describe personal and professional achievements within the last five years that are good indicators of your potential for a successful management career. (2) What qualities are you looking for in a business school? How well does Michigan fit your needs? (3) During your years of study in the Michigan MBA program, you will be part of a diverse, multicultural, multiethnic community within both the Business School and the larger university. What rewards and challenges do you anticipate in this campus environment, and how do you expect this experience to prepare you for a culturally diverse business world? Please draw on your own experience in your response. (4) What professional and/or personal goals have you tentatively established for the next five years of your life, and how do you see the MBA helping you to reach your goals? (5) If there is any other information that you feel is important to our assessment of your candidacy, feel free to add it to your application.

« *A housemate of mine from the program had been an aerospace engineer with NASA before coming to Michigan. His biggest reason for wanting to get his MBA was to be able to present his ideas and plans better to an overly bureaucratic agency. He wanted to know how to refine his projects and make them presentable for others' review. He wanted to be able to market his projects to the agency itself and then be able to follow through with implementation. Most important, he wanted to become a manager of people and projects, and not just another cog in the wheel. He wanted to become the bridge between engineering and other departments — and when you deal with projects such as the Shuttle combustion engine, with its thousands of parts and operating variables, there is a tremendous need to be able to communicate between technical and nontechnical personnel. He felt that a Michigan MBA would benefit him, and the school agreed.* »

Although at first glance these questions may seem to be straightforward, their purpose is to gain insight into how you as an individual think as well as how you operate and react in various environments. Acceptance is a two-way street; the school wants to know what you have to contribute to your potential fellow students in addition to what you expect to gain from your choice of Michigan. Each top ten business school has its own unique atmosphere, and Michigan is not alone in wanting to maintain its well-known reputation for producing well-rounded team leaders who have the motivation and experience to become future corporate managers and executives.

Interviews are not now required, although prospective students are invited and strongly encouraged to visit the school and tour the facilities with a current student. Students applying to business schools should realize that schools are professional as far as recruiting brochures and other informational pamphlets; business school is a significant commitment of time and money. Students who visit Michigan can see for themselves that Michigan doesn't just look good on paper, and they are encouraged to speak with current students and observe classes and professors. Appointments may be made with the assistant dean of admissions or with various admissions counselors, but the meetings will be for informational purposes only. There is growing pressure from the administration as well as from current students, faculty, and alumni/alumnae for interviews to become an integral part of the application process.

As Michigan follows a "rolling" admissions policy, students are strongly encouraged to apply as early as possible. There is an early-decision option available in which those who have all materials completed by December 1 will have a decision by February 15.

Otherwise, consideration of applications begins February 15, with preference given to those received by March 1. Remember, impressions are everything — don't wait until the last day. Deferrals are extremely limited and should not be assumed.

ACADEMIC ENVIRONMENT

MOST students probably find the first term or semester to be the most difficult. The vast majority of students have been out of school for several years. Not only is there the adjustment to no paycheck, but having to open textbooks and course packs to read, to take notes, and to be prepared for class is also a major adjustment. First-term required courses include Financial Accounting, Microeconomics, Marketing Management, Statistics, Corporate Strategy, and International Business. Courses are taught using a combination of case method, lecture, and seminar. Given the nature of the topics covered, Accounting and Statistics are traditionally taught through lecture, although cases can be and are used when deemed appropriate. Michigan gives its professors great flexibility in determining and using the method that best suits a particular topic. You can rest assured that no matter what the class, chances are extremely high there will be group work, which accounts for a significant part of a course's requirements. By the middle of the first term, everyone religiously carries their HP calculators and is prepared to crunch numbers at will.

« We'd all seen Paper Chase and heard horror stories about professors who would carry around index cards or sheets of paper with pictures and backgrounds of all the students on them. They would pick several cards at random and have those students begin the day's discussion. Before class, students would nervously joke with one another, hoping that they weren't wearing something that would draw attention to them or hoping that their card did not have a tear or crease in it that would make it stand out from all others. Nobody came to class unprepared.

Little did we know the benefits of the case method — once you were on the hot seat, you knew that you had to think before you spoke and understand all and any ramifications of your decisions. As that *professor told us, it was okay to make mistakes in the classroom as long as we learned from them and corrected ourselves — but mistakes in real life were often irreversible.* »

The second term at Michigan is more of the same: number crunching with Financial Management, Managerial Accounting, Operations Management, Organizational Behavior, and Computer Information Systems. But there are also several big differences. Students know what is expected of them, have had experience working in group projects, and have gotten over the thoughts of why they are paying so much money to have such demands and time constraints made on them. Study groups have often been formed, and your "section" becomes your home away from home. Oftentimes you know more about your sectionmates than you might want to! But it is nice knowing that you always have someone you can commiserate with — and from whom you can seek help and advice.

Additionally, the classes in the second term begin to touch on some real business management skills rather than simply the fundamentals. By the end of the second term, students feel they have been exposed to the basics of general management, a trait for which Michigan is well known by recruiters and corporate sponsors. While you might not feel yourself to be an expert, you know enough to know when you are outside your bounds of safety — you can identify a problem and potential solutions, even if their implementation is beyond you. Also during the second term, the search for a summer internship begins in earnest, with interviewing and networking among fellow students and alumni/alumnae.

While the University of Michigan Business School continues to exhibit a dedication to excellence, its academic environment has changed significantly in recent years. Starting two years ago, a new grading system was instituted based on four levels instead of the more traditional nine point scale from A+ on down with a bell curve. This system uses the "grades" of Excellent, Good, Low Pass, and Fail instead of letter grades. The idea is to deemphasize individual competition and stress the importance of working in teams and groups of fellow students. Based on feedback from students and faculty, this system will be kept with some modifications.

Regarding popular acceptance of the system, the jury is still out. Most students agree that the new grading system promotes learning for the sake of learning and that it cuts down on the pressure and intense individual competition experienced with the old scale. Others say it promotes mediocrity instead, since almost everyone gets a Good, while Excellents are hard to come by. Equally difficult to receive are Fails, although it does happen if someone tries hard enough! Given the motivation and determination of students, it is difficult but not unheard of to flunk out of the program. But no matter what scale is used, it is clear that the course work is demanding, and each grade must be earned with a great deal of time-consuming and dedicated work. Most students come to Michigan to learn about business anyway, and grades are secondary.

« *I'll never forget our first marketing exam. It started at 6:00 P.M. and was scheduled to last until 10:00 P.M. We were handed a case to analyze, with a list of questions and scenarios. You could hear the groans from throughout the room as everyone opened the exam packets. The product was chicken hot dogs. Soon the scribbling started and continued until hands started cramping and beyond. I did scenarios for break-even analysis based on untold numbers of variables: price, promotion, market segmentation, and product mix to begin with. We had to allow for the product life cycle, competitive reaction, as well as the various available marketing channels. Four hours of solid writing didn't even guarantee getting to the last question, and more than one of us walked out of that room with a sinking feeling that our sore hands and arms didn't help us pass the test. It was only after I left the exam that I began to realize that the intensity of the program and the depth of my learning would pay off in the future. I now have great confidence in my ability to develop a situation analysis, and from that, analyze the problems and opportunities presented and evaluate various options, then make the best decision.* »

The students in the B School are extremely bright and have high personal standards, which help to create a stimulating atmosphere. They are friendly yet at the same time competitive. The competitiveness is not cutthroat, however, and tends to be hidden — although we all know it is there! Overwhelmingly the students are cooperative, and you can always count on someone helping you out in a bind. This is probably a result of the many group projects required during a term. Classmates must count on one another and work together to complete the projects. Students who don't pull their weight are quickly "branded" and find it more difficult to recruit willing group members the next time groups are formed. Final course grades are usually derived by combining the results of group work and class participation with the outcome of individual tests or other homework and projects.

« *The first group paper of your graduate career can really teach you a lot. Second-year students were kidding us not to spend too much time arguing over every word and comma. At the time we thought it would never happen to us but soon found out we were wrong!*

The project was simple: provide a descriptive analysis of the management hierarchy as described in a video on the Walt Disney Company we had seen earlier in the week. Individually, we could have finished it in probably an hour or two. Not so with our first experience in writing a group paper. We finished that paper at about 3:00 A.M. simply because we were still finding out how to work as a group. We did not know how to delegate authority or how to work efficiently as a group. The most important lesson we learned was to trust one another and spend time only on the important things. Needless to say, we were the ones doing the kidding the next year! »

The Business School population is composed of students from all around the world and from a variety of ethnic backgrounds. This can be a double-edged sword, since both the benefits of interacting with people of different races and backgrounds and the difficulties sometimes associated with misunderstanding each other's heritage are increased. But each section reflects the diversity of the class, and lasting friendships are made with classmates from across the globe. Students spend their first year in classes with their sectionmates unless they place out of required classes and enroll in electives with other first- and second-year students.

The facilities at the Michigan Business School can only be described as outstanding. The library is among the largest business libraries in the United States and contains several different CD-ROM research data bases. A large computing lab supports several of the most popular business and word processing software packages. Hardware includes 486 microcomputers as well as Macintosh computers. Generally there are plenty of computers available, as the lab is restricted to Business School students only, although there are still lines for the units when final papers are due! For night owls, the university also has several large computing facilities with much of the same software as at the Business School and that are open twenty-four hours. Recently new audiovisual equipment was added to all of the large lecture rooms, to allow projection video and networking between rooms. The library has also outfitted many of the group study rooms with computers and printers.

It is hard to characterize the typical teaching style at Michigan. Few of the professors at Michigan teach with a straight lecture method. Most of the classes are a combination of lecture and case discussions, with some goodies such as videos, computer simulations, and guest speakers thrown in. Professors will lead discussions. They generally have a list of items that need to be covered in the hour-and-a-half class but will leave the meat of the class up to the students. The success of this method of learning from other students' opinions and experience is highly dependent on the skill of the professor in leading the discussion. Discussions in section (or core) classes tend to be more lively and spontaneous due to the added depth of knowledge about your fellow students' opinions and backgrounds.

Is there a lot of pressure at Michigan? The answer to this is both yes and no. Yes, because you are expected to complete the work no matter how many other classes and extra activities you may be responsible for. You are expected to think and offer insights and opinions and not just to read and regurgitate information in the class discussions and assignments. Some professors make sure that no matter what, you are prepared for their classes by employing the "on the spot public grilling" technique in which you are asked to justify and back up every statement you make. In addition, fellow students/ friends count on you to contribute your part to projects in group situations. It all takes a tremendous amount of time management and prioritization, and the pressure can be quite intense at times.

The good news, though, is that the professors make office time available if you have questions and, for the most part, are very human and approachable. You do not operate in a vacuum. You are not a number. The pressure is to learn and contribute, but not to do it all on your own under adverse conditions. As Professor Suslow tells her first-term Economics classes, you can only fall so far off the floor! The importance is in learning the tools adequately and sufficiently so you can build on them and gain invaluable assets. And ultimately, the real value of the Michigan MBA, given a very strong educational base, comes from developing your own sense of style and an ability to work with others. Like a lot of things in life, the more you put into Michigan, the more you'll take out — a very hands-on approach to business and management.

SOCIAL LIFE

« *Our Economics professor let it slip one day near semester break that some professors were talking about our section in the faculty lounge. Upon further urging from us, she let us know that some of the professors were "dreading" getting our section the next semester because we were so socially active and always made quite a few announcements before class! Sometimes it became the joke that she would ask us for permission to start class — but only if it wouldn't be interrupting our social plans for the day. She did tell us, though, that they all agreed that "we worked as hard as we played"!* »

Social activities tend to center on your section for most of the first year. Although Michigan has a large entering class of approximately 420 full-time students, everyone gets a chance to know one another; the second-year sections will indoctrinate their first-year "sister sections" into the social life of the Business School within the first couple of weeks of the semester. Generally the year starts off with a barbecue in a nearby park, complete with food, tennis, volleyball, other activities, and, of course, beer. And what would Orientation be without an introduction to those infamous turkey sandwiches from Executive Education! With Orientation activities, section parties, and schoolwide events crammed into the first few weeks, it's not uncommon to form lasting friendships immediately.

« *My best friend from school was a woman who related the story of her experience at Michigan during the first days of Orientation. Within the first two weeks of arriving at school, she and her husband had met three other couples, and it turned out they all got along great! They formed a rotating dinner club where each couple was responsible for feeding the others one night every fourth month. They quickly came to count on their monthly evening together as a welcome break from the hectic pace of school. They tried a wide variety of new foods from Japan, Europe, and the United States. The dinner club lasted through both years, and no matter how many other friendships they formed, those friendships started in the first few weeks were, and still are, among the closest and most valued ones they took away from the program.* »

Throughout the year many clubs and organizations sponsor events for the whole school. Generally there is at least a Halloween party, a holiday formal at a nearby hotel, a welcome-back party in January, and an end-of-the-year formal before graduation. In January, students also put on a variety show called *The Follies*, which pokes fun at every aspect of Business School life. Students, spouses, faculty, and staff all take part in the skits and songs and provide a funny and sometimes scathing look at the Business School and corporate America. Professional lighting and sound help to sell out the three performances of this "traditional irreverence."

« *This year's* Follies *had a skit put on by faculty members — primarily Accounting Department professors. Not only did they satirize student "gunners" — those students who feel they need to sit at the front of every lecture and dominate any discussion — but also the truth came out that many papers and projects are graded by the janitorial staff at the B School! (You had to be there to see the dean come to school on a Harley-Davidson.) Seriously, though, it was also a way for faculty members to acknowledge some of the day-to-day pressures that students face and to let them know that the whole process is meant to be a learning experience, not just another ritual. Besides, the school is ready for some amusement after the month of January, when the weather can start to become quite tedious, even for those who love snow! Everyone — students, staff, and faculty — looks forward to this annual gathering.* »

As for other social pursuits, there are endless possibilities — if you look for them — at Michigan. Since the Business School is part of the larger Big 10 campus, with more than thirty-five thousand students in Ann Arbor, there are campuswide groups to get involved with and activities from canoeing to old-movie-watching to keep you busy. Don't be surprised, however, when people from other schools faint when they hear you're from the Business School — we tend to have the reputation of sticking to ourselves, since our buildings are self-contained and there is so much to keep us busy close to home. (Some like to explain it by saying that they're resentful because we're going to be their bosses!) Football mania sweeps the campus in the fall, and many business students will form seating groups in the stands. Around Ann Arbor, bars are abundant, although some are populated mainly by undergraduates. There is always at least one B School happy hour scheduled each week at one bar or another. If something more "refined" is desired, Detroit or suburbs such as Birmingham and Southfield are only forty-five minutes away for dancing, theater, or major-league sports. Canada, the Great North, is also nearby.

The level of social life ebbs and flows throughout the year. A flurry of activity occurs at the beginning of each semester and just before graduation, while parties can be pretty sparse from midterm through finals. It is no myth that the program can eat up all of your time if you let it (and many people do). There is no avoiding the overwork at times when *everything* is due and you can't get around the long, frantic days.

« *I'm still shocked at my lack of surprise when I agreed to my first 10:00 P.M. meeting! It becomes increasingly difficult to get four to six people together for a group meeting as finals grow near. Everyone has their calendars completely filled, and sleep becomes a commodity that you trade away to complete projects. Socializing can be limited to quick meals or working happy hours.* »

If you're married, any commitment by a spouse to attend school can put a strain on the marriage. Second-year students often tell new students to "write to your spouse often," since students tend to spend so much time at school! Unfortunately, these predictions are quite true, and during busy times a couple can go weeks without seeing very much of each other. On the positive side, every effort is made to include spouses in as many events as possible, including parties, Orientation activities, and special speakers. Also, a group called "Section 7" was formed so spouses could meet, talk about topics other than classes and projects, and offer moral support to each other. Although not intentionally and certainly not exclusively, married couples tend to socialize with other couples. A casualty of the commitment to school is definitely time alone with your spouse, let alone any time for yourself.

Housing in the Ann Arbor area ranges from mediocre to extravagant (and expensive)! Limited graduate dormitory accommodations are available. For married students, plenty of married student housing is a bus ride away, on North Campus. This housing is admittedly small and Spartan, but the rent can't be beat. On-campus apartments are generally small, expensive, and hard to come by. The biggest problem can be parking. It is common for roommates to seek each other out in January and sign leases then for the following fall. If you want to find anything in the way of an apartment, it is important to make a visit to Ann Arbor early in the summer and by July at the very latest. While there is no shortage of apartments in Ann Arbor, there can be a shortage of those that are affordable and convenient.

Leases are almost always for twelve months, and Ann Arbor realtors/landlords are notoriously unyielding. Farther away from campus, apartments are available that are generally kept up at a higher standard, but limited options for parking on-campus and the long days required in the program can make living off-campus difficult. In other words, finding housing can be a daunting task as students prepare to begin their graduate program. Putting it into perspective, your new home is going to be the Business School anyway, and between the work and the lifelong friends you'll make, two years of "slumming it" doesn't seem that bad!

RECRUITING AND JOB SEARCH

GRADUATES of the Michigan Business School are highly respected and sought after by many Fortune 500 companies (or so the Office of Career Development has drilled us into believing). Recruiters are impressed by the solid general business background that each graduate receives, which is rooted in hands-on experience of solving real-world problems. The Michigan Business School prepares its graduates for hard work, action, and comprehensive group interaction. As many before have said, Michigan grads are well known for their willingness to roll up their sleeves and get down to work. If this is not your type of personality, Michigan might not be the place for you.

The placement record at Michigan is outstanding. Last year, although many companies were downsizing or not hiring, the Michigan Business School recruiting system still brought in nearly 400 companies. Approximately 150 companies recruited for internships as well as full-time positions. By July 15, a total of 85 percent of the most recent graduating MBA class had accepted job offers, with a mean salary of $57,600. Forty-one percent took jobs in the service sector, mainly in consulting and in commercial and investment banking. Fifty-nine percent accepted offers in the manufacturing sector, with the majority in the automotive, consumer goods, and chemical/pharmaceutical categories. Of the graduating class, 93 percent worked in a professional position during the summer between their first and second years. Geographically, about half of the student body remained in the extended Midwest, from Colorado to Ohio. One third of the students located to either coast, with the remainder accepting jobs elsewhere — more than 10 percent outside the continental United States.

To achieve these successes, the recruiting system at the Michigan Business School begins grooming you for the extended job search almost before you set foot on the campus for Orientation.

« *We couldn't believe our ears when we were told on the second day of Orientation that résumés for the first-year résumé book were due within the month. Most of us had just left jobs, and here we were being reminded that we would have to start looking for another job almost right away! There was another set of us who hadn't rewritten our résumés since high-school graduation. Then again, there was an even smaller set of persons who had never even written a résumé.* »

Throughout the year, the Office of Career Development holds many workshops and seminars, especially for the first-year students, to prepare them for their upcoming job searches. The workshops focus on such things as self-assessment, cover-letter and résumé writing, positioning, making a career change, networking, and interviewing techniques. Videotaped mock interviews and counseling are offered by second-year MBA student placement counselors to help prepare peers for actual interviews. Occasionally, alumni/alumnae or guests will take part in more official mock interviews to give feedback from a corporate perspective. The Dean's Office has also begun what they call Executive Skills Workshops taught by faculty and visiting lecturers throughout the year that provide an excellent way to gain some of the less traditional tools sought after in executives in subjects ranging from teamwork, leadership, and creativity to ethics and diversity.

Most first-year students search for internships between their first and second years. This serves as training for the more intense job search that takes place in the second year. For both internships and permanent positions, the process is roughly the same. Starting about the beginning of October, corporate representatives come to the Business School to give presentations about their companies. Some of these take place in lecture halls in the Business School, while others are off-campus. On some nights there are so many presentations that students will try to get to two or three. Most presentations are followed by hors d'oeuvres and plenty of chitchat and brown-nosing. Some presentations are followed by dinners at fancy restaurants for select students who have sent their résumés to the recruiters weeks before the presentations.

« *Another friend of mine lived off-campus and during the "presentation season" would rarely see his wife. I lived less than a block from school, so he would keep a suit and other essentials at my house, since he didn't have time to return home to change during the day. He would leave at 7:20 A.M. for classes and would return at 11:00 P.M. or later after the presentations were done. Then he would start his homework. It was incredibly exhausting, but necessary to land a great job.* »

Two weeks before the interview they are interested in, students must put in a bid card prioritizing their choices for that particular week. The results are posted the week before the interview, when each person finds out if and when he or she got on the interview list. Popular companies invariably have a waiting list of interviewees ten times as long as the slots available. About the only way to get around the bidding system is to obtain a spot on the closed interview lists that some companies have. This is done by contacting the company in the fall for first-year job hunters and in the summer for second-year students — and by not missing the company presentation. An invitation to be on a closed list means that you don't have to take your chances in the random bidding card process.

For first-year students, interviews actually start in late January, although presentations have taken place the previous term. For second-year students, interviews begin in October and continue until mid-December. They resume in January and continue, although not as often, until a few weeks before graduation. It all makes for an extremely busy and hectic schedule, balancing interviews, fly-backs, daily course work, and ongoing projects.

« *Maybe its because we've been in school during a "recession," but they neglected to tell us in the school brochures that if you're not careful, this place can turn into a two-year job search. What with presentations, bidding for interviews, having the interviews, thanking people for interviews, and on top of it all, conducting an off-campus search to augment the interviews on campus — a person can get swamped! Students begin to wonder if they will have time actually to get the degree they returned to school for. Don't get me wrong, it's definitely better than not having a recruiting office at school at all, but it gets to the point where it's ridiculous if you do everything they suggest.* »

Outside of arranging for on-campus interviews, the Michigan Business School also offers a variety of resources to contact smaller and/or nontraditional companies. Company, regional, and city information is kept at the Career Resources Center in the library, and a job posting board is maintained outside the recruiting office. Several special events, such as the Small Business Forum, the MBA Forum, and the Executive Recruiter Forum, in which students get the chance to network with decision makers face-to-face, are hosted at the Business School. The alumni/alumnae network is also a growing tool that the administration seeks to keep involved. With more than twenty-six thousand alums, the possibilities are endless — with long lists of alums who have agreed to advise and encourage current students in their job search. The school recently implemented a new computerized networking system called M-Track, which has greatly eased the search for current students as well as alums. Plans are under way to implement a continuing placement and counseling service for grads as they grow in their careers. The school recently hired in the Office of Career Development additional staff, whose sole job is to travel throughout the country promoting Michigan to potential corporate recruiters.

Other new programs initiated at the school include regional re-cruiting forums such as the one held in New York City this past year for MBAs; it attracted more than thirty-five companies that have not traditionally recruited at Michigan. Additional forums have been proposed next year for Los Angeles, San Francisco, and Atlanta. In a recession year, the Office of Career Development also sponsored a five-day career program the week after graduation for MBAs who were continuing their job search.

ON THE JOB — FIRST YEARS OUT

« I was one of the older students at Michigan who decided to come back to school after eight years of work experience. It took a lot of soul-searching for me to leave a very well-paying job and security for the unknown. But I knew that I needed the MBA and the education behind it to reach the management levels I sought. Was it worth it? Most definitely! I'm making almost twice the salary I made before going back to school. But more important, the friends and the re-sources along with the connections are invaluable. The first time I had a problem at work, I had a list of professors and friends I could call for advice. One professor has even made a point of keeping in close contact with me for evidence of the latest trends he is research-ing. Friends who I now work with tell me that I have to promise them never to go back to school, though — I graduated from undergrad in a recession, and did the same this past year from Michigan. I never thought I had such power! »

The first job is often marked by a certain urgency among students to "try out" a lot of the theories and experiences they've received in the previous eighteen months. You can't blame them, because they've analyzed so many cases and studies to the point that it becomes habit-forming. Students know how to identify a company's core competencies (thanks to Michigan's guru, C. K. Prahalad) before proceeding further. They know to ask a thousand and one questions from as many people as possible before attempting to resolve a problem. Associate Dean Tom Kinnear was infamous for starting his class in Strategic Marketing by asking the question "What's your plan?" — fully expecting a detailed and exact outline of the scenario and its implications, past, present, and future.

Michigan prepares you for real life. It's not learning for the sake of learning, but learning for the sake of knowledge and understanding. If there is one distinguishing factor, this is it: the ability to throw 110 percent of yourself at a problem, and draw upon courses, experiences, as well as acquaintances to resolve it. The MBA program at Michigan teaches you to think and to react like business managers. The fundamentals of teamwork, time management, and prioritization are stressed. Michigan gives you the tools and confidence with which to make a difference. The rest is up to you.

« *Another friend recently recounted how satisfied he was with his Michigan MBA while at his new job with a leading international telecommunications firm. Six months into his job, he was promoted to the position as marketing coordinator for North America based on his ability to analyze and quantify trends and identify growth areas properly. Sure, this friend came to Michigan with exceptional background and experience — he was truly a genius — but Michigan enabled him to broaden his background and gain exposure to new ideas as well as to gain access to corporate insiders. The Michigan MBA provided him with more than just an entry ticket.* »

SUMMARY OVERVIEW

THE majority of students enjoy their two years at Michigan. For most, it is a whirlwind of strong emotions and hard work. No one ever said that it would be easy, and looking for a job is *never* fun, particularly in the midst of a recession. But by gaining a very strong business foundation based on hands-on performance and actual field experience, students are one up on the majority of potential rivals.

One of Michigan's greatest strengths is its ability to change with the times and be innovative in its implementation of academic policy. The administration is continually assessing the needs of students and faculty while analyzing current business and professional trends to keep the curriculum up to date. The school strives to be proactive and not reactive. Flexibility is inherent in the system. The challenge is not only to meet but also to surpass this moving target. The Michigan Business School is only as good as its faculty, staff, students, and resources. It is reassuring to know that as each year passes, the quality of each of these human elements at Michigan keeps increasing.

It goes without saying that the students at Michigan are a major strength. Coming from all over the world and with as many backgrounds, it is hard not to find someone in your class who has not dealt with a problem or situation being covered. At times it can mean intense pressure on that individual to help provide insight or additional analysis in class, but it means that classroom teaching can be supplemented by personal experience. Classes are meant to be thought-provoking; professors seek to give students the ability to analyze situations and come up with effective and successful solutions.

Michigan's hands-on approach to management is the culmination or result of this interactive policy. Students leave Michigan having been part of the Global Citizenship Program and hopefully with a new perspective on business ethics and responsibilities. With a mandatory field project similar to medical internships, students gain real-world experience in addition to leading-edge classroom teaching. As a result, students are able to put their ideas to work on completion of their two years in Ann Arbor, and they have a real foundation from which to "hit the road running."

No school is perfect, however, and the Michigan Business School has its problems. They are inevitable when you speak of an institution with more than twenty-five hundred students at one facility including BBAs, MBAs, PhDs, and full- and part-time students. It is virtually impossible to keep everyone happy at all times, and occasionally there is intense competition for limited resources among the three academic programs and a world-renowned executive facility.

A price must also be paid for attempting to attract professors who are the best in their fields. There is always the professional issue of the emphasis between research and teaching. Are faculty as accessible as they should be, or do they emphasize their connection with executive education and private consulting at the cost of the students? Is it a case of "Do as I say, but not as I do"? While in the past, teaching was not as strong as it could have been in some cases, the Dean's Office has made great strides in improving the quality of teaching, particularly among the core courses.

Another concern for some grads as well as prospective students has been in the areas of recruitment and placement. A significant number of students remain in the Midwest after graduation. The University of Michigan is not located in the heart of the financial district, and students must work that much harder to open new doors for corporate recruiters who are on either coast. If you are set on becoming the next Wall Street whiz, perhaps a school nearer the center of action might be better for you. But as with any negative, there is also a positive — Michigan has made great strides in overcoming what some see as its geographic disadvantage. The school has hired in the Office of Career Development additional staff whose sole purpose is to publicize the school's ability to train and deliver business managers. And rest assured that the quality of education is by no means affected by geographic location — if anything, the quality of life in the Ann Arbor area is a great advantage to the school in everything it does.

Chapter 8

THE STANFORD GRADUATE SCHOOL OF BUSINESS*

« *The glow from my Caribbean vacation faded fast when I returned to Connecticut and found the message on my bedroom door:*

"Call Wayne Forester, Stanford's director of admissions, at his office or at home."

Shoot! I had mailed in my application a few weeks before — what had I left out? Maybe they wanted to interview me. Maybe they thought my application was a joke.

I gathered up my courage and called California. "Hello, David," *Wayne said in a cheery tone. "I am pleased to inform you that we've decided to offer you a place in the incoming class."*

"What?" I asked. I made him repeat the good news. I didn't even try to disguise my surprise. Five minutes later, Wayne had finally convinced me that I was in. I let out a hoot when I got off the phone.

Reality quickly set in. Now that my what-the-heck-I-might-as-well-give-it-a-shot application had been accepted, I had a serious decision to make. Did I want to move across the country for business school, or should I stay closer to home?

In the weeks that followed, Stanford proved that it knew something about marketing. In contrast to the apathetic attitude of another top ten business school that had accepted me, Stanford showered me with attention. A half-dozen Stanford alumni/alumnae and students

* BY DAVID HESSEKIEL, MBA

called me with unsolicited offers of help. Did I have any questions? Did I want to visit the campus?

When the time came to decide, I found that Stanford had made the choice easy. »

To start with the obvious, the Stanford Graduate School of Business has some awesome credentials. Year after year, its rigorous MBA program attracts many of the country's most outstanding business students. The general management education Stanford imparts is so highly regarded that hundreds of recruiters storm the campus each year. And competition for GSB graduates is so fierce that the school's average starting salaries regularly surpass those paid to graduates of the other leading programs.

All of that would be enough to recommend Stanford to anyone seeking a top-flight business school, but there is something more to the Stanford experience, something not measured in dollars and cents. Stanford is a great place to go to school. The GSB sits a few hundred yards from the center of one of the most beautiful campuses in the country, the eighty-two-hundred-acre former farm and racehorse-breeding ranch of the illustrious Stanford family. The campus vibrates with the entrepreneurial spirit of Silicon Valley and the joie de vivre of the San Francisco Bay area.

Earning a Stanford MBA is as tough as earning one from any of its sister schools. The Stanford difference is that when you need a break from the grind, you can run, bike, or walk into the northern California foothills or jump into a friend's hot tub — and still make it back to campus in time for the next study group. My classmates' appreciation of the fringe benefits of living in northern California can be easily discerned from a quick look at where they settled after graduation. At last count, more than half of those surveyed were ensconced in the San Francisco/San Jose region.

The temptation is strong, but this insider's account will not be a northern California travel guide. If you have the record of achievement, the potential, the pull, whatever it takes to get into one of the nation's top ten business schools, however, life-style should be an important factor when choosing a place to spend two years. And in my book, no other top business school comes close to offering the quality of life on "the Farm."

But a stint at the GSB should in no way be confused with a trip to nirvana. The first year is the academic equivalent of boot camp for the 350 entering students. It's a challenge for the quant jocks, the engineers, and the analysts fresh from investment banks who arrive knowing an HP-12C keyboard like the backs of their hands. It can be hellish for the "poets," the English and political science majors who went into journalism, nonprofit fundraising, or street performing after college. The academic work load diminishes in the second year, but the added responsibility of finding the right job keeps shifting the center of gravity in this two-year balancing act.

Since the 1960s, the GSB administration has prided itself on following a philosophy of "balanced excellence" between teaching and research. As is common at so many academic institutions, GSB students sometimes accuse the administration of weighing research more heavily than teaching ability in making tenure decisions. That sentiment also produces some discussions of teaching quality in school assemblies and on the pages of the school newspaper.

The bottom line, however, is that the overwhelming majority of GSB students are glad they chose to spend two years in Palo Alto. A recent GSB poll asked students what they would do if they could make the choice to come to Stanford again. The results: 90.2 percent said they would make the same choice, 7.1 percent said they would choose another business school, and 2.7 percent said they would choose not to go to business school.

Unlike "that school in Massachusetts," as Harvard is often jokingly referred to, Stanford is not committed to the case method. Core and elective classes are taught in a variety of styles ranging from fairly strict case method (Marketing Management) to straight lecture. Most classes combine lectures with case studies and class discussion. Teaching quality, like most things in the business school, seems to follow a normal distribution: some professors can breathe wonder and elegance into the driest material, most get the job done in a competent manner, and a few make you curse the day you mailed in your application.

The relative popularity of GSB professors is never so obvious as at course-selection time. It is not unusual for sections taught by popular professors to close out. Among the perennial favorites: Grousbeck for Entrepreneurship, McDonald for Investment Management, Van Horne for Corporate Finance, and Collins for Small Business Management.

The strongest departments at the GSB are Accounting and Finance. The Accounting faculty counts such big names as Charles T. Horngren, author of one of the most popular accounting textbooks; George Foster; and William H. Beaver. Among the Finance stars are James C. Van Horne and Nobel Prize winner William F. Sharpe, authors of leading corporate finance textbooks; George G. C. Parker; and Myron S. Scholes, codeveloper of the groundbreaking Black-Scholes option pricing model. Overall, the faculty is one of Stanford's strongest assets.

Strategic Management is an increasingly popular department, thanks to rising student interest in entrepreneurship and some extremely popular professors, including H. Irving Grousbeck, William C. Lazier, Steven C. Brandt, and Robert A. Burgelman. Operations Management has improved with the addition of William Lovejoy and Seungjin Whang. As for Marketing, Northwestern's marketing professors probably don't quake in their boots about threats to their preeminence from Stanford, but some hardworking junior faculty at the GSB are trying to return that area to its former glory.

The school has made a concerted effort to expand its course offerings in International Management during the past few years. International issues make up approximately one quarter of the material covered in the core strategic management and marketing courses. A bolder gesture is the opening of an overseas campus in Kyoto, Japan. There, a limited number of second-year students have the option of spending a quarter taking courses and undertaking an internship with a Japanese company.

That overseas venture is just one of the new programs and facilities the GSB has unveiled in recent years. The most visible is the recently dedicated Edmund W. Littlefield Management Center, a sixty-thousand-square-foot building housing faculty offices and meeting rooms. That construction helped free up space in the adjacent GSB building for, among other things, a product design laboratory intended to encourage exploration of new ways of solving design problems. The GSB is also dedicating significant resources to beefing up fellowships and new courses designed to attract more physicians to the MBA program. This stems from a belief that management training will help physicians deal with many of the problems they face in delivering medical care.

In addition to these new and traditional strengths, Stanford is one of the few top schools to offer a concentration in public management. The Public Management Program (PMP) awards a certificate in public management to students who successfully complete three PMP core courses as well as the rest of the GSB graduation requirements. About fifty students per class qualify for the PMP certificate, but far more get involved with PMP activities. A new director and a committed group of students began to reinvigorate the PMP in 1987 after several years of decline. One of their biggest successes was the establishment of the Public Management Initiative, a program that focuses attention each year on a single public-policy issue. Speakers and panel discussions, independent study projects, and trips were organized to get students and faculty involved. PMPers, many of whom have a public- or nonprofit-sector background, add to the GSB's diversity.

Stanford continues to be a leader in management education. From its rigorous academic program to its unmatched quality of life, Stanford excels. While other top MBA programs are good in one area or another, Stanford's commitment to balanced excellence truly sets it apart as a great program.

GETTING IN

ANOTHER part of the Stanford difference is size. The GSB student body is dwarfed by those of most of its competitors in the top ten. For years the incoming class was limited to 318 students because that was the seating capacity of the rooms used for the core curriculum. (The administration is experimenting with slightly larger class sizes to take advantage of the handful of empty seats in core classes caused by student exemptions.) GSB students get to know (or at least recognize) nearly all of their classmates. That lends a sense of intimacy and community to the GSB experience.

It also means that getting admitted to the GSB can be tougher than at larger prestigious business schools. There were 4,592 applications for the 342 places in a recent class. With that tight a screen, the students who do get in inevitably have some impressive accomplishments under their belts.

« I had met so many people in pre-enrollment math and computer classes, on the Orientation scavenger hunt, and on the restaurant and bar-hopping trips, yet I couldn't seem to find any of them as we filed into Bishop Auditorium. As I looked around, I kept getting people's backgrounds mixed up. The facebook, with its directory of my classmates' accomplishments, had been too depressing to study in depth. It made me feel as though I were the only newcomer who had not gone to Harvard, Yale, or Stanford and had not worked on Wall Street or for a consulting firm. I found a seat and waited for the director of admissions to begin his welcome.

"This year's class is a really outstanding mix of people with great academic skills and fascinating backgrounds," he began. "The bankers are present. There are fifty-six students who worked in investment banking after getting their undergraduate degrees and forty-six consultants, plus the president of a steel company. But the class also includes students who never have seen the outside door to an executive boardroom, let alone written a business plan.

"There's even one motorcycle-gang member, but he was the leader of the gang."

Among the other enrollees he described were a minister and a rabbinical student, three journalists, a California winemaker, and a fellow who produced films for major league baseball.

I was still nervous by the end of that assembly, but I didn't feel nearly as alone. »

Stanford certainly opens its doors to a heaping helping of excellent traditional candidates. It would be no sweat for the school to fill each class with such people, but it doesn't. Stanford strives to inject an element of diversity into each class. My friends, for example, included a woman who had helped manage a windmill generator company in Colorado, a billboard salesman, a physician, a college textbook marketing manager, and a nonprofit fundraiser, along with many former bankers and consultants.

Adding to the GSB's diversity — and the competition for admission — is the school's international reputation. A recent class admitted applicants from thirty-four countries. Foreign students have made up 19 to 22 percent of recent classes. That gives the GSB a multicultural flavor, a decided advantage when you consider the global nature of the business world. The GSB does not use quotas to admit students.

The personal preferences of each admissions director are reflected in the classes they admit. Nevertheless, the basic criteria for admission remain constant. Stanford looks for solid academic aptitude (but has no minimum GMAT score or GPA cutoff); proof of strong managerial potential through work, academic, and outside activities; and something unusual in an applicant's background that would enrich the GSB community. "We weren't looking for people who followed the safe, well-lighted path," the director of admissions told my class. "We were looking for people with real intellectual curiosity and demonstrated success in management roles."

Those criteria, combined with the avalanche of applications that hits Stanford each year, mean no one really knows if he or she is going to get in. Don't rule Stanford out if you're an Indian-rights activist with weak board scores. And don't assume you're a shoo-in if you're a Harvard grad with great boards and a stellar job on Wall Street.

Stanford does not interview candidates for the MBA program on- or off-campus. To get in, your application and letters of recommendation must shine — and that's not easy in such a brilliant applicant pool. The application requires three very broad essays dealing with your personal development and career goals, painful professional experiences, and personal ethical dilemmas. My advice: make that application sing. Take chances. Put something in there that will make the admissions officer laugh, cry, gasp, salute you, or run for cover. Give 'em something to remember, something they can't forget when it comes time to make the cut.

Even the most outstanding college seniors will have an extremely tough time getting into Stanford. The administration strongly believes that MBA students should have several years of work experience under their belts. As a result, recent admittees have tended to be a little grayer than their predecessors. The average age of the most recent class was 27.3. That class included sixty-six members over 30 and only four under 23.

Women are still outnumbered by men at the business school, but the trend is generally up. Women took 106 of the 342 slots in a recent class, the largest number ever admitted in one year. Minorities made up 25 percent of recent classes.

ACADEMIC ENVIRONMENT

THE first question most students are asked when meeting a recruiter is "What are you concentrating in?" Stanford students do not have an easy answer to that question because the Stanford MBA program has no majors or minors. (The one exception to that is the increasingly popular certificate in public management.) Once you have fulfilled the twelve core requirements, you must take another thirteen elective courses. Students are free to pick from approximately one hundred business school electives and hundreds of non-GSB courses. Many students concentrate by taking a number of courses in a particular discipline. The average GSB student does exactly what the curriculum invites: takes a little bit of this, a little more of that, and walks away at the end of two years with a good basic education in the disciplines useful to a modern general manager. The choice is yours.

Choice, however, is not a big part of the first-year experience for most GSB students. That's because you must take eleven of twelve required courses in the first year, unless you pass exemption exams. But don't be too optimistic: only a small percentage manage to place out of core courses.

Graduation requirements are the same for students who exempt core courses and the rest of us mere mortals. Everyone must complete one hundred credit hours of course work (twenty-five four-credit-hour courses). Up to sixteen credit hours may be taken "across the street," as GSB insiders call the rest of Stanford University. Popular non-GSB courses include public speaking, acting, art history, writing, and virtually everything offered by the physical education department. (I learned to sail at the tiller of a fourteen-foot vessel of the Stanford flotilla.)

The school year is broken into three periods, and, in spite of the fact that no one takes business school courses over the summer, the GSB calls each marking period a quarter. (First-year students — "first-years" — are expected to take four courses the first two quarters and five in the spring. Most second-years take four courses per quarter.) No classes convene on Wednesday. Those wonderful classless Wednesdays give students opportunities to catch up on their work, interview with prospective employers, and, on occasion, play a round of golf.

The GSB brochure describes the core as "especially rigorous, intense, and rewarding." In retrospect that is a fair assessment, but while you're going through it the last adjective rarely comes to mind. The core courses are:

Autumn	*Winter*	*Spring*
Economic Analysis and Policy	Accounting II	Operations
	Finance	Strategic Management
Accounting I	Marketing	Business and the
Decision Support Models and Information Systems	Management Decisions and Data	Changing Environment
Organizational Behavior		Human Resources Management

Students most likely have complained about the core curriculum since the beginning of time (at the GSB, time began in 1925). To its credit, the GSB administration has been working with student groups to improve communication between first-years and the faculty teaching the core and has recently revised part of the core curriculum. It remains to be seen whether that system actually will improve the core's palatability.

The GSB's forte is providing an excellent general management education in a stimulating academic and preprofessional environment. Much as a liberal arts education is designed to teach students how to think and express themselves, the Stanford MBA program seeks to equip managers with the skills necessary to tackle diverse problems. The school describes its goals as:

"Fostering innovative thinking and problem solving. Providing an awareness and understanding of the economic, political, and social environments in which business operates. Teaching basic analytical skills. Strengthening interpersonal skills for effective and productive working relationships. Building self-confidence and the capacity to make effective use of experience, learning situations, and skills. And finally, imbuing a sense of intellectual incompleteness that stimulates a pattern of lifelong learning." Stanford does all this very well.

« *"Real classes haven't even started, and already I'm confused," I said to myself as I sat, white-knuckled, in the first session of pre-*

enrollment math, one of two skill-sharpening courses offered before official Orientation began. "What hubris," I thought, "trying to learn calculus in a week, a decade after my last high-school math class."

Two days later I realized that if anyone could get me through, it was Professor Jerry Miller. What an incredible teacher! A senior member of the faculty, he had made a personal crusade of devising exercises, supporting materials, and new teaching techniques to prepare even acute "math anxiety" sufferers for the challenges ahead. His infectious good humor gave us courage. By the end of class, I had publicly taken a derivative, a feat my classmates greeted with applause.

On the last day of class, Jerry gave us a sort of valedictory address. Tackling the core, he warned, "is like being asked to take a drink from a fire hydrant. There is so much coming out you can't possibly take it all in without drowning." »

The first formula every Stanford MBA should learn is: P = MBA. Roughly translated, that means that all you have to do is maintain a P (Pass) average to receive an MBA at the end of two years. While other classic equations will teach you how to determine a rate of return, analyze market research, or control inventory, good old P = MBA will help you maintain your sanity, and even enjoy learning, during the rough-and-tumble first year of business school.

P is the middle ground in the GSB grading system of H, P+, P, P−, and U. Unlike a C in your undergraduate days (if you ever got a C), there is no shame attached to a P. It is the mark that Stanford MBA students receive most frequently. It means you tackled the material competently, satisfied the course requirements, and are ready to move on to your next business school challenge.

The GSB attitude toward grading is one of the healthiest aspects of the institution's philosophy. There is no enforced bell curve requiring a certain number of students to fail, no public display of grades, no class ranking. Under no circumstances will the administration distribute grades to prospective employers. Stanford recognizes that it has admitted an entire class of bright and talented people. Its grading policy encourages them to cooperate to get the most out of the program.

Flunking out is extremely rare. In my class, 306 of the 318 students with whom I started received diplomas on time. Most of those who were missing from the graduation procession were scheduled to finish the following year. Two fellows, for example, took a year off to help found a rock-and-roll museum in San Francisco. Of those students who do leave, most are not forced out, but decide they'd rather be doing something else.

Even so, a self-induced feeling of academic pressure, an almost hysterical fear of failure in some cases, is common during the first year. The core can be a brutal experience. Most Stanford students populated the tops of their undergraduate classes and met few academic challenges along the way that they could not master. For many, especially "the poets," the nontraditional MBA students, crashing into the core is a humbling experience.

Every year, second-year students tell first-years not to worry about surviving the core. "Everyone who works hard," they counsel, "makes it through." And every year, first-years continue to fear that they will prove the exception to that rule. Shirzad Bozorgchami, a thoughtful classmate of mine, was so concerned about the unnecessary anxiety the core provokes that as a second-year he wrote an open letter to the first-year class titled "Pain or Pleasure at the GSB." (That class must have liked it because they reprinted it the next year.) The heart of Shirzad's message was this:

« You have a higher chance of getting into a serious car accident or coming down with a serious disease in the next two years than you do of not making it at the GSB. . . .

This is not to deny that you will need to work extremely hard in the next year. Most of us did. But some of us had a lot of fun working hard; some of us were miserable at it. What made the difference was our perspective. If you work hard because you have to, because you are afraid of not passing, because an ugly monster in your nightmares keeps reminding you that the world will come to an end if you don't pass, you can easily resent the experience and find it painful. But if you constantly remind yourself that passing is not the issue, that you are here because you want to learn and grow, that every minute of hard work is making you a better, tougher, and more capable person, your experiences will be much more enjoyable. »

Shirzad's letter exemplifies the spirit of cooperation common at the GSB. Many students volunteer to tutor classmates. Some work as teaching assistants and hold weekly help and preexam cram sessions.

The core curriculum is a frequent subject of debate at the GSB. Few would deny, however, that the core has at least one valuable by-product: it forces students to pool their talents and work in teams. Study groups are key to taming the core in the first year and managing the conflicting demands of finding a job and taking classes in the second year.

« Two A.M. on the Saturday before finals week, first quarter. I'm locked in a pale green romance languages classroom on the Quad with Brad and Mike, my study group comrades. Each of us is battling our own core enemies. I can't make heads or tails of the probability problems we will face in our Trees exam. Mike's having trouble getting his Financial Accounting grade into P range. Brad is just plain worried about everything.

At times one or all of us feel so dumb that we yell and curse into the foggy darkness enveloping the university. Sometimes we're infected with laughter so hysterical that tears come to our eyes. We break the tension by shooting hoops with balled-up pieces of paper covered with problem sets.

If I'd been on my own, I would have called it quits and gone to bed an hour ago. But we are a team. Just being with these guys gives me a lift. It feels as good to help them solve a problem as it does to solve one myself. And the feeling is mutual. »

Study groups come in all sizes and flavors: high-powered, competitive groups that pull all-nighters in order to master a case in the most minute detail. Angst-ridden groups united by their inability to crack the cases. Synergistic groups that bring the varied talents of their members together to tackle problems collectively and efficiently.

Life in the classroom is just as varied. One professor uses a randomized computer program — nicknamed the wheel of fortune — to select the lead-off group for case-study discussions. Talk about intense. It's bad enough worrying about whether you really know all there is to know about a complicated case. Add to that the worry of whether yours will be the first group called on, and you've got the makings for a real headache.

The average class is not intimidating. Most professors promote classroom cooperation and try to make learning an adventure. Many use Stanford's prestige to lure executives to the campus to give guest lectures or to comment on class discussions. Speakers from start-up Silicon Valley companies, Napa Valley wineries, old-line manufacturers, and other ventures around the world are regular classroom visitors.

Don't make the mistake of thinking that Stanford is exclusively the domain of interesting professors. You will run into your share of droning monotones who offer some nonthreatening — and downright boring — lecture classes. And there are young wizards who try to compensate for their lack of teaching experience by dazzling — and in the process losing — their students with high-powered mathematics. Fortunately, outstanding professors significantly outnumber lousy ones. Most GSB students can point to at least one professor who opened their eyes to a new way of solving problems, a new approach to building a career, or a new attitude toward the future.

« *If anyone had predicted that Financial Accounting would be the highlight of my first quarter of business school, I would have laughed. Yet here I was, scrambling to get to class on time. I didn't want to miss the latest installment of "The Professor Smith Show."*

Smith, a balding, wiry little man who always wore eyeglasses and an infectious smile, had made it clear on day one that this was going to be more than an academic look at balance sheets and income statements. It was going to be an exercise in which a professor and sixty students of varying backgrounds and abilities worked together to get the most out of a class period. "If we succeed, then we will share the credit for the success," he had told us. "If we have a bad day, I'm not going to take all of the blame."

Every class had a sense of drama. Sometimes we were able to conquer complicated accounting problems. At other times, Smith would realize that most of us were lost. Then he would stop, retrace his steps, and explain things in what he called "slow-motion, big-picture" style. Preexam study sessions were all-day affairs that were overcrowded because students from other sections wanted a taste of the professor's magic.

The quarter had its ups and downs. Smith wanted to take us way beyond the standard approaches of our textbook, so he prepared a series of handouts that went into much more complexity. Some were helpful. Some were awful. Smith, however, was always upbeat and willing to work overtime to make up for any inadequacies in the materials. His final exam was a killer, a bitter way to end an exciting quarter. It rocked so many people that the prof's immense popularity was temporarily shaken.

Most of us recognized — once we stopped reeling from that exam — that Professor Smith had taught us a lot more than just accounting. During my second year, Smith was voted outstanding teacher. True to form, his acceptance speech was inspiring. He reminded us of the pact we had made to share the credit and the blame for what went on in the classroom. "You will be outstanding leaders rather than just good managers," he said, "if you appreciate how dependent you are on those with whom you work." »

SOCIAL LIFE

THE best feature of the Stanford GSB is the student body. Don't take my word for it. That was the hands-down top response to a survey of my classmates back in the spring of our first year. The GSB attracts and admits an amazing group of people from all over the country and the world. They're a great bunch to work and play with.

Finding time to play is not easy during the first year, especially during the first two quarters. Married students are torn between dedicating insane hours to study-group meetings and giving their spouses a minimum of attention. Biz Partners, a support and social group for spouses and significant others, helps to alleviate some of this stress. Among singles the pressure contributes to the termination of some long-distance relationships. Most unattached students find it difficult to spend much time finding Mr. or Ms. Right during that first-year squeeze. On the upside, many lifelong friendships are forged in the heat of the core.

The second year is much better socially. Students are beset with fewer academic demands and have developed the confidence to know they will make it through. They have also developed a solid network of friends with whom to work, play, and plot careers. Married students have more time and energy to put into their families. Many single students find that their social lives rise phoenixlike from the ashes. By the time graduation arrives, announcements of new relationships, engagements, and impending births are as common as tales of breakups and other social headaches were during the core.

The GSB social scene holds something for everyone. There are college-style gatherings with kegs of beer for the hard-core partyers. There are potluck dinner parties and quiet evenings shared by a few close friends. Several times a year, the social committee holds formal and informal dances such as the Black and White Ball, a formal costume party depending on your inclination. Some people do it all. Others make only occasional appearances at GSB functions.

A popular informal social function, really almost a time-honored institution, is the "Arjay." Each Tuesday, the Friends of Arjay Miller (FOAM) gather at the Old Pro, a bar near campus, to drink beer, play pool, and socialize. The group's name comes from the fact that on graduation day members of the top 10 percent of the class are named Arjay Miller scholars, after the former dean; the Friends of Arjay Miller allegedly don't expect to make the top ten, so they feel free to blow off Tuesday nights.

Liquidity Preference Functions, Friday evening bashes in the GSB courtyard, are even better-attended than Arjays (possibly because the GSB Social Committee pays for the beer, soda, and chips).

Whatever your taste, there is no shortage of places to go or things to do. The campus is beautiful and crawling with interesting people. Athletic facilities are available for practically every sport, and the GSB is famous for the intramural teams it fields each year. There are numerous tennis courts, running and biking trails, an enormous outdoor swimming pool teeming with students, an excellent and inexpensive golf course, weight rooms, squash and basketball courts, and football, softball, and soccer fields.

The campus is also a renowned cultural center that hosts everything from student performances of original one-act plays to visiting symphony orchestras.

But social life and entertainment do not end at the university gates. Palo Alto is an attractive town with good restaurants, shops, and movie theaters. Some culinary standouts include Watercourse Way, a combination restaurant and spa where you and a friend can rent a small room with a hot tub and sauna and then enjoy some excellent sushi; the Oasis, a classic burger-and-beer joint; and Pearl's Oyster Bar, a seafood eatery founded by a Stanford MBA. If the shops along University Avenue, Palo Alto's main drag, don't carry what you're looking for, the Stanford Shopping Center, built on university-owned land adjacent to campus, is one of the finest upscale shopping malls in northern California.

Housing is the bane and the joy of Stanford students. The problem is that off-campus housing is expensive (expect to pay at least $850 for a two-bedroom apartment) and good on-campus housing is in short supply. If you are willing to bite the bullet, however, the hilly towns surrounding Stanford harbor some absolutely gorgeous houses equipped with hot tubs, pools, and breathtaking views. Groups of students band together to split the rent on these pleasure palaces. The admissions office serves as a clearinghouse for housing information, but most students find their digs through the want ads in the *Peninsula Times-Tribune*.

Automobiles are another popular form of indulgence among Stanford students. I, for one, could not resist the charms of a 1973 Fiat Spider convertible, a vehicle I felt would enable me to live the California dream. It was great on the road but hell on the wallet.

Parking around the GSB can be a hassle, especially if you're the type who regularly arrives on campus two minutes before class. Many students pay more than $200 a year for an "A" parking permit, which gives them access to special parking lots near the school. The more common "C" permit costs only a fraction of that.

Looking farther afield, a great part of Stanford's charm is its location in northern California. It's only forty-five minutes to San Francisco, four and a half hours to the ski resorts of Lake Tahoe, and two hours to the vineyards of the Napa Valley. Organized and informal trips to those hot spots, to Yosemite National Park, and to other natural wonders occur frequently during the school year and intersession breaks.

The numerous attractions on- and off-campus constantly beckon, but they don't stop GSB students from spending tremendous amounts of time on school-related extracurricular activities.

« *(Sing to the tune of "If I Only Had a Brain" from* The Wizard of Oz.*)*

> *I would punch 'em, I would lunch 'em,*
> *The numbers I would crunch 'em*

> *I'd crack the case with verve.*
> *Every challenge I would take it*
> *The world I would shape it*
> *If I only had the nerve.*

Of all the crazy things I did in Business School, dressing up in a bright orange lion's costume, a blond wig, and booties was perhaps the wackiest.

I wasn't interviewing for a job with Disney. That was my costume, and the lyrics constituted part of my solo in The Wizard of Biz, *the second-year show. Each year the first- and second-year classes take their turns writing, directing, and performing in musical parodies of GSB life with the financial support of corporate underwriters.*

Close to half of my class spent the better part of a month writing and rewriting that script, rehearsing, and erecting sets for that show while juggling job interviews and fly-backs and, oh, yes, attending second-quarter classes. »

Too much to do. Too little time. Not enough sleep. Typical business school. Exhilarating and exhausting. If they have nothing else in common, GSB students share a propensity for doing. That is why the business school hums with all kinds of extracurricular activities: social, career-oriented, charitable, political, and athletic.

Most students belong at least peripherally to several career-oriented clubs, and each club has a nucleus of dedicated members who make things happen. There is a club for almost every interest, and if your interest isn't covered, it's a cinch to start a new group. Among the clubs' themes are marketing, advertising, manufacturing, business and the arts, real estate, finance, women in management, black business students, Hispanic business students, and students who hail from or are interested in Asia.

Most of these clubs sponsor guest speakers and at least one major activity or conference each year. The Finance Club, for example, runs a popular stock market investment simulation game that challenges financial wizards and neophytes to make the most of an imaginary $100,000 stake. The manufacturing and entrepreneurship clubs are among the groups that organize conferences that attract leading national and international business leaders to campus.

Student-organized study tours to foreign countries have become very popular in recent years. GSB groups have taken off during spring break for Japan, Korea, Taiwan, New Zealand, India, Nigeria, Mexico, and the Soviet Union. In many cases, student organizers have arranged for American and foreign companies to subsidize the trips.

GSB students have also found many ways of disproving the stereotype that MBAs are heartless, money-grubbing rascals. Hundreds of students participate in the annual Challenge for Charity, a weekend of competitions between teams of West Coast business school students, to raise money for the Special Olympics. The GSB Volunteers have raised money for and worked in soup kitchens, sponsored picnics for disadvantaged youngsters, and recycled newspapers and cans. A recent class "adopted" fifty-six at-risk students in an "I Have a Dream" program. Successive generations of MBA students will see them through college.

Each year the Stanford Management Internship Fund (SMIF) asks first-year students to pledge a portion of their summer earnings to help support classmates working for nonprofit organizations. The Business Development Association matches students with companies and nonprofit organizations that have requested help on specific projects.

Keeping track of all of these groups and more is the *Reporter*, the irreverent GSB newspaper. The *Reporter* features articles on all sorts of school activities, carries a well-read gossip column, and sometimes gets into serious discussions of GSB issues.

RECRUITING AND JOB SEARCH

IF the idea of being wined and dined by corporate recruiters is offensive to you or the prospect of facing daily a mailbox full of invitations to learn about the nation's leading companies turns you off, Stanford may not be the place for you. The competition among recruiters for Stanford MBAs is absolutely mind-boggling; it is perhaps the best indicator of the value American big business places on the school's graduates.

Many students enter the GSB without knowing exactly what they want to do when they get out. Some may go back to investment banking, consulting, or whatever business they left to go to school, although this trend is decreasing. And that's okay. In addition to being valuable academic institutions, business schools are useful transition devices.

An MBA provides students with tools with which to position themselves for a new career or to relaunch the career they left. A Stanford GSB degree is particularly valuable because the institution's prestige is so great that it will open many doors for job-hunting students. That is not to say that a Stanford degree guarantees that you will get the job you want. Far from it. But it can help you get in to see potential employers. It's up to you to persuade them that you have what they want. Finding the "right job," even with a Stanford degree, is a serious, time-consuming business, especially if you want to enter a field that doesn't send many recruiters to campus.

Almost all first-year students take a summer job to help them learn more about an industry or type of work. High-paying summer jobs can also be a big help in making ends meet during the second year. The highlights of some of my classmates' summer jobs included helping to shoot a television commercial for a consumer products company; crunching some of the numbers necessary to evaluate a big deal for an investment banking firm; writing speeches for the CEO of a major computer manufacturer; and traveling to Asia as part of a management consulting case team. About 10 percent of the class take summer jobs with nonprofit organizations.

The two industries that have swallowed up the most Stanford MBAs for full-time jobs in recent years are consumer products and management consulting. The number of Stanford graduates heading to Wall Street dipped from over 21 percent five years ago to about 8 percent in recent years. Management consulting, especially with such large firms as McKinsey & Co. and Boston Consulting Group, attracts roughly 25 percent of the graduating class, with more offers than there are takers.

Manufacturing is another popular field for Stanford students. Consumer products have attracted the greatest percentage, followed by electronic equipment and computer firms that have lured graduates to Silicon Valley, Massachusetts, and in recent years to the Pacific Northwest in increasing numbers.

More than 210 companies sent recruiting teams to Stanford recently, and they conducted approximately 7,200 interviews. Students looking for specific jobs with firms that don't send recruiters to campus conduct "tailored job searches" using tools such as electronic résumé books, computerized job lists, and regional recruiting receptions that match students interested in a specific geographic area either within the United States or internationally with alumni and firms in that region. The tailored search can be nerve-racking, since job offers from on-campus recruiters pour in long before most independent job seekers receive responses to their initial query letters. On the other hand, the payoff can be tremendous: a job in the industry you want, a position you feel good about, and the knowledge that you made it happen. Among the classmates I know who made their own way are a pair who bought a records storage business; a fellow who lined up investors to fund his search for a publishing acquisition; a duo that received venture capital funds to develop sophisticated financial trading software; and a woman working for a small advertising agency.

You have to see the on-campus recruiting spectacle to believe it. Firms employ all sorts of gimmicks to arouse student interest. Food companies will stuff student mailboxes with coupons for free samples of their products. Top executives give noontime on-campus talks (called Meet the Company or MTCs) about their companies. Many firms sponsor cocktail parties and sit-down dinners in local restaurants and hotels. During the heat of the recruiting season Stanford students are absolutely besieged by invitations to eat, drink, and rub elbows with company executives.

« *The shrimp are jumbo, the miniature quiches are light and fluffy, the servers circulating through the hotel ballroom graciously bring whatever beverage you desire. A typical night out on the recruiting circuit.*

Tonight I want to speak with some of the younger members of this top management consulting firm. Consulting sounds fascinating, the money is fantastic, but the life-style sacrifices sound pretty heavy. What's it really like?

This was billed as an opportunity to get acquainted. It's not so easy, however. Hordes of classmates have turned out for this event, and each consultant is surrounded by a gaggle of students trying to appear simultaneously impressive and nonchalant.

In one group I get into a good discussion of international assignments with a fellow who spent most of the last year helping reorganize a mining company in Indonesia. The conversation goes well until I ask him about balancing family life with that kind of professional travel schedule. "Oh, it can be done," he assures me. Pretty soon, however, he has spotted an old acquaintance across the room and excuses himself.

Perhaps consulting isn't for me. »

The MBA Career Management Center is in charge of choreographing the on-campus dance between companies and students. The recruiting season for second-year students starts in October. To help the first-year students focus their attention on the core, the CMC keeps recruiters from contacting first-year students until February.

A computerized bidding system is used to divvy up interview slots among students. Students are given 1,000 points at the beginning of the interviewing season to allocate among the companies they want to speak with. Some companies prove so popular that their schedules are oversubscribed.

Stanford does not permit on-campus recruiting firms to refuse a first interview to anyone who submits a winning bid. This permits some students to speak with companies that might not have otherwise given them a hearing. First interviews take place in small offices in the Career Management Center; sometimes the schedules grow so crowded that interviews spill over into other business school and campus facilities.

Firms make an initial cut after these first-round interviews and invite several students back for a second round in a nearby hotel, or back at company headquarters. (A rejection letter is called a "ding." An invitation to visit the company is a "fly-back" in GSB parlance.) Most students amass a good number of dings before they sign on the dotted line with a company they like. It is common to get multiple offers.

In the topsy-turvy world of campus recruiting, competition for student attention is so intense that some firms complain that Stanford students are not sufficiently appreciative of the executive time and expense being lavished on them. Outright rudeness is probably very rare. On the other hand, Stanford students may not be overwhelmingly responsive to the "red-carpet treatment." Going out on the town with potential employers gets to be quite a grind when you're doing it night after night, week after week.

Most students do not limit their job hunting to companies that recruit on-campus. The CMC provides guidance to students embarking on independent job searches. The school's alumni/alumnae relations office has voluminous computerized lists of Stanford alumni/alumnae broken down by industry, job classification, firm, and geographic location. They are generally very open to inquiries from students seeking advice on breaking into a new industry.

Sixteen percent of the most recent class was undecided when the annual June placement poll was taken. That seems to reflect a trend to look carefully at alternative careers and entrepreneurial ventures. However, by September almost everyone (92 percent) was engaged in gainful employment.

ON THE JOB — FIRST YEARS OUT

« *"Mike, what's it like for a Stanford MBA to live and work in San Francisco?" I asked my old study-group partner during a long-distance call several months after hitting the real world. "Well, it's pretty wild," he said. "I get on the bus each morning and by the time it reaches the Embarcadero Center I'm riding with at least a dozen of our classmates.*

"What's it like in Des Moines?" he asked. "Any good sushi places?"

"Well, I don't see any classmates, that's for sure. In fact, I'm the first Stanford MBA to come to Iowa in nearly a decade. And sushi isn't real big out here. They're more into pork tenderloins." »

Stanford MBAs' experiences are extremely varied following graduation. If you're living in the Bay Area there is a tremendous network of graduates to call on for business and social activity. Stanford has healthy alumni/alumnae groups in Los Angeles, Chicago, New York, and several other major cities. But northern California is where it's at if you want to get the ultimate payback from your Stanford contacts.

Those contacts can be especially helpful if, like so many MBAs these days, you find yourself looking for a new job a year or two after graduation. Eight months out of school, I already know of half a dozen people who have quit their jobs or are actively looking for an alternative to their present situation.

One classmate lasted a few weeks at a small investment banking firm before realizing that the job was a far cry from the position that had been described months before. Another put in six months with a real estate company before calling it quits. Classmates at major consumer products companies that have merged or been acquired recently live in fear that their positions may be axed in the next round of layoffs.

But eight months after graduation, the majority of my classmates are still plugging away in the jobs they landed at school. Most are working very hard to prove that they merit their high salaries. The median salary for members of the class who went into consulting was $72,000, reportedly the highest in the land. The median investment banking salary was $55,000. The 2 percent of my classmates who went into venture capital started life after Stanford with a median salary of $70,000. A median salary of $60,000 was offered to those who went into electronics or computers, pharmaceuticals and biotechnology, commercial banking or financial services. Consumer goods producers awarded my classmates a median paycheck of $58,000.

Job-hopping grows even more prevalent two and three years out of business school, but control, not compensation, is usually the key factor. "I hardly know anyone still in their first job," a graduate of the class three years earlier told me. Many of his classmates had left jobs with large companies to take on bigger roles in smaller, more entrepreneurial firms.

The Stanford MBA is not a substitute for years of on-the-job training, nor is it designed to be. It provides bright and intellectually curious people with a solid academic background in management science and some useful analytical tools. That background can be useful on a day-to-day basis for people who go into consulting or corporate finance, but few other recent MBA graduates use their academic training that regularly. If the MBA program fails students in any area it is in underemphasizing interpersonal relations, communications skills, and organizational behavior in the curriculum. (Stanford does have a management communication program that provides training in oral and written communication, but its workshops are brief.)

One of the major lessons that the school does teach effectively is that modern managers must remain intellectually curious, that they must dedicate themselves to learning throughout their careers. It may be that emphasis on intellectual curiosity that contributes to the high turnover among Stanford MBAs in the first few years after graduation. The real world of work in a major corporation can be a disappointment after two years of anticipation. Much of the course material taught in business school looks at problems from the point of view of a high-level manager. Few students working within large corporations deal with such earthshaking issues in their first few years on the job. Stanford would do employers and future employees a great service if it helped students develop realistic expectations of their first years on the job.

SUMMARY OVERVIEW

THE Stanford GSB is a wonderful place to spend two years getting mind, body, and soul prepared for the rest of your professional life.

The school has more than its share of notable scholars and gifted teachers on its faculty, many competent professors, and only a few duds. The 350-plus new students Stanford attracts annually to Palo Alto are perhaps the most incredible collection of highly intelligent, highly motivated individuals you will ever work with in one place. The Stanford campus and northern California environment are among the most beautiful and stimulating locales in the country. Finally, the Stanford GSB imprimatur is a powerful credential that can help open many doors.

That highly positive endorsement is given with the benefit of hindsight. Many students spend much of their first year at the GSB in an academic daze, often wondering what the heck they are doing there. Former liberal arts majors can find the core curriculum brutally difficult. Even the more quantitatively adept students have been known to complain that the core throws too much material at them at one time. Many argued that the load for students taking the core should be lightened and that the curriculum should be shifted a bit farther away from the academic toward the real-world management end of the educational spectrum. The school has made efforts to do this.

And yet, the completion of the core is worn like a badge of honor.

Virtually all of us got through it and felt we were tougher for having survived. And we learned a great deal in the process, thanks to the help we gave one another and to some professors who raised teaching to a high art form.

An exciting world opens up to GSB students once they realize they are going to clear the academic hurdles. The flow of high-profile speakers, inspired entrepreneurs, and recruiting company road shows through the GSB is staggering. Increased emphasis on international management and the reinvigoration of the Public Management Program continue to expand the GSB experience. The student body is so compact that there is room in any school organization for someone who wants to be involved in virtually any type of social, academic, or professional activity.

The world immediately beyond the GSB's walls offers excellent opportunities to get your body in shape or abuse it. The social life is laid-back Californian with a touch of collegiate beer bashing. People really do go hot-tubbing, spend weekends in the wine country comparing chardonnays, and hit the road for Tahoe when the snow falls. In fact, prospective students who envision themselves spending two years at Stanford and then leaving northern California should be forewarned. Leaving the San Francisco Bay Area is difficult once it gets under your skin.

The strength of the Stanford network in California is another powerful reason for staying in the West after graduation. East Coast applicants should recognize that a Stanford MBA may be somewhat less potent east of the Mississippi than a Harvard Business School diploma.

A high rate of job turnover among recent graduates is not unique to Stanford GSB alumni, but it is a concern. Ironically, Stanford's exalted place in the business school hierarchy and industry's seductive recruiting efforts may contribute to the problem by creating unrealistic expectations of life immediately following graduation.

In the long run, however, GSB graduates continue to make significant marks on the American and foreign business scenes. The generous support of school alumni and the premium salaries companies pay new graduates indicate the value placed on a Stanford MBA. Most important, Stanford graduates believe that the degree was worth the effort it took to earn it.

—————————— *Chapter 9* ——————————

AMOS TUCK SCHOOL OF BUSINESS ADMINISTRATION (DARTMOUTH COLLEGE)*

THE PROGRAM

So you want to go to Tuck. That's somewhere in New England, isn't it? Part of . . . Dartmouth? You probably didn't know that Dartmouth College had any graduate schools. You probably heard that it's pretty small, a bit isolated, cold. From Boston, take Route 93 northwest to Concord, New Hampshire, then Route 89 northwest. Then pull over at the first town on the right. Still interested? Read on.

The Amos Tuck School at Dartmouth College offers much more than an MBA program. Any school can do that. Tuck offers a two-year experience that combines top-notch academics, a very close community of classmates, and a fantastic outdoor environment in the New England countryside into a quality of life and learning that is unmatched by other top programs. For people seeking the opportunity to learn, have fun, and grow personally and professionally, Tuck is a dream come true.

Located on the New Hampshire-Vermont border about two hours northwest of Boston, Tuck is part of Dartmouth College's beautiful campus in Hanover, New Hampshire. The alma mater of Daniel Webster, who endeared himself to generations of alums by stating in a landmark U.S. Supreme Court case that Dartmouth was "a small

* BY FRANK HUNNEWELL, MBA

college, but there are those who love it," Dartmouth is rich in its Ivy League traditions, academic distinction, and love of the outdoors. Only a short distance from New Hampshire's White Mountains that Webster loved, Tuck gets you back to the basics fast: crisp country air, cookouts, and exercise. Ski areas, jogging trails, golf courses, horseback riding stables, Dartmouth's canoe club on the Connecticut River, and similar attractions all beckon as Tuckies busily calculate ROIs, NPVs, and the probability that they will get called on to open Professor Shank's accounting class the next morning.

Tuck was founded in 1900 as the world's first graduate school of business. Today, continuing this long-standing commitment to management education, Tuck remains one of the nation's premier graduate business schools. It boasts an excellent, extremely demanding academic program supported by a dedicated faculty of teacher-scholars (the student/faculty ratio is about 10 to 1). Tuck graduates command among the highest starting salaries of all recent MBAs; they can be found as the CEO of many corporations and in the highest levels of the public sector as well.

Of course, at least a couple of other schools can and do rival Tuck's superb academics, distinguished faculty, high starting salaries, and successful alumni/alumnae. However, as any good business strategist would, Tuck has created a unique position for itself among the ranks of these top schools by offering a very practical, hands-on approach to management education that includes the development of strong interpersonal and leadership skills. This is accomplished by emphasizing team projects and outside consulting assignments for actual companies and organizations, which gets Tuckies working together, building consensus, and testing classroom theories in real business situations.

« *I was amazed at how quickly Tuck got us working in the business world. Within one week of arriving, we were assigned to small groups analyzing specific business problems for actual companies for the Managerial Economics and Management Communication course. My group had to design a new pricing strategy for a canoe and wind-surfer rental business on the Connecticut River (which, of course, required quite a bit of product testing). Other groups worked with Public Service of New Hampshire and Vermont Yankee Nuclear Power Station.*

This hands-on approach continued during the second year. For example, in the Marketing Research course, my team and I executed a nationwide survey of fifteen hundred high-school career guidance counselors for an entrepreneur who had an idea for a product they might need. In the Real Estate course, we developed a viable proposal to build a parking garage in Hanover, which involved meeting with property owners and Hanover's town manager and zoning board. In Technological Innovation in Manufacturing, we helped a local maker of high-tech torches and welders improve its manufacturing process. For me, this emphasis on group work and outside projects made Tuck more realistic and practical rather than an "ivory tower" experience. »

What else makes Tuck different? Its rural location and small size (170 students per class) combine to create an extremely close-knit, supportive environment of students, faculty, administration, and staff, as well as the spouses, children, and domestic pets of each of the aforementioned demographic breakdowns. Each quarter, the first-year class is divided into three sections of 58 students. As a result, by the end of the first year you will not only know, but also have been in the classroom with, almost everybody in your class. You will know many second-years by name as well. You will also know who is interested in whom.

Although there is always room for privacy, Tuck is not the best place for those seeking anonymity. It is a place for sharing your time, thoughts, and efforts with people who will, I guarantee you, become some of your best and closest friends.

If you go north early for preenrollment week, the Tuck program starts with a low-key introduction to the school and the main characters of this true-life drama. Professors are there to teach orientation sessions and introduce some major quantitative concepts (just remember that marginal revenue should equal marginal cost) of the first year.

« *I couldn't believe the second-years. They seemed to have thought of everything. They went all out to make us feel welcome at Tuck. They hosted cookouts and parties at their off-campus homes and organized informal discussion groups covering everything from how to use the HP-12C (the standard business calculator we all use) to what it's like to be a foreign student at Tuck. They wanted to incorporate us into the Tuck community as quickly as possible and to get the year off to a good start.*

As I got to know my own classmates and the second-years better, I discovered to my relief that they were not MBA weenies — the type that refer to beer parties as "liquidity certainty equivalents." Instead these people were cool — from Olympic skiers, fighter pilots, and marksmen to ministers, architects, and musicians — our class covered the whole nine yards. »

The Tuck MBA program gives the student a general management education rather than a narrow, specialized view of the business world. The goal of the MBA program is to develop "a concern for the management of a total enterprise." Because the Tuck curriculum looks at all aspects of running a business, this approach is particularly attractive to students interested in a career change but uncertain about what field to enter. As a result of this philosophy, Tuck students do not receive MBAs in specific fields, such as marketing or finance. All our diplomas look the same.

Given this approach, the school believes that there is a core of fundamental business knowledge that every general manager should have. The first-year curriculum forms the foundation of this knowledge base, and it is, to say the least, extremely structured.

Tuck is on a quarter system, and all thirteen of the first-year courses are required. These courses are loosely grouped around four parallel work streams. The Accounting module includes Financial Accounting in the fall, Finance in the winter, and Managerial Accounting in the spring. Quantitative Analysis includes Decision Science, Applied Statistics, and Management Science. The Economics module comprises Managerial Economics, International Business Environments, and Political Economy. The fourth grouping includes Ethics, Marketing, Organizational Behavior, Operations Management, and Management Communication.

It is possible to skip a first-year course by demonstrating sufficient prior experience in the field, in which case you take a second-year elective. However, to ensure an even distribution of the fundamental business knowledge contained in the first-year curriculum, most professors are reluctant to let you place out of classes. Some flatly will not consider it.

« *I thought the Tuck approach was phenomenal. By going through the structured first year with the entire class, I felt that we all learned the business basics together. The courses were designed so that even the "poets" (Tuckies with little business experience) could embrace the material and move forward with the rest of the class.*

I was certainly a poet in statistics — I mean, I didn't even know all the Greek letters the quant jocks were throwing around on the first day of class! To me, zeta times sigma divided by e and all squared just meant disaster — not the formula for Required Sample Size for Tolerable Error and Confidence Level When Estimating the Population Mean. But Tuck didn't let me down. There were extra study sessions, accessible faculty, and second-year tutors, all of which formed a safety net below me. It took some extra work, but I learned statistics. »

The second year is composed of elective courses. Building on the foundation of the first year, you can further your knowledge in specific fields as your interests become more focused. In addition, new topics such as Entrepreneurship, Technology Policy, Agribusiness, Business Law, and many others are introduced. (Note: if you don't take New Hampshire Supreme Court Justice Johnson's Business Law course, at least audit the last class session to hear his fatherly advice on how to succeed and have a happy life — he's right on the money.)

Given the general management approach, Tuck does not strive to have any particular academic specialty. There is, however, some variation in the experience and overall quality of the professors. During the second year, most students base their choice of electives at least as much on the professor as on the material, if not more.

Since Tuck does not have a reputation as a highly quantitative program, most people are surprised by the strong emphasis on numbers in a majority of the courses.

« *I was frankly amazed at the amount of number-crunching at Tuck, especially during the first year. Even though I had come from a Wall Street bank and felt comfortable with numbers, it was almost overwhelming at first. In Decision Science we created a very complex decision tree computer model (the famous Green Cap case), which took an IBM PC about twenty minutes to calculate the net present value of the optimal strategy. Man Ec (Managerial Economics) uses some calculus, and some of us worried about this until we learned that it doesn't go beyond taking first derivatives of relatively simple equations.*

I found that most professors are quite sensitive to students who are uncomfortable with numbers and will go out of their way to help if you go to them with questions. Quant jock study group members, however, proved to be the best resources to the numerically handicapped, and they were more likely to be available for help at 3:00 A.M. the night before an exam. »

During the second year, class size is mostly a function of the popularity of the course and can range from ten or fifteen to fifty-five. If a class is widely subscribed, the professors will almost always offer to teach a second section to keep the class size small.

Teaching methods vary by course from straight lectures to the traditional case-method approach, wherein students read a description of a management situation and are expected to prepare their own response. Most courses, however, use a combination of the two methods. In the first year, only Marketing, Finance, and Managerial Accounting use cases predominantly. Decision Science, Managerial Economics, International Business Environments, Political Economy, and Statistics tend to be taught by lecture. Organizational Behavior, Operations Management, Management Science, and Management Communication use a combination of the two methods.

GETTING IN

So you're still with me. Good. If you've made it this far you might as well stick around and see what it takes to get the nod from the Tuck admissions committee.

Getting into an excellent business school requires a lot of thought and effort, and Tuck is no exception, particularly since the school has been getting more publicity in recent years. In fact, last year the school received more than 2,100 applications for 170 openings, so they can be pretty selective about whom they accept. Even though the Tuck admissions package will, at first glance, appear less complex than those of other schools, don't make the mistake of treating it lightly.

In its simplest form, getting into Tuck is a two-step process. First, do the market research. Understand fully what Tuck is all about and why you want to go there. Just reading this book is a step in the right direction; it's not enough to want Tuck because of the great skiing nearby. Second, go into execution mode with your marketing plan. Convince the school that you are the perfect match for the learning environment it offers. No problem, right?

Here's a hint to help you ace first-year Marketing: know your customer. Think like your customer. Eat, sleep, and breathe like your customer. Who is your customer? The admissions committee. They are selecting from a wide range of your competitors, each claiming to have a distinct competitive advantage. Even being the best isn't good enough if you don't know what they're really looking for. It's actually not very complicated.

Tuck classes are made up of individuals of varying ages and backgrounds. It doesn't matter what college you went to, because everybody has to demonstrate the intellectual ability to handle the material; the admissions committee will review your academic credentials very carefully. It doesn't matter what your job is because all the lawyers, architects, ministers, and medical doctors in my class did just as well as the former bankers.

Some statistics. Last year, the average age of entering students was 26.6. About 20 percent of the class was married, and 98 percent had one year or more of full-time work experience. Only 2 percent entered directly from college. About 10 percent had advanced degrees in other fields. Minority and foreign students accounted for 9 percent and 24 percent respectively.

Most entering students actually have at least two or three years of significant prior work experience of some kind, and Tuck will base a lot of its decision on your discussion of that job. What did you learn? What would you do differently if given the opportunity? What will you be able to contribute to Tuck and to your classmates as a result of that experience? Perhaps most important, they will want to know why you think you need an MBA, and a Tuck MBA in particular.

« I discovered that my previous work experience served me very well at Tuck. With a three-year background in business, I felt I was better prepared to ask questions and to understand the difference between management theory and practice. My classmates' extremely diverse business experiences proved a great opportunity for learning about different industries and management situations, and it felt good to be able to share my own business perspectives with them.

For example, one day in the International Business Environments class we were discussing some of the risks in investing in foreign countries. I was able to describe a situation in which a former client of mine operating a subsidiary in South America was dealing with raw material import quotas and tariffs, domestic price controls, peso devaluation, and lack of foreign exchange. I like to think that this added an element of reality into a discussion that otherwise might have been only theoretical.

Even though many of us had had traditional "business" jobs before school, there were a number of people in my class with architecture, medicine, armed forces, and other nonbusiness backgrounds. This added greatly to the diverse fabric of our class and contributed other examples of "real life" experiences as frameworks to understand the complexities of modern organizations. I remember how an architect helped us understand the common conflict between marketing and manufacturing functions. He described how architects (the marketer) can develop incredibly creative designs, only to be frustrated by builders (the manufacturer) who say it will be very expensive or impossible to build. The example was so simple, but it really helped a lot. »

Brains, check. Job, check. But there's more to it than that, and the hard part is that only you will know if Tuck actually is the right place for you. You see, it all boils down to your personal qualities and, if you will, your values. Tuck is looking for that rare person who can combine demonstrated leadership abilities with a willingness to embrace a close-knit academic and social community. These are people who are mature enough to realize that no matter how good you are, you can always learn something from the next person. As a result, most Tuck students check their egos at the door. And that's why you'll find that Tuckies in general are very good listeners.

For the purpose of the application, this means demonstrating personal qualities that are consistent with working in small groups and sharing knowledge and expertise generously with peers. Tuck is looking for people whose goal is to succeed with their classmates, rather than at the expense of others — people who are competitive but can also remember what team they're on.

Tuck also seeks a willingness and an ability in its students to ask questions and contribute actively in class discussions. This process is an important part of your own learning experience and (although it's hard to believe sometimes) that of your classmates. You will find yourself challenging and being challenged by professors and fellow students alike in almost every class. And since it can represent a substantial portion of your final grade, you should be confident in your ability to contribute.

While the application process itself is relatively straightforward, it is a time-consuming and often stressful period. I mean, how would you feel if you were in the sixty-fourth percentile on the quantitative portion of the GMAT the first time around — or asking a college professor you haven't spoken to for two years for a recommendation?

Tuck "strongly recommends" a personal interview as part of the admissions procedure, although it is not required. Last year, 65 percent of the applicant pool interviewed, 84 percent of the admitted pool interviewed, and 85 percent of the enrolled students interviewed. My analytical skills may not be great, but those numbers tell me that interviewing has a positive influence not only on your chances of getting in but on your final decision as well.

If at all possible, get up to Hanover to visit and attend a few classes. Walk around. See what it's like. While you might use the interview as part of your market research to learn about the school, be sure to take it as a marketing opportunity as well. Here's your chance to sell yourself as a dynamic person, great personality, well-informed, lots to contribute, established goals. If you don't like the winter weather, I think you should just keep that to yourself.

If you can't get away for an interview on-campus, admissions officers scour the country on published dates, interviewing candidates in major cities. In addition, alumni/alumnae often are called on to pinch-hit, and many are very active in the interviewing process. Be prepared for a heavy dose of Tuck spirit when you interview with a Tuck alum.

« *I approached the optional interview as an opportunity to differentiate myself further from the thousands of other applicants. The director of admissions was in New York for a week, interviewing candidates. I remember being very nervous as I walked over from work to meet with him. But it went fine. It was more like a conversation than an interview. He told me a lot about Tuck and I told him a lot about myself and why I wanted to go there. I could tell that his objectives were to determine how committed I was to business and management education, and if I was up to the Tuck academic standards. But I sensed that he was also trying to see how well my personality and interests matched with the Tuck academic and social environments and thus how happy I would be once I got there.* »

A final word: marketing. As you flip through the admissions bulletins of the major business schools, you will note that most schools, including Tuck, say that they seek what is generally termed a "diverse class of motivated, talented individuals." That's great if you're a rock star or a fighter pilot. But if you are not, your application needs to jump up and scream "Choose me!" Work hard to make sure your application honestly describes you as the individual you really are. Then, if you are convinced that Tuck is the place for you, relax — you'll get the nod.

ACADEMIC ENVIRONMENT

YOU made it. At some schools, that's the hard part. At Tuck, the fun is just beginning. You see, it would be wrong to think that the school achieves its collaborative learning environment and fun life-style at the expense of demanding academic requirements. Nothing could be farther from the truth.

Tuck's academic standards and faculty are top-notch, and they really demand a lot from the students. Usually, every hour of class requires at least two to four hours of preparation and analysis for you to feel fully prepared. Classes themselves can be extremely challenging. And, since almost every class introduces significant new material and concepts, you rarely have time to slow down.

As discussed earlier, the Tuck academic environment is not at all bookish or overly theoretical, notwithstanding its relatively remote location. The group projects and consulting assignments add a heavy dose of reality to the experience. In addition, Tuck's Executive-in-Residence program draws senior managers from diverse industries to the school for visits of one to several days. Students can take the opportunity to interact with these executives in a variety of ways, ranging from one-on-one meetings to classroom discussion, meals, and even afternoon exercise. In the recent past, the program has included executives from Time Warner, Eastman Kodak, Hershey Foods, McKinsey & Co., Morgan Stanley, National Semiconductor, Price Waterhouse, Procter & Gamble, Texaco, the U.S. Treasury, and many others.

During the two years, the work load varies widely, from extremely intense to pretty manageable. Even for those coming out of the most competitive investment banks or consulting firms, the fall quarter of the first year can be a shocker. During this period, students are anxious to prove themselves and get off to a good start. And since most Tuckies are very bright and highly motivated, there can be a lot of self-inflicted pressure to get good grades.

The transition from the working world to academia can be a difficult one at first, especially if you're used to setting your own agendas and goals. From the moment you register and pick up the two-page schedule of fall quarter due dates, you can kiss a lot of that control good-bye.

« I remember being shocked as I left the registration area the evening before the first day of class. As I walked back to my room carrying huge bundles of course materials, I looked at the schedule and couldn't believe what I saw. It seemed as if every minute of the next three months had been planned for us. Exams, papers, presentations, and group projects in topics I knew nothing about were looming up in a matter of days — and it was all in addition to daily class preparation. It was a very intimidating prospect because at that point I thought I was going to have to do it all on my own. »

Those gruesome work loads. You try rubbing them out. You try soaking them out. And you still get — not enough time to go skiing. Try your study group. If you could bottle all the energy, fun, and learning that goes on in a week's worth of study group meetings, you'd, well, never have to earn a living selling detergents.

One of the basics of the Tuck experience, study groups are nothing more than groups of four to six students who get together daily to prepare for classes, exams, and group papers. They are the most important aspect of the academic environment outside of the classroom, and Tuck really encourages them actively as a way for students to learn from one another and debate the business issues actively before class.

You will depend on your group a lot, and it's key to get into one you're comfortable with. Most groups develop during the first few days of school, and since you don't know each other very well at that point, it's a bit of a crap shoot. In my class, some groups stayed together for the entire two years, while the composition of others changed a bit every quarter.

« *I was so lucky with my study group; we became good friends and ended up living together in a rented house in Vermont during the second year. I was a little scared at first when I heard that the group I was interested in joining was practically screening résumés, but we were actually less intense than others.*

We would meet for several hours every day to prepare the next assignments, and we really had a good time. It was impossible to be glum in study group, because we knew we were all in it together and doing at least as well as the others — and we laughed a lot. Everybody contributed and taught the others based on his or her own skills, be they accounting, marketing, or just telling jokes.

The best part was that everybody participated because you could ask any question you wanted. (Just how did you get that number?) It went without saying that our goal was to prepare each other, not just ourselves. We would rarely break up unless everybody felt equally prepared for the next day. »

A typical first-year day might look something like this. Up at 7:30 A.M. Frantic shower, dress, and sprint down to the dining hall for breakfast. First class at 8:00 A.M. After second class ends at about 10:55 A.M., coffee break. Discuss (argue, actually) with professor the correct strategy for German fastener company just analyzed in class. Third class. 12:30 P.M.: lunch. Get mail. Mad drive to meet with project client in nearby town. Back to study before 6:15 P.M. dinner.

More study and study group meeting. 11:00 P.M. to midnight: hockey practice. Then, if you're lucky, sleep.

During the second year the schedule is not nearly as structured, and it tends to be less intense than the first year. However, this depends primarily on the courses you select, and it is certainly possible to pick elective courses that will dump a work load on you that is as demanding as or more so than that of the first year.

With few exceptions, the grading at Tuck is very fair. The grades are: Honors, Satisfactory Plus, Satisfactory, or Low Pass (known as a "loop" or in verb form as "to loop" or "to be looped"). Evaluation criteria are slightly different in each course, depending on the professor, but you will always be told what those criteria are at the beginning of the course. Final grades are usually a weighted average of performance on class participation, projects, papers, homework, and exams.

As I have mentioned, class participation is an important part of the Tuck learning experience, and it can count for as much as 50 percent of the final grade, particularly in courses that use the case method. Tuck professors really encourage you to stop them to ask questions, especially if you prove yourself able to ask good questions that take the analysis to a deeper level.

Tuck does not have an arbitrary cutoff that forces some students to "hit the screen" (get the boot) after the first year. In fact, as long as you participate actively and intelligently in class, you probably won't fail or even get looped. Not many students flunk out of Tuck; most of those who leave do so for personal reasons. It's rare that somebody sincerely interested and trying his or her hardest is ever asked to leave.

Professors. Some are funny. Some aren't. One throws chalk. One brought his dog to class until people said that her barking and chewing the carpet were distracting (I thought it was funny). When you think about it, the Tuck professors are as diverse as the student body. Very approachable, all of them operate at high energy levels, and some are extraordinarily dynamic. I mean, try making an hour-and-a-half-long statistics class fun and seem like it went by in twenty minutes — that's tough!

Teaching styles vary quite a bit. Some professors prefer the more intimidating approach of cold calling on students to open cases, and might keep going back to that student for the entire first half of the class. Others ask for volunteers but will notice if you're not speaking enough and will call on you sooner or later.

Whatever the teaching style, most class sessions at Tuck are pretty exciting. The best ones will combine great humor, interesting material, and a strong feeling of accomplishment; fortunately this happens most of the time. Although initially there is a lot of apprehension as students start to figure out "the system," it doesn't take long for that to wear off and for students to feel at ease contributing in class.

One of the highlights of the Tuck academic experience is "Tycoon," a four-day computer simulation business game during which all other classes are put on hold. Part of the required first-year Business Policy course, Tycoon really summarizes the Tuck experience: group work, long hours, fun, and the "management" of a total enterprise. You and your management team spend twenty-four hours a day for four days managing a clock-making company in a dynamic computer environment of volatile interest rates, touchy labor unions, changing technology, and management kidnappings.

The first step is to give your company a name appropriate to a clock manufacturer, such as "Chronomeisters," "Nervous Ticks," or "Tocking Heads." The second step is to annoy the other companies by printing hostile tender-offer tombstone ads on a Mac, posting them all over campus. But when the decision deadlines start to approach, you have some serious thinking to do. How do we make the sales force more productive? Should we invest abroad? What about raw material sourcing, patents, insurance, and advertising? Just remember — goodwill amortization is not tax-deductible, and positive retained earnings are required to win.

So although Tuck is demanding, the academic environment is not threatening and offers an ideal opportunity for learning and professional growth. The faculty will challenge you every step of the way, and even though some classroom situations can get pretty intense, most professors are very friendly and easily accessible. As in corporate America, everybody (well, almost everybody) operates on a first-name basis. One of the best things about the faculty is that the professors strike a balance between teaching and research that, with few exceptions, actually makes the students feel as if they come first.

SOCIAL LIFE

WHEN you graduate from Tuck, you get to keep your business knowledge, your diploma, and your friends. In twenty years, when the diploma is lost and you can't remember how to do regressions, you'll know that it's the people at Tuck who make a long-term difference. If you are the kind of person who belongs there in the first place, it would be almost inconceivable for you to graduate from Tuck without a good handful of friends for life, and the social life has a lot to do with that. For most, Tuck's small size and location in New Hampshire more than make up for the lack of more cosmopolitan social distractions to be found in the urban environments of other major schools.

During the first days of a typical week, particularly during the first year, there are few organized social events. By Thursday evening, however, people begin to anticipate the approaching weekend. Students who have finished Friday's preparation gather at about 11:00 P.M. to down a few beers.

While the hard core may start at Pub Nite on Thursdays at Café Buon Gustaio, nearly everybody joins in for " 'tails" (cocktails) on Friday evening in the lounge of one of the first-year dormitories. This event starts after class and goes until dinner. Like all Tuck social events of this kind, the entire community is invited. 'Tails always includes a healthy dose of student spouses, friends visiting for the weekend, and often faculty members and administrators.

Twice a year, the social committee organizes talent shows for which anybody can sign up to perform a song, skit, stand-up comedy routine, or whatever. The whole campus gets psyched for the coffeehouses, and it is truly amazing how much energy and creative talent lurk in the hearts of number-crunching Tuck MBAs.

« *Some student groups, such as the Tuck Executones, an a cappella singing group of twelve men and women, rehearsed for several hours a week preparing for performances. Often there were contributions from students, faculty members, spouses, and even students' children. However, the best performances were frequently by impromptu groups that didn't prepare for more than a couple of hours. One of the best was a group called the Moving Violations, whose rendition of "The Lion Sleeps Tonight" was one of the funniest things I have ever seen. You had to be there, but it felt great being associated with people like that who were creative and expressive, not just MBA digitheads.* »

The social committee also organizes large-scale dances and theme parties at least once a quarter. One of the best is the Winter Formal, a dinner-dance that takes place at some off-campus establishment, such as the fashionable Hotel Coolidge in White River Junction, Vermont, where trains carrying vacationing Bostonians arrived forty years ago.

Another student organization, the Quality of Life Committee (QLC), organizes social events geared toward contributing Tuck energy and volunteer time to the local community. One of these is the Run for the Kids, a 5K run to benefit area services for children and teenagers. Tuck students also volunteer as teaching assistants in local public school systems, work on projects to feed the homeless, and have volunteered in an activities program for children at Dartmouth-Hitchcock Medical Center, three miles from campus.

The QLC also organizes student-faculty dinners at which second-years prepare and host informal and delicious dinners for about ten students and one faculty member and spouse. These popular events provide an ideal opportunity for both faculty and students to get to know one another better.

Although major events such as these form the foundation of the Tuck social scene, there is no explicit pressure to participate if you'd rather not. It goes without saying that some of the best fun and most rewarding times come from spending time with a smaller group of closer friends. Be it staying up half the night talking politics in the dorm rooms or running the Rip Road loop together, the opportunities to get to know your classmates as individuals are endless.

During the second year, most students live near the Tuck campus in groups of four to six in rented houses, many of them beautiful contemporaries or restored farmhouses with hot tubs and other amenities. In terms of distance, these range from a two-minute walk to a twenty-minute drive. Most houses develop descriptive names, such as "The Enfield Sailing Club" or "The Dude Ranch." Those lucky enough to have snagged the best houses are under a moral obligation to host cookouts and dances for the whole school.

« *One of the best off-campus parties I remember was in the fall of first year at Deer Run Farm. The farm is situated on the brow of a hill overlooking the upper Connecticut River Valley, and the clear October day was truly spectacular. We were all just getting to know one another then, but most people appeared pretty relaxed. It seemed as if everybody in the school, including married students and their children, was there, having a good time. The party went well into the evening and concluded with fireworks and bonfires.*

The evening did not pass without incident, however, as one person accidentally knocked over a woodpile with his car on the way home. Enter a representative of the local constabulary, who, upon examining the skid marks and noticing a point where they seemed to leave the ground, remarked with classic New England dry humor, "Mr. Smithand, I believe you were airborne at this point." »

The social life extends well beyond parties, however, and the great outdoors play an important role in the Tuck experience for almost everybody. Many, but by no means all, students are pretty athletic, and there is a lot of informal walking, running, basketball, tennis, skiing, and skating. The athletic facilities at Dartmouth are all new and easily accessible to Tuck students, and there is usually an aerobics class open to all, taught every afternoon in Buchanan Lounge.

Tuck stands apart from the other schools, however, in organizing and hosting formal, inter–business school athletic events. The Tuck Winter Carnival, which includes a fully organized ski meet at the nearby Dartmouth Skiway, draws teams from nearly every top business school around the country. The Hockey Tournament takes place during a weekend in February and is held at Dartmouth's Thompson Arena and neighboring rinks. In the spring, most schools send teams to compete in the annual Soccer Tournament. Tuck students plan and execute all aspects of these events, including drumming up corporate financial support. These events are highly competitive and very well managed. Get involved if you can.

Because the Tuck community is so small and welcoming, married students and their spouses usually choose to participate in the social life just as much as or more than the single students. Most organized activities, from the Executones to the Tuck athletic teams, include Tuck spouses, who can quickly become as much a part of the community as the students.

« *One of our study group members who is Japanese described this sense of community when he said, "My son was born at Dartmouth-Hitchcock Medical Center on October 16, just four days before my first midterm exam at Tuck. I cut his navel cord like American fathers do. When I returned to my house from the hospital, I was surprised to find congratulation messages from my study group members on the answering machine. Just after the midterm exam, seventy people gathered in front of Tuck Hall to give me cards and presents. By the way, my baby's name is Takuo. The meaning of the name? Of course I named him after Tuck, my favorite school!"* »

Married students can choose to live off-campus in rented homes or in Sachem Village, a small compound of modest homes (rumored to have been built to house soldiers during World War II) for married graduate students and their families, located about a mile from Tuck. Sachem is a community that is both part of and distinct from the rest of the college, which gives married students a common ground in which to live that part of their lives, and it forms a great support network for Tuck spouses and children. Sachem residents include representatives of Dartmouth's undergraduate program as well as all of its graduate programs, including medical, engineering, and business students. Many a future Tuckie has been born in homes on Sachem's "Fertility Row."

RECRUITING AND JOB SEARCH

OF course, the whole point of all of this is to find a great job that's right for you — and those student loans. Tuck has historically done extremely well in placing students in the popular industries, such as investment banking and consulting. However, Tuckies also land fantastic jobs in manufacturing, marketing, operations, and other fields at small and large companies across the country. Whatever your interests, you will find that the resources allocated to career planning and recruiting are tremendous and go a long way toward compensating for Tuck's small alumni/alumnae base and relatively isolated location.

The Office of Career Planning and Placement, in the Murdough Center on the Tuck campus, is the main resource for the job search.

Its most important function is to maintain relationships with companies that recruit Tuckies and to organize on-campus corporate presentations and interview schedules. For those who seek it, Placement also offers tests and guidance to help you make career choices that match your interests and personality. The Career Resources Library contains files on most recruiting companies. These files are bulging with company literature, industry reviews, and recent newspaper articles that are invaluable in preparing for interviews.

Tuck in general is very supportive of students' efforts to get the best jobs they possibly can, and the placement office works with each student individually to make that possible. During the second year there are no classes on Friday in the winter and spring quarters so you can leave Hanover for interviews without missing classes. The airport in nearby Lebanon, New Hampshire, has regular direct flights to Boston, New York, and other cities. Although these flights can be expensive, recruiting companies usually pick up the tab.

Because an established system is in place to facilitate the job search and to avoid compromising the integrity of the academic program, most professors are very reluctant to excuse you from class for a job-search reason. This can be frustrating for students, particularly if they feel micromanaged by Tuck's structured approach and rigid attendance policies, because sometimes it's tough to schedule interviews only for periods when you don't have academic commitments.

Days after you arrive at Tuck for the first time, the process to rehabilitate you as a productive member of society begins. Almost everybody gets a summer job after the first year, and the first step is to prepare your résumé for the class résumé book, sent to all recruiting companies. The Office of Career Planning and Placement, as well as second-years, can help you develop effective résumé styles and polish those important interviewing skills. You might not realize it, but you probably learned most of these skills long ago: clean your fingernails, smile, look your interviewer in the eye, don't scratch.

On-campus interviews for summer jobs can begin in December or January of the first year. You can tell when the season has started when the people who always look like they just fell out of bed turn up for class in suits and shined shoes that would make a drill sergeant proud.

In a move not hugely popular with some students, Tuck does not permit recruiting companies to host receptions, a practice common at other business schools. Some people claim that this restriction on recruiting activity, combined with Tuck's out-of-the-way location, put us at a competitive disadvantage to students at other MBA programs. Other students welcome the opportunity to be free from having to attend countless receptions, wearing plastic smiles, fearful that not showing up for a legitimate reason will be interpreted as a total lack of interest.

Throughout the fall and winter quarters, representatives of about 100 companies travel to Tuck to deliver presentations describing their companies and to recruit interested students. Hundreds more send information and/or post job listings. In addition, dozens of companies participate in panel discussions focusing on particular industries. That's not bad for a school with only 170 students per class! Often recruiters will be Tuck alumni or alumnae themselves, and you can find them later at popular running routes and local watering holes when their corporate responsibilities are over. All students are invited to the corporate briefings that take place on-campus at lunch or in the late afternoon.

« *My interest in consulting developed after the Consulting Club hosted an open panel of consultants from some of the best companies, during which they discussed the industry in great detail (actually, it was only the money . . .). I followed up by reading articles in the Career Resource Library and started to understand more fully some of the major differences among the firms. Finally I spoke with fellow students with consulting experience to get some firsthand impressions.*

Armed with this information, I felt pretty well prepared for the interview process. I understood what made each firm unique, and I had developed arguments as to why I could make positive contributions at each. It would have been impossible to succeed in the interviews without this preparation. »

Typically, the first round of interviews takes place on-campus in study rooms in Murdough. Interview formats range from informal and fun to incredibly structured ("Tell me, in order of importance, the five main reasons why you want to dedicate yourself to the chemical industry") and boring. Second- and third-round interviews might be at the Hanover Inn or perhaps at the company's offices.

« *Appearing relaxed and poised, even if you're trembling inside, is a key to interviewing success. During the final round at one of the major consulting companies, I found myself in a small room as several consultants and partners came through to speak with me. The interviews were pretty intense and often involved a case in which the interviewer would describe a business situation and ask how I would approach the problem as a consultant. Having a sense of humor, and getting along with the interviewer as an individual, however, proved to be just as important as having the "right" answers. Although it's easier said than done, be yourself.* »

ON THE JOB — FIRST YEARS OUT

AFTER business school, your life will change from that of the more or less carefree student to that of the (more or less) responsible employee. Gone are the opportunities to go running in the middle of the afternoon or to spend hours quietly working in the library on some interesting project. You are no longer paying for the privilege of learning, you're being paid to perform. Most important, you can forget those generous, academic-style vacations you were getting used to — try two to three weeks per year for starters.

A Tuck MBA can jump-start you into any one of a number of career paths that are probably out of reach without the extra boost. Your diploma will open the corporate door and get you into the interviewing process much faster than you would be able to otherwise, and it makes a great paper airplane as well. But what does it really get you once you're wearing your suit and power tie and you look like all the people from the other top schools? The answer is: it does not give you the answers. Tuck gives you a framework and a practical way of thinking about business situations that can do nothing more than help you come to your own conclusions and take action accordingly. In addition, because Tuckies tend to develop easygoing interpersonal skills, you will find that many people really do enjoy working with us.

There is no question that Tuck will teach you the business fundamentals you will need for a successful start at almost any company. Although it is not the school's objective to make you an "expert" in any one field, you will leave Hanover knowing the most important fundamentals, and usually much more, in every major business topic (and in bad-weather driving). This is particularly true in highly quantitative subject areas such as statistics, where the stated course goal is to make you an intelligent "consumer" of statistical information, but not a statistician (no self-respecting Tuckie would want to be a statistician, anyway).

On the job, such an educational philosophy means that Tuck students develop a way of thinking about business situations that is truly comprehensive. As business issues arise, the key questions seem to surface very naturally as you think back to the fundamentals you learned in the business school.

« *I had been consulting for less than one year and had already been exposed to a variety of business topics such as strategy and tactics, marketing, operations, and international economics. In each case, I felt comfortable entering the assignment because I could remember the fundamentals from my Tuck experience — even those 8:00 A.M. midwinter classes. Usually I could quickly identify the key issues and ask the most leveraged questions to isolate the problem and get the analysis started (I hope my boss is not reading this). Interestingly, I have found myself thinking more about the "people issues" in management now than I was before attending Tuck.* »

Base salaries the first year out are largely a function of the industry you enter, and for the most recent class ranged from $28,000 to $120,000. In general, the large service firms, such as consulting and finance, offer the highest initial base salaries, followed by the food and beverage industries, which offer brand management and marketing opportunities. If you're lucky, your firm may also offer you bonuses, tuition reimbursements, and signing bonuses. For most Tuckies, even those with the most extravagant habits, compensation at these levels meets expectations. However, it's important to remember that many students come out of Tuck with large tuition loans to repay, which can have a substantial negative impact on your personal statement of changes in financial position. In the early years, these payments can even rival "capital expenditures" (for VCRs, houses, and baby gear) and "dividends to parents" as the number one outflow.

This sounds pretty good. Tuck will make all kinds of job opportunities accessible, teach you the business basics, and bring you into a community of bright, talented people. Compensation, even during the first year out, is often more than generous. What's the catch?

« Tuck can teach you almost anything you need to know except one important thing: to choose the job that is truly the best fit with your talents and interests. Although there are resources available at Tuck in terms of testing and professional career guidance to help you make the best choices, it is up to you to take advantage of them.

In discussing jobs with classmates six to twelve months out, I noticed an unfulfilled desire on the part of many to work for smaller companies with less structure and fewer politics and often ones that make a physical product they could throw at someone. Manufacturing sometimes takes a bad rap during the MBA years, but the urge to design, make, market, and ship a real product is shared by many would-be entrepreneurs who ended up at service firms crunching numbers.

If you think you'd be happier at a small manufacturing company making some interesting product, don't just talk about it — do it! Don't go to investment banking or consulting just because everybody else is. »

SUMMARY OVERVIEW

TUCK was just what I was looking for in a business school, and I continue to recommend it highly to anyone I think would fit in well there. Coming from three years in a New York City bank, I was anxious to learn about all aspects of running a business, not just the financial stuff. Tuck gave me an excellent general management education, a true appreciation of effective people skills, and a high level of technical abilities without overspecialization. The group consulting projects for local companies got me out in the field with real entrepreneurs and management and allowed me to roll up my sleeves and test classroom theory with actual management situations. Most of the work during my two years at Tuck was extremely interesting and challenging, which made the whole experience very rewarding as well.

By the time I graduated, I had accepted a consulting job that would in fact allow me to participate in a variety of management functions with my clients. And because consulting is such a people business, I find myself constantly drawing on experiences in study group and group projects where I had learned to work effectively with diverse types of people.

In addition, after three years in a large, impersonal city, I welcomed the chance to start with a clean slate in a more rural area within a smaller, more intimate community. I found myself eager to learn and to contribute. The other students were motivated, smart, and friendly, and our class really did have a good time together. On a personal level, Tuck helped me to loosen up a bit and not to take myself quite so seriously.

Tuck's exceptional academic program really sets it apart from most of the nation's other business schools. Within the ranks of the very best, Tuck differentiates itself further by stressing group work, interpersonal skills, and frequent "reality checks" with the actual business world. Tuckies emerge with not only a great education, but also with excellent communication skills and values that help keep things in perspective.

But the most unique features of the Tuck School have their origin in its small size and location in northern New England. These two attributes, as well as others, make Tuck an ideal learning environment (for the right people). Student-faculty interaction is frequent and genuine. Most of the students themselves are extremely supportive, and with few exceptions will really go out of their way to help you and to learn from you as well, because at Tuck everything is a two-way street. In addition, the "remote" location causes all of the characters in this situation to gel into a genuine, close community.

The Tuck spirit also carries over into the alumni and alumnae, who usually remember their Hanover days very fondly. Recent graduating classes have demonstrated their enthusiasm with near-100 percent participation in the annual alumni/alumnae giving program. This is a participation rate unheard of at the other top business schools. For job-hungry MBA's, these loyal alumni and alumnae are a gold mine of information, tips, references, and anything else you need to find the right job.

« *I bought off on the community aspect of the Tuck experience* 100 *percent. From the day I arrived I found fellow students, faculty, and staff making sincere efforts to improve our education, job prospects, and quality of life. And they expected a lot of me, too, because you can't live in an environment like that and only take without giving something back.*

The best thing is that you can contribute to Tuck in so many ways while you're there, not only in the classroom. A lot of people spent huge amounts of their limited free time doing things such as organizing events and participating in Tuck athletic teams, and in many other activities. I think it was the few people who didn't want to contribute to the community in some way who probably didn't enjoy the experience as much. As for the alumni and alumnae, I am confident I could call anyone at random with a career-related question and get a helpful, thoughtful response. »

While the Tuck community and its small size are major selling points, there can also be disadvantages. Faced with a small student body, Tuck simply can't offer as many different courses as the larger schools can. Although the breadth is there (i.e., no gaps in the basic business topics covered), larger schools may offer deeper course offerings that go into specific business topics in much greater detail.

In addition, although the Tuck alumni/alumnae network is undoubtedly one of the most loyal and supportive, it can't compete with the sheer size of the alum pools of the big schools. Every seven years or so, schools the size of Harvard turn out more new graduates than Tuck's entire alum body. As a result, it has taken longer for Tuck's excellent reputation to become widely known in the business community.

When it comes to job-hunting, this means that foreign firms will be less likely to have heard of Tuck than larger schools. Even in the United States, many West Coast firms find it costly and time-consuming to recruit Tuckies actively when other top schools are more easily accessible. This is not to say that these job markets are off-limits to Tuckies — only that it will take a bit more effort and expense by the student to get that initial interview.

« For most of my classmates, the many obvious strengths of the Tuck program far outweighed these negatives. The vast majority were extremely satisfied with their academic education, their job prospects, and their decision to pursue an MBA. Seventeen months out, we are still a very tight group. I speak to somebody from my Tuck class almost every day, and if I need support or some good advice, I know where to find it. »

Remember, Tuck offers much more than an MBA program. Tuck offers a two-year experience in life. A great deal will be expected of you from the faculty, from your peers, and even from yourself. It will be fun and exciting. It will be a challenge. Accept it if you dare.

Chapter 10

THE WHARTON SCHOOL (UNIVERSITY OF PENNSYLVANIA)*

THE PROGRAM

« Our marketing case concerned a large industrial fabricator of manufacturing metals whose senior management faced the problem of capacity shortage and late deliveries. To make problems worse, not only did the firm have more business than it could currently fill, it was also losing money. Flushing out the problems in the case was easy. The case was rife with them. Solutions abounded, too. The professor solicited recommendations from around the class, which ranged from adjusting the pricing structure to hiring more welders. Each recommendation that was offered seemed to confound the problems rather than solve them. The number of variables was making my head swim.

Faculty from various departments sometimes attend other departments' classes. Today I noticed our operations strategy professor paying particularly close attention to the discussion from his perch in the back of the class. At one point the discussion faltered, and he put up his hand to ask whether he could make a suggestion to the class. The next thing I knew, the operations professor began leading our marketing discussion!

His solution involved breaking our marketing problem down into three parts: a microeconomics, an operations, and a human behavior component. Taken separately, each component only offered insight as to what caused the problem. By combining them, however, he sug-

* BY CHRISTY KALAN, MBA, AND BURNETT HANSEN, MBA

gested a framework by which we might arrive at a series of solutions.

Reaching the operation professor's level of analysis did not require extraordinary technical expertise or advanced mathematics. On the contrary, it involved thinking about a managerial problem from several different perspectives and combining the results. I remember this class because it taught me how powerful integrated thinking can be to solving real problems. »

After two years of research incorporating the insight of alumni/ alumnae, recruiters, CEOs, students, faculty, and administrators, Wharton designed an integrative curriculum with the goal of educating the next generation of business leaders. Wharton was already known as a finance powerhouse that in recent years has expanded to include general management. The new program goes a step farther, by expanding the breadth and depth of Wharton, achieved by keeping eight key components in mind: functional knowledge (i.e., a major), integrative learning (e.g., how a decision in marketing affects operations), global perspective, interpersonal skills, problem formulation, "real world" learning, creativity, and enthusiasm for learning. Students continue to benefit from Wharton's well-established strengths in specialized fields such as finance and entrepreneurial management, and everyone selects a functional major (depth). The core courses simply broaden the knowledge base and increase the integration and application of that knowledge (breadth).

To deliver this kind of program, the core design includes "real life" simulations and cases, a year-long leadership skills course, new electives, better coordination among faculty in different departments, and an optional month-long trip to Japan, Germany, or Brazil. A preterm component gives everyone the opportunity to learn basic skills in accounting, statistics, and microeconomics so everyone starts out on a more even footing when the first semester begins. Wharton believes the program offers learning opportunities critical to training managers for the twenty-first century. Most important, students learn to think critically, both about their studies and about themselves. Students have the opportunity to explore and understand some of the subtleties of business — how functions relate to each other, how to apply management tools, and how to consider career management within the context of life interests and personal development.

The first-year curriculum builds on a foundation of fourteen required core subject areas, most of which are broken into six-week modules. Students who demonstrate proficiency in a core subject area may waive the course and substitute an elective instead. For example, by taking a waiver exam or submitting sufficient academic credentials, students can waive out of the first part, second part, or all of a core course. Breaking semester-long courses into two modules increases the flexibility of Wharton's program, a feature appreciated by most students. In addition, some core courses are tracked so that students can take beginning or more advanced versions, depending on aptitude and experience. In theory, the waiver and tracking processes mean that students of roughly the same proficiency end up in classes together. In practice, the system works well most of the time.

Unless you waive courses, the core classes are the same for everyone: Accounting, Statistics, Microeconomics, Macroeconomics, Management Science, Operations Management, Managing People, Organizational Design, Business Strategy, Global Strategic Management, Legal Studies, Finance, Leadership Skills, and Marketing. Beyond the core, Wharton offers nearly two hundred courses in eleven departments. The course offerings are extensive, and impossible to exhaust in two (or even three or four) years. Prominent departments include Finance, Marketing Research, Strategy, Health Care, Real Estate, and Entrepreneurship. In addition, sixteen research centers and programs provide specialization in areas such as global competitiveness and service-based industries. If you are focused, Wharton is the place to find the facilities, faculty, and students who share your interests.

In fact, one of the standout features of The Wharton School is that it offers so many academic and social options. Wharton students have to be able to set priorities and make choices. Guidance is available if you ask for it, but you're essentially responsible for setting your own agenda. However, given its size, Wharton does a good job of fostering a sense of community, primarily through the cohort system.

What is a cohort? It's a concept Wharton developed a few years back to create a friendlier, more manageable environment for the 750 incoming first-year students. Each cohort (the dictionary calls it a band of soldiers or colleagues) is designated by a letter and is made up of about 65 students who meet during Orientation and take all of their first-semester core courses together. Cohorts also form teams for intramural sports; elect academic, social, and athletic representatives and historians; and give themselves nicknames such as "E pluribus unum" or "I think, therefore I M." Your cohort is a tightly knit "class within a class," and friendships formed from these groups spill over into extracurricular and non-school-related activities.

These activities might include taking advantage of all that Philadelphia has to offer. The city boasts an excellent symphony, the Barnes foundation (a huge private collection of Impressionist paintings), spirited professional sports teams, several great museums, and every kind of food imaginable, including cheesesteaks (order yours "wiz with" and argue with friends over who makes the best). Or try exploring spacious Fairmount Park, the Franklin Institute, or rafting down the Delaware. The rents are cheap, the city is friendly, and with a little exploring, it's possible to compile a long list of favorite places in a short time.

Even though the architect who built Vance Hall (home to graduate students and famous for its inability to regulate room temps) mistakenly thought he was supposed to build a factory, students attracted to Wharton are anything but "cookie cutter" products. In addition to the expected parade of engineers, consultants, and investment banking types, there are theater directors, sky divers, orchestra conductors, photographers, pro football players, and dancers with the New York City Ballet. The school also has a decidedly international flavor, with about 30 percent of the student body coming from abroad. Wharton's international recruiting efforts make the classroom a dynamic place. If a professor doesn't have firsthand experience with a specific foreign culture or company, one of the students in class surely will.

The diverse student body means many opportunities to share expertise. Whether you fall into the category of "gearhead" or "poet," you'll be able to contribute to group projects and learn from your classmates. Although the gearheads would appear to have an advantage at Wharton, poets shouldn't despair. Conceptual thinking underlies most business decisions, and professors want to see ideas communicated articulately and concisely in writing. Besides, the quantitative learning curve is steep, and after taking core classes it is possible to fashion a program that won't tax your calculator batteries.

Professors teach classes using a combination of case method, lecture, and discussion. A typical approach is to present an analytical framework in a lecture format, then ask students to apply that framework in the next class to a case. In each course, the aim is to take advanced management theory and apply it to real problems. The practical application will reveal where the theory is strongest and in what situations it is weakest. Wharton students learn that there are seldom "right" and "wrong" answers, but rather better and worse arguments about the many competing factors that a manager must understand.

A series of computer simulations brings to life the complexity of day-to-day decision making. Even though these simulations are computer-generated, they take on a "reality" of their own. Teams of students have to divide up mountains of information; share their expertise; and reach cohesive financing, marketing, and operations decisions. The MBA program includes additional opportunities for hands-on experience through group class projects that entail studying local companies or through advanced study projects in which students consult to corporations around the country.

Overall, the program is a challenging experience. Students learn to think about problems from different angles and to avoid the pitfall of pulling solutions from a single discipline. Students are trained to think across functions when making decisions. This training means that a student shouldn't forget the skills of one course once the class is over. A concept learned in one class is sometimes fair game for a professor in another class, even on exams! The faculty here are committed to teaching and challenging students to think integratively.

« One day while I was sitting outside in the Wharton Quad studying for a final examination, the vice dean of the school wandered over to say hello.

"So, how is everything going today?" he asked.

I was seated amid a sea of notebooks, assimilating job design characteristics and production management concepts while heroically attempting to quell the usual panic that generally seizes me right before a test. "Oh, pretty good," I answered.

"Only pretty good?"

"Well, things will be going better once this exam is over."

"What exam is that?"

I drew a blank. For a moment I couldn't remember. I knew Professor Fisher was giving the exam in this class, but I was looking at notes from Professor Cappelli's class. Hmmm, this was an embarrassing situation: the vice dean was asking what I was doing and I didn't have an answer. "Professor Fisher's class, but I'm not sure what subject it is."

He nodded. "You're learning."

By second semester, however, preparing for cross-functional classes seemed easier, and I was able to talk about an operations issue from an organization design standpoint without the same anxiety. In fact, the integration became second nature. The Wharton program was working. »

GETTING IN

GETTING into Wharton isn't easy, but it's worth a try. Each year, the vast majority of the applicant pool is qualified for admission, and about 20 percent make it in. Wharton doesn't have a formula for admissions, so there's no point in telling the admissions office what you think they want to hear. The school attains its student profile by marketing the program to students they want to reach. Because the statistical profile of the admitted class will mirror the larger population, and because so many students are qualified, the admissions committee is free to look for, as they put it, "a compelling reason to take somebody."

So how does the committee make its selections? Your candidacy will be evaluated in four areas: academic experience, work experience, personal qualities, and overall presentation. How you present your "overall package" is the key to admissions, because the school is looking for well-rounded candidates who have clearly and carefully thought through their reasons for applying to business school in the first place. Apply to Wharton as if you were applying for a job. Because students come from so many backgrounds, each component of your application — GMATs, GPA, essays, work experience, recommendations, comparative salary progression, and evidence of achievement — will be evaluated within the context of your particular job or career path. Contrary to popular belief, applicants are not categorized based on their experience or background. This outlook enables the admissions committee to assess individuals relative to the general competition. In other words, the committee conducts its evaluations so they are able to compare apples with oranges.

The first thing admissions looks for is evidence of your potential as a manager and leader. If you have little else to offer, a few years in a training program with a big-name firm will not get you in the door. The committee is interested in why you chose a particular path, what you got out of it, and where you are heading. Good grades (average GPA, 3.4) and top GMATs (average, 640) are important, but by themselves they won't guarantee admission.

« I applied to Wharton in late March with little hope of ever being admitted. My background included eight years in a small Swedish student travel and language company, an undergraduate degree in English, and very faded memories (nonexistent, really) of a calculus 101 class taken ten years ago. My grades and GMATs were adequate, but nowhere near the top.

I visited the school in February and sat in on a packed macroeconomics class. Topic: the monetary equation of exchange identity and hyperinflation. I didn't understand a word. There was no way I'd get in.

One year later, I was sitting in that same class, taught by the same professor, thinking, "Okay, this makes sense." Maybe I wasn't an admissions mistake after all. Still, out of curiosity, I asked the (then) admissions director why I got in. After reviewing my dossier, he said it was because my essays were direct and honest, and my work experience showed good potential for managerial success. (As a matter of fact, he was reading from portions of my application that I had considered editing as being too "chancy.") All along I'd assumed I wasn't business school material because I wasn't at the top in every category. My admission is evidence that at Wharton the whole can be greater than the sum of the parts. »

Although there is no typical admissions experience, certain procedural steps may help your application en route to a decision. First, it's up to you to make sure that everything is in your file, including recommendations and grade transcripts. Don't assume that items have been sent directly to the school — follow up on each detail. Second, apply early. This especially holds true for foreign students. Postal systems can be slow, so it's best to allow plenty of time. Third, if you choose to interview, it's highly recommended that you do so before submitting your application.

The interview is treated as a chance to meet you without the bias of having read your application. The admissions committee gets to know a person rather than a piece of paper, and you can ask questions and raise concerns (e.g., I have a 2.8 grade average; what does that mean for my chances?). Procedurally it helps to interview first because when your application comes in, it can be added to an already active file, and the results of the interview become part of the application packet. Otherwise, because of Wharton's rolling admissions policy, it's possible for the committee to review your application, and perhaps reach a decision, before the interview is held.

Graduate assistants help with some first-round readings and offer valuable insights to the admissions committee regarding how certain industries and companies work. Second- and third-round readings are conducted by full-time admissions officers, and applications go through a cyclical distribution process so that new eyes see an application each time it is read. Given the large number of applications to review, Wharton has an excellent turnaround time of four to six weeks, although joint degree candidates may have to wait longer for a decision.

So, who eventually gets in? Through its rigorous admissions process, Wharton creates a diverse student body of which roughly 29 percent are women, 12 percent are minorities, and almost 30 percent are foreign. About 22 percent come from engineering, 16 percent from business, 20 percent from economics, and 42 percent from the remaining liberal arts and science fields. Most of these people have excelled in school and at work, and they expect to excel at Wharton, too. Most also appreciate and take advantage of the opportunity they've been given to work with and learn from fellow classmates. The atmosphere is both friendly and competitive. On the whole, Wharton does a good job of recruiting genuinely nice people.

ACADEMIC ENVIRONMENT

« *"Do you agree with this pricing strategy?"*

The professor's voice rang in my ear, and I could feel my face reddening. Some faculty incorporate cold-calling students without warning as a means of ensuring that everyone in class is prepared. Today was my day, and I was on the spot in front of my sixty cohort peers.

"No, I don't," I answered, and proceeded to give what I thought was a lucid explanation of my point. The professor did not seem to share my optimism. At each of my assertions, he would press me for reasons and would question the assumptions I had made. Questions were coming at me so quickly I did not even have time to be embarrassed about making mistakes. It was a struggle to keep all the issues in mind as well as defend the assumptions behind my answer. Moreover, my position was becoming less tenable by the second.

"Do you mean to say that these buyers are not price-sensitive?" he asked me.

"Of course they are, but they are considering performance factors as well as price."

The professor then solicited discussion from other members of the class. "Do any of you believe what Mr. Hansen is telling us?"

Some of my peers threw themselves into the fray, building and strengthening my argument. Others took the professor's view that pricing ought to be the primary consideration. The professor did an excellent job of dividing the class into two major positions on this pricing issue. Given the heated discussion, everyone in class had strong and well-founded opinions on this case.

At last, our professor presented his view on the pricing strategy and unfolded a cogent argument based on his research. However, answers per se do not matter much in most case discussions. The value of the lesson lies in the debate leading to the solution, not in the solution itself.

It was a challenging experience to lay myself on the line in front of my professor and the people whom I would see several more times that day and four more days that week. But over time, a spirit of trust develops within which students and faculty can begin to learn from one another. By speaking up and contributing, I became part of the collective learning process. »

Students generally collaborate when it comes to academic work. It doesn't take long for the sixty-five students in a cohort to know one another quite well both socially and academically. Faculty encourage students to study together and require that much of the assigned course work be done in groups. Group work reinforces a collegial air. For one course, students self-select into a learning team, a study group that remains together for the entire first year. This experience mirrors the workplace and allows students to explore the complex issues of group dynamics. Frequent faculty and peer feedback and self-assessment make these teams a powerful part of the Wharton learning experience. Learning here happens as much from your 750 classmates (1,500 if you include first- and second-year students) as from faculty. Ask almost any Wharton student what they value about school and the answer will be some version of "my classmates."

Integration and cross-functional training at Wharton also mean applying classroom learning in the real world. Wharton's Northeast Corridor location provides students with access to New York, Washington, D.C., and a vibrant Philadelphia business community. Many firms actively seek Wharton students to carry out research projects. These arrangements have proven most successful: businesses gain information they might not otherwise access, while students complete course requirements and face complex organizational problems.

« Within four weeks of arriving at Wharton, I found myself with my learning team in the president's office of one of the nation's most prominent nonprofit organizations. We proposed a study of employee motivation and job satisfaction. Our team consisted of two members with health care backgrounds, two engineers, a former financial services marketer, and a banker. Upon negotiating a mutually agreeable project with the president, we quickly discovered that our project would require us to draw on all our collective expertise and would need some faculty support. In the vernacular: we had our work cut out for us!

A few days later, two of our team members were designing and precoding a motivational survey. Another was making arrangements with the personnel department for interviews and survey distribution. Another two prepared a statistical model to analyze the data. And *one sat down with our management professor to borrow a stack of books and journals from which we would develop the framework for our study. Three weeks later we actually had a fair understanding of the nonprofit organization.*

By December we had loads of information, which had to be distilled into a manageable thesis and series of recommendations. We all appreciated how complex employee motivational issues could become. We were buried in statistical analysis and interview transcripts. The process of assembling our research into some semblance of order made our usual class case analyses seem like pleasure reading. We finished the project and presentation at 5:00 A.M., sufficient time for us to get a few hours' sleep before the presentation was due.

Our team made the required presentation before faculty members of the Management and Communication departments. We then traveled to the organization to make our presentation to the president. The most memorable part of the whole experience was neither the hours spent agonizing over the project, nor the Management Department's favorable comments. Rather, it was the letter we received on the day we returned from our holiday break in January: a warm letter from the organization's president thanking us for our contribution. We had made a difference where it mattered, in the real world of business problems and decisions! »

Wharton strongly emphasizes teaching quality and supports this emphasis with published student rankings of professors' performances along dimensions of clarity, presentation, and ability to inspire interest and to make material relevant to the "real" world. Many students use these published rankings to select their courses. With almost no exceptions, professors teach all classes, with PhD or graduate student assistants. Most professors are accessible and are genuinely interested in how the class is going. Many form small "teaching quality circles" with students to get feedback on their teaching style and exchange ideas about future classes and possible topics. Some faculty members can also be found at the Wharton Pub on Thursday nights, chatting with students.

The Wharton faculty have studied and consulted to businesses all over the globe. Most of the core classes feature a significant international perspective. For example, in our Marketing class, only four cases focused on the U.S. domestic market. For a more in-depth international experience, the Joseph H. Lauder Institute, which offers a joint MBA/MA in management and international studies, may be appealing. This demanding program requires proficiency in a foreign language and includes studies overseas. Another global exposure program is the joint MBA/MA program with The Johns Hopkins School of Advanced International Studies (SAIS). Even without opting for these special programs, students in the core curriculum can participate in numerous opportunities for overseas study and cultural immersion trips offered every year.

Outside the traditional course offerings, independent study projects (ISPs) are an opportunity to study a subject of your interest in depth. Such a project can be started by asking professors for a topic or by making a proposal to a professor. It is an opportunity to work closely with a faculty member. Professors can sometimes arrange funding if the project is sufficiently complex and will entail special travel or materials. Other kinds of studies are Advanced Study Projects (ASPs), often completed by a group of students. ASPs usually involve a consulting-type project for an outside company, some of which are Fortune 500 firms that are leaders in their fields. Some majors at Wharton require an ASP or an ISP; others do not. No matter what one's major, students in all disciplines can take advantage of this opportunity for personalized study and learning.

The Wharton academic program abounds with resources and activities. To support the work you will do in any of over two hundred courses, the school's Instructional Technology Department offers IBM and Apple labs, a DEC mainframe system, and free training at all levels. Free training and support are also available for the university's host of on-line data bases, some of which can be conveniently accessed twenty-four hours a day within the privacy of your own home. Wharton and its many clubs sponsor guest speakers from prominent business areas to supplement classroom experience. Students also participate in the immensely popular Wharton Foreign Language Jump Start Program. These noncredit courses are competitively priced, conveniently scheduled, and available to students, faculty, staff, spouses, and significant others. Finally, most Wharton faculty make themselves available to students outside the classroom for job talks, research interests, and social gatherings.

The first year of Wharton's program has a decidedly different flavor from the second year. To support the cross-functional goals of the program, first-year classes are largely divided into six-week mini-courses. Students gain exposure to many faculty members and subjects areas and develop problem-solving skills using multiple disciplines. The pace is fast and the work load intense. Although it's difficult to face final exams nearly every six weeks, most students find it helpful and an effective way to learn core disciplines. During the second year, students have only one core obligation — an Integrative Management class that pulls together the subject areas learned in the first year. The rest of the classes are traditional semester-long electives and courses toward a major. The pace is more relaxed, exams are more spread out, and the focus is on more in-depth understanding of a particular subject area.

Most students are not overly concerned with grades, although competition does exist at the upper end of the scale. Wharton faculty assign grades of Distinguished (DS), High Pass (HP), and Pass (P), with class distributions being approximately 10 percent, 25 percent, and 65 percent, respectively. Students who fail receive a grade of No Credit (NC); however, a professor isn't required to fail a percentage of his or her class. Academic honors are based solely on the number of DS grades. (There are no calculated GPAs or class rankings.) This grading system alleviates academic pressure because the majority of students earn P's. In fact, the group work required in the Wharton program tends to foster a spirit of cooperation among students. Still, this is not to suggest that grades are unimportant here or that there is no competition. There is. First, Wharton students can disclose grades to recruiters, and getting a DS looks better than an HP. Second, most students at Wharton have excelled professionally and academically and expect to do so here. It's fair to say that Wharton students work hard and push themselves to achieve their best no matter what the prospective grade may be.

The chance of failure at Wharton is small for several reasons. First, the admissions committee is highly selective, culling from an extraordinarily capable applicant pool. Second, there are lots of safeguards in place: professors are available during office hours and by appointment for extra help, teaching assistants have regularly scheduled hours for extra help in either private office hours or during public review sessions, and professors will often seek out students who are not doing well. However, students can't coast through the program. Lack of attention to trouble signs or weak areas can lead to the dreaded grade of NC (no credit). A student's best advice is to prepare for each class, ask questions, and expect to be challenged.

Furthermore, Wharton students are expected to take some risks. Let's face it: the cost of making an error in a class is far lower than making the same error in a real business situation. Professors insist that students question accepted assumptions. In class discussions, students often take what may be an unpopular opinion. Learning here happens not only through textbooks, journal articles, and lectures but also in rigorous discussions among students and professors.

SOCIAL LIFE

SOME professors grouse that Wharton students must not have enough work because they appear to have too much fun. Although students would disagree about the work load, most do manage to have an active social life. There is something here for everyone. As a matter of fact, one of the first skills you learn is how to manage your time to fit everything in.

« Carving out a social life at Wharton depends on your own expectations and priorities. I was happiest cooking dinner with friends, going to the movies, swimming, catching guest speakers at school, and doing assorted other non-school-related events. I met people primarily through classes and a part-time job I had at school. My roommate, on the other hand, filled his date book with numerous lunches, school events, and parties, made it to the symphony at least once a month, and also managed a long-distance relationship. Two married friends commuted from New York City. One worked part-time at the Small Business Development Center, fit in squash games, and still made the 7:05 P.M. train back to New York. Each of us split our days among studying, socializing, and personal time in ways that worked for us. »

It's theoretically possible at Wharton to study all the time, and a few students do, but it isn't recommended. Even during extra-busy times, informal socializing goes on between and after classes in Sun Lounge, Zellen Snack Bar, the Quad, and the Anvil Club. Everyone is invited to join the Anvil Club, touted as the preferred lunch place for Wharton grads. For less that $500 students receive a two-year membership, seventy-five lunches, and the convenience of eating at a nearby, slightly upscale school cafeteria. Not quite the dark-paneled private dining room hinted at in the invitation, but still a good place to meet friends and fill up on hearty food. Anyone with a robust appetite will appreciate the all-you-can-eat policy. In addition, numerous "working" lunches happen at the Anvil Club. If you want to broaden your culinary horizons, you can do so by sampling the fare at lunch trucks conveniently located around campus.

News travels fast at Wharton, and students keep up by reading the weekly newspaper and checking their mail folders religiously — sometimes three times a day. The mail folder is a Wharton student's lifeline to the rest of the school. On any given day you can find memos from professors, frantic notes from study group mates (as in "Where are you? The rest of us are in Steinberg-Dietrich 207."), a coveted letter from a corporation recruiting on campus, administrative information, activities announcements, or a note from a friend or roommate.

A second source of information is the *Wharton Journal*. Besides featuring the all-important menu at the Anvil Club, the paper covers school news, dean's forums, corporate presentations, speakers, upcoming events, and an exposé of who was seen with whom during the previous week. If "TalkTalk" (the *Journal*'s gossip column) isn't your cup of tea, try "Financial Statements," a column about amusing behavior by Wharton profs. Articles for the *Journal* can be submitted by anyone, and regular columns and good reporting keep students current on happenings around school.

The Student Affairs Office is the focal point for coordinating cocurricular programs such as the Zweig Executive Dinner Series, Executive Life-styles, Food for Thought, and Take a Professor to Lunch, as well as numerous VIP presentations. Student Affairs is also responsible for publishing the student directory that everyone thumbs through repeatedly during their first few weeks of school. Extracurricular events and clubs are organized through the Wharton Graduate Association (WGA), run exclusively by Wharton graduate students.

WGA activities run the gamut from A to Z and fall into three broad categories: student government, professional development, and social life. Although some activities are for students only, most can be enjoyed by friends, spouses, and children as well. With fifteen hundred students and over a hundred clubs and affiliations to choose from, it's impossible to say what most people do, but the following paragraphs should provide a sampling of what's available.

The end of the school week (Thursday) brings the start of one of the more popular WGA events — happy hour ("the Pub") at the MBA House. Each Thursday from four-thirty on, students who pay a one-time admissions price can drink beer (or wine or soda) to their heart's content. And by about seven o'clock, hungry men and women can be seen lunging for slices of lukewarm pizza. Don't stand in their way. Many students consider the Pub one of the best values at Wharton — and spouses, friends, and kids seem to have a lot of fun, too. During the week, the MBA House is a quieter place, where groups of students can eat lunch, study, play billiards, or watch TV.

Another tradition is the Walnut Walk. Once each semester, students who choose to can wear business attire above the waist and boxer shorts below, and parade through Center City on a tour of local bars. Some groups stop for dinner and dancing along the way, but the diehards and drinking enthusiasts make it to the end of the line, where they eat a 2:00 A.M. breakfast and hope for a taxi to take them home.

To celebrate the end of each semester, students can trade in their jeans and dress up for the Holiday and Spring balls (or work on the committees that put them together). But the event most waited for is probably the *Follies* — Wharton's spoof of itself, produced and performed by some multitalented students. *Follies* is special because most of the school participates in one way or another, either by being onstage or in the audience. Practice starts in the fall, with performances held in February in both Philadelphia and New York.

Sports-minded students can participate in any of about twenty athletic clubs, ranging from ice hockey to squash to roadrunners and more. And for those who like to take cohort rivalries onto the field, intramural football or softball games pit the Killer B's against the Special K's. Sometimes even the deans and professors join the fray by inviting students to show their stuff on the basketball court in the highly touted student-faculty game. Nearby, Gimbel and Hutchinson gymnasiums offer the opportunity to swim, play squash and tennis, or work out with weights between or after classes. The hours could be better, but the facilities are good.

Although Wharton students clearly like to have fun, they also show a strong interest in charitable events. Students and professors join forces for the annual Wharton Olympics to raise money for The Mayor's Commission on Literacy, and Say YES to Education teams Wharton graduate students with underprivileged high schoolers who need tutoring. Volunteer opportunities abound. Perhaps the best-known annual fund-raising event is Christmas in April. Close to three hundred students (with the help of skilled laborers) repair and renovate homes in West Philadelphia that belong to people who are unable to tackle the projects themselves.

Nearly all of the groups that thrive under the WGA umbrella are student-initiated, and many celebrate Wharton's cultural diversity. Over fifteen cultural affairs clubs — from AAMBA (African American MBA) to WHALASA (Latin American Student Association) — operate on both social and professional levels and welcome all students to their programs. International students are well represented, and West Coast natives even have a club to make networking from three thousand miles away a little easier. All of the clubs come together for the International Festival to celebrate cuisine from around the world, but the hands-down favorite event is any dance party sponsored by WHALASA.

On the professional front, twenty-one clubs reflect the range of careers available to entrepreneurs, wheeler-dealers, and the undecided alike. Clubs from Arts Management to Venture Capital — sponsoring activities from alumni/alumnae career forums to plant tours — offer a terrific opportunity to learn more about areas that interest you. The professional clubs also work closely with Career Development and Placement to arrange recruiting presentations and compile industry and career information packs.

The social activities at Wharton also provide support and social opportunities for spouses. Throughout the year, Wharton Partners is an active agency that coordinates many programs dedicated to the student's spouse. These include lunches, and job search help for newcomers to the Philadelphia area. Wharton Partners also sponsors a Saturday program called "A Day in the Life of a Wharton Student." This day features classes taught by full Wharton professors in several areas of business. Wharton Kids, another group, tailors activities to families with children.

Last but by no means least is the city of Philadelphia itself.

« *Too many students I met viewed living in Philadelphia as something they'd have to endure to get their degree from Wharton. West Philly (the area surrounding the campus) isn't paradise, but the city has lots to offer, and during my two years I sampled as much as I could, including the ballet, the zoo, free concerts by Curtis Music School students, coffee at Ray's, South Philly's Italian market, breakfast at the Down Home Diner, the Franklin Institute, ball games, and the Art Museum. Before you opt for an Amtrak ride out of town, try Philadelphia; it grows on you.* »

Wharton students have three basic housing options: West Philly, Center City (downtown), or on-campus dorms. For convenience and proximity to campus, many choose to live in West Philly. Although the area is a bit run-down, it's possible to find roomy accommodations at reasonable rents. Campus vans are available to shuttle students home at night when safety is a concern.

For students who don't have time to search for a Philadelphia apartment (or for those who like to roll out of bed and into class), there's Grad Tower B. Twelve floors have been reserved by Wharton, and the building is two blocks away from most basic necessities of student life: school, library, gym, laundry, ATM machines, fast food, and WaWa. Married students can find a similar setup in Meyer Hall.

Choosing to live in Center City generally means finding an old Philadelphia row house or heading for a high rise, one of which has been dubbed "Grad Tower C" for the huge number of Wharton students who reside there each year. The rents are higher than in West Philly but are still affordable, even on a student budget. Living downtown generally means a ten- to twenty-minute bike, bus, or subway ride to campus, or a twenty- to forty-minute walk. Few students drive, since finding a parking space on or near the campus can be more trouble than it's worth. A fairly common pattern is for students to start out in Grad Tower B and then move to Center City for their second year.

Married or single, living downtown or on-campus, Wharton students perform a juggling act. Yes, it's possible to have a life. No, it won't be the life you led before school. At least at Wharton the choices are there, and you can fill your plate — or not.

RECRUITING AND JOB SEARCH

FOR better or for worse, preparation for the job search begins shortly after students arrive. One of the required first-year management courses on leadership skills is coordinated with the Career Development and Placement office and the Communications Department. This course begins with rigorous self-assessment, since knowing oneself well is the natural starting point for any job search. The Management Department administers a series of diagnostic evaluations to assess career interests and personality profiles. Such assessments provide data for students to think critically about themselves and for faculty to offer constructive feedback about career choices.

Including career management in the curriculum helps students to balance business, career, and life interests. The course progresses through résumé-crafting, letter-writing, and the job offer negotiation process. This whole class process is coordinated with the business recruiting season for summer jobs, which generally begins in February of the first year. For those who take it seriously, this course can be one of the most valuable job search tools.

« I sat at home one night preparing to write a personal development journal entry, a required exercise in the core first-year management course. The results of a Myers-Briggs Type Indicator test, a Strong Interest Inventory test, and a Life Interest survey lay in front of me. At first I rebelled against these tests because they told me little about myself that I did not already know. What a waste, I thought!

Then I realized that these evaluations were some of the first objective and yet nonquantitative data I had ever seen on myself. GMAT scores and GPAs both represented my quantitative performance. But these evaluations that I was resisting compared my opinions, interests, and reactions to huge data bases of people from around the world. This awareness helped me open myself up to self-evaluation.

Four months later, in a job interview, a recruiter asked me, "What is your biggest weakness?"

The stock answers to this question are laughable and legion (I work too hard and am too committed to my employer), and not without reason. The question is difficult to answer without digging oneself into a hole. I thought back on the objective data I knew about myself.

"I am an introvert," I answered, "at least according to the Myers-Briggs test. I derive much of my creativity internally rather than from outside sources. I have to make a conscious effort to socialize in large groups. For instance, most of the business school's social life revolves around large parties. Since I prefer small, more intimate groups of people, I have to make a concerted effort to attend."

"You strike me as quite outgoing. Are you going to try to become more extroverted?" the interviewer probed, skeptically.

"I think I am generally outgoing. But my sources of inspiration and motivation tend to be personal. I am not, however, trying to change my personality. On the contrary, I think such a personality trait has probably contributed to my academic success and the small-group leadership skills that you see on my résumé."

After pursuing this subject for another minute or so, the interviewer said, "You've thought a lot about this, haven't you?"

"Yes, I have." In fact, if I hadn't thought about those personality tests, I probably would not have even considered working for this company! Data from the Strong Interest Inventory encouraged me to explore a career in this area. »

Most Wharton MBA candidates take a summer job between their first and second years. Many students find it an opportunity to "try out" a different profession. Such an opportunity can be especially important for students who plan to change careers. Some students prefer to continue with their full-time studies during the summer and graduate in December of their second year. This option may be viable for students who are taking a leave of absence from work to pursue an MBA.

More than 730 companies recruit MBAs at Wharton for summer jobs and for permanent positions following graduation. The office of On-Campus Recruiting Services (OCRS) has a modern complex and capable staff dedicated to orchestrating the recruiting process and making the experience as easy as possible for busy students.

Some ten thousand interviews take place in the OCRS complex, and thousands of others happen in local Philadelphia hotels. OCRS also administers a computer application on the Wharton mainframe computer to keep students abreast of additions and changes to the recruiting calendar. This system can be accessed confidentially from most computers on-campus and through a modem in the convenience of student homes. The system reminds students of deadlines for applications, posts name-and-address information of companies recruiting on-campus, and serves as the vehicle by which some companies select which students to interview through a competitive "bidding" process. Between 40 and 50 percent of students get jobs through OCRS.

In addition to all the on-campus recruiting efforts, Career Development and Placement (CD&P) supports students' independent job searches by maintaining an extensive library of student résumés, past job placements, and current press articles, including Nexus scans of more than eleven hundred companies. They compile information both by field (e.g., finance or marketing) and by geographic region (e.g., Asia or U.S. West Coast). To supplement these data, Wharton's business library has on-line data for thousands more companies. The network of more than twenty-three thousand Wharton alumni and alumnae listed and kept on file at CD&P makes access to industry experts worldwide easy. CD&P's more than twenty-five development and resource publications on top of the weekly newsletters provide yet more information. All these resources can be overwhelming at first glance. Perhaps most valuable of all are the fifteen full-time staff who help students use these data efficiently. Student access to counselors is flexible, either by appointment or as a walk-in for quick questions. These professionals offer everything from résumé critique and job-hunting tips to salary negotiating strategies and job-acceptance protocol.

Finance, banking, management consulting, consumer products, and marketing companies seem to find Wharton MBAs welcome additions to their firms. Students do not have to major in their chosen career field, but many do. Although not all students who become investment bankers study finance, many students desiring to change careers find the major an opportunity to learn some of the skills and vocabulary of the new business. Moreover, a major can be a credible signal to recruiters that one is committed to starting a new career. Attending the several hundred company presentations held for Wharton MBAs can also prove a useful information source.

« Corporate presentations not only provide career information to job-hungry students, they also frequently host some lavish receptions and ply cash-poor MBAs with copious amounts of food and drink. During the recruiting season, I admit to feeling hunger pangs and attending presentations with the intent of quelling my grumbling stomach. In spite of my culinary (rather than career) curiosity, I gained useful insights into corporate culture from these parties. »

Mock interviews conducted by CD&P and the professional clubs help prepare students for the real thing. Interviews tend to be specialized by profession; for example, a management consulting interview may center on a "case analysis," especially in the early rounds. The interviewer presents a situation for the candidate to assess, and after asking questions, the student is expected to present diagnoses and recommendations. Such specialized interviews can be disastrous if walked into "cold." Individual counseling sessions, seminars, job panels, and corporate presentations are also invaluable research tools for the taking.

If a student's career interests extend to the international realms, Wharton's active offices in Tokyo and Paris may be of assistance. Wharton's global management focus attracts overseas employers, who hire about 17 percent of the graduating class. For students who want the entrepreneurial route, some 4 percent of the class bought or started their own businesses upon graduation.

The diverse companies that recruit here evidence a patently capable and diverse student body. Given these diverse, sought-after students, what does the Wharton experience prepare the newly minted MBA to do that makes him or her so desirable?

« During my first year at Wharton, I took a job to broaden my business school experience. I was plunged into an unfamiliar job setting in an unfamiliar industry, management consulting. All I had to go on was my one semester's worth of classwork and my previous work experience in banking.

To my surprise, I was able to make a contribution quickly to the consulting firm's efforts. Specifically, I was able to apply techniques from my *Problems in Financial Statement Reporting* and my *Security Analysis* classes to a valuation we were completing for a client. My *Leadership Skills* class helped me assume a directing role for a team on which I was the youngest and newest member. Another class, on the strategic uses of information technology, helped me analyze and formulate a solution about another client's eroding competitive position. Many of the skills I amassed at Wharton during my first semester were of real value to my company and its clients.

I also spoke with a recruiter of MBAs. He summed up his perspective on hiring new employees as follows, "We recruit here because Wharton MBAs do numbers, they think across functions, they know how to be practical managers, and they can hit the ground running." »

ON THE JOB—FIRST YEARS OUT

A Wharton education gives you a useful analytical tool kit and a chance to practice skills that are vital to success on the job: setting priorities, managing your time, understanding your leadership style, and working as part of a team. Wharton graduates are in a prime position to overcome an oft-heard lament that MBA students are overpaid, underexperienced, and too narrowly focused. Students who get through the Wharton program not only know how to analyze and calculate, they've also learned how to ask the right questions, think integratively, and handle teamwork. This education applies to many different first jobs. Over the past five years, 40 percent of Wharton graduates have gone into consulting or investment banking, and the remaining 60 percent vary across all professions.

« My first job out of Wharton was a free-lance stint doing marketing and operations for a small wholesale bakery. After a couple of days, I began to suspect that the letters "MBA" secretly stood for "Massive Buzzword Accumulation," but the fun part of the job was seeing how some of the concepts I had learned applied to a small business. Much of what we talked about in cost accounting and entrepreneurial was directly applicable to the bakery, and although I never considered myself a numbers person, I felt comfortable analyzing their production needs and brainstorming about marketing strategies. The harder part was developing rapport and trust with the owner and getting the baker and finisher to work more cooperatively, for which I relied on skills developed in my previous job. All in all I felt prepared for the position, and I loved being part of a small business.

A friend of mine felt similarly about his position at a premier Wall Street investment banking firm. As one of nine MBA recruits and the only one from Wharton, he found himself to be more than prepared for the analytical requirements of the job. On his first day at work he was asked to write an internal marketing sheet for an initial public offering, and a few days later he was called on to prepare a financial model and projections for a paper company looking to recapitalize. His ability to handle the quantitative aspects of the job is actually helping him earn good-deal assignments early on, although an equally important factor is his ability to work well with superiors and colleagues.

Another friend parlayed her summer experience consulting in Eastern Europe into a short-term marketing project for a major consumer goods company. Her assignment: to take the pulse of the East European teenager. »

An MBA degree is not an entitlement. What counts is what you've learned and how well you're able to apply that learning to business situations. However, an advantage to attending a "name brand" school such as Wharton is to gain credibility, meet people, and perhaps have access to doors that might otherwise be closed. The payoff of a Wharton degree can come when you land a job, start your own business, or exchange expertise with a colleague ten years down the road. Still, as good as Wharton's reputation is, most MBA students face a dose of reality on their first job.

You've just had two years of professors telling you you're the CEO and that you need to make some big decisions. Now you're in the trenches, working on spreadsheets or conducting focus groups. It's easy to forget — especially in the rush and pressure of recruiting — that first jobs are exactly that: places to start. Wharton encourages students to think big, when in fact most starting MBA jobs call on students to use functional and analytical skills. Working at a big company sometimes means being a small fish in a big pond, and the climb to the top (if that's your goal) can take years. Lots of students find themselves readjusting their expectations during the first year out.

It is in fact typical for most Wharton students to change jobs after four or five years. Factors determining how long you stay with a company will depend on the industry you've picked as well as your personality and other needs.

« *I have a friend who took a job with a management consulting firm a few years back. He started out by working on a small piece of a larger project — living in New Mexico for three months and collecting manufacturing data to help with the factory planning and relocation of a bus division of an auto giant. The next step, about a year later, was to take full responsibility for a small project, followed by a promotion to the position of actually pitching business and managing the associated project himself. Although he found consulting intellectually challenging and was happy with his progression in the company, he also found it physically taxing, and he was very receptive when a former colleague offered him a chance to add a new capability to the MIS department of a large pharmaceutical company. He never planned to make a career of consulting, but his experience in that job gave him the connections and expertise he needed to move on.* »

The business school skills that are most useful will also depend on your chosen industry and previous work experience. Typically, graduates seem to remember the classes in areas that were most unfamiliar to them or were the most challenging when they arrived at Wharton. Those influential classes will vary from person to person. For instance, another friend looks back on what she found most valuable about her Wharton experiences and how they relate to her current job in food industry brand management:

« *I remember difficult class discussions that I found frustrating at the time because there was no resolution. Those same conversations happen here at work. I used to think that decisions in the real work world would be easier because I'd have more information. Wrong! Every day I deal with making decisions in high uncertainty situations. This time my job performance is based on the results I achieve. Another memory two years out of Wharton are the professors. I thought I'd never learn finance. I was afraid of the Finance Department and feared bland-personality academics lecturing about esoteric theory and higher mathematics; I wasn't good at math, and I didn't want to learn it. That's what I thought until the first day of class. The professor's personality and real-world approach made the concepts tangible for me. I remember that class because people here at work will sometimes ask me to help them sort out a financial problem. It is a great feeling. »*

SUMMARY OVERVIEW

A Wharton education will put you through your paces. You will crunch numbers, you will juggle study groups, and you will be all too ready to return to a "normal" life. You'll also have great friends and a learning experience that can't be taken away or found anywhere else. Once you've made it through the core, Wharton's flexibility and many choices allow you to dive into a subject or sample a topic that has piqued your interest. Regardless of your background or career choice, the program's analytical rigor, integrative learning, and emphasis on practical managerial skills will be invaluable. Wharton continues to move well beyond its original niche as a finance powerhouse, and it intends to remain a forward-thinking school for graduate management education.

Wharton is a great school, but it's not for everybody. Four features could be considered potential drawbacks for some students. First, Wharton centers its program around quantitative skills as a foundation for management education. Although this emphasis is now balanced by integrative learning and "softer" managerial skills, Wharton students still do numbers. The quantitative portion can be handled by anyone admitted to the school; the question you have to ask yourself is if you want a quantitative program to begin with.

Second, Wharton is big and part of an urban university campus. As with any large institution, you'll run into some bureaucracy intended to ensure students have equal access to facilities, courses, and resources. The obvious advantage to Wharton's size is the huge number of resources at students' disposal. The disadvantage is that all these opportunities can be overwhelming. And a word of warning: although you can choose from more than 200 classes, pick carefully and plan ahead, because not everything is offered each semester. The key to managing potential sensory overload is to talk to second-year students, faculty, and Wharton staff. These people will be your guides through the host of possibilities here.

Third, there are no bucolic hills surrounding the immediate campus, so do not come to Wharton expecting pastoral beauty through the classroom window. Philadelphia is a big city with big city problems. Students here recognize this fact and look out for one another. Carpooling, shared cab rides at night, and groups waiting for the university's shuttle service are common events. On the other hand, students can take a short bicycle ride down by the Schuylkill River to read, cycle, run, or watch the crew skulls.

And fourth, while the school is making some progress, women and minorities need to be proactive to ensure that the school listens to their needs. There's no getting around that it's a male-dominated environment: male faculty far outnumber female professors, contrary to the impression given in the promotional video; also, you'll find only two women among the group of academic and business leader portraits hanging in Steinberg-Dietrich Hall. However, staff- and student-initiated efforts are beginning to bring about change. Recruiting of women to the faculty, for example, has increased over the past two years, and Wharton now has the highest percentage of women who are tenured faculty among the top ten schools. Nevertheless, more can be done.

The strengths of Wharton greatly outnumber the weaknesses, however. Students find the resources at Wharton and the University of Pennsylvania to pursue literally anything imaginable. Few business schools anywhere can boast the number of courses or the cutting-edge research that Wharton offers. Remember that flexibility is one of the program's features. Some students design their own curriculums and majors by combining the array of offerings in new ways. Creativity pervades a diverse and well-rounded student body. These people can be a source of learning, inspiration, and support.

Wharton's new program forces students to think critically, both about their studies and themselves. For many students, this program is the first time that they have considered career management within the context of their life interests of family, leisure, and personal development. This critical thinking underlies all the integrative class teachings and synthesis that happens here. The thinking is not easy, but such efforts can be richly fulfilling.

Wharton has developed a humane grading system and group project requirements that encourage students to pursue excellence while not encumbering them with undue competition. The rich Wharton social life is also testament to the spirit of cooperation that builds within an MBA class. Most students find that Whartonites work and play hard.

Finally, thinking, hard work, and new friendships can all be important components of a rewarding job search experience. The number of recruiters interested in hiring Wharton MBAs is enough to boost most students' confidence and clearly sets Wharton apart from most MBA programs. Students and faculty with firsthand experience with corporations all over the world supplement the Career Development and Placement Office's extensive resources.

MBAs from Wharton join the longest tradition of business education, which started back in 1881. Singularly capable people apply to and accept admission from this school. In spite of their innate gifts, few of these students can claim that they "did it alone." The Wharton experience really is an example of collaborative learning.

Chapter 11

SUMMARY OVERVIEW

THE nation's top ten business schools share a similar mission: to prepare the best and the brightest for the world of corporate America. The programs are tough and the hours overwhelming, but the rewards are enormous. Graduates of the top schools leave with the skills, contacts, and credentials needed to succeed at whatever they choose to do. They may decide to work for a corporation or start up a new venture. It is this excellence in training and placement that distinguishes the top ten MBA programs.

There are basic elements common to all the top ten schools: a strong set of required core courses ranging from Accounting to Human Resource Management, a very heavy and demanding work load, a bright and aggressive student body, an emphasis on both formal and informal student interaction, a distinguished faculty with renowned expertise in one or more areas, a university with a reputation for and obsession with excellence, and an active recruiting and placement program.

Beyond these common elements, however, each school has its unique set of characteristics and special areas of competence that define its niche within the top ten. For example, one business school may be noted for its finance program and another for its training of top-level general managers. All the top ten schools provide an excellent basic business education, but each does it in its own way.

COMMON THREADS

Required Courses

Required courses are to a business school student what exercise is to an athlete: basic training. The courses are long and they generally require a lot of work. They tend to be less interesting than many other courses in the program. But all in all, they do provide the basics necessary to compete in business.

Almost all the schools require courses in eight core areas: accounting, finance, statistics, marketing, human relations in an organization, production, economics, and business policy. In addition, all the top schools now require computer literacy either through courses completed or demonstrated proficiency. Sometimes there is a choice among a number of courses in a core area; most of the time there are no options. Occasionally core courses can be waived, but usually the exemption exams are very difficult. The core courses are the heart of the business school program and provide students with the basic skills and knowledge crucial to their education and future careers.

Work Load

The top business school programs are tough and demanding. Long hours are the rule rather than the exception. Generally, more work is assigned than anyone could possibly do, and that is the method to the madness. To complete the work, it is necessary to manage time exceedingly well and to work cooperatively in groups. These are precisely the abilities that business schools want to inculcate, because time management and cooperative effort are key to succeeding in the business world.

Students

It is often said that the top business schools accept such high-level achievers that these students would have succeeded regardless of whether they went to business school or didn't. To a large extent, it's true; the top business schools can't fail. Students at the top schools are all bright and aggressive. They all graduated at the top of their class, have great business boards, and have done something unique and outstanding that sets them apart from the other thousands of unsuccessful applicants. They also are willing to put in the long hours and hard work required during business school.

The schools provide the structure, environment, and training; students make or break the program. Given the students' abilities and willingness to work, the programs succeed very well.

Student Interaction

While Greek mythological heroes and Western cowboys may go it alone, students at the top business schools rarely do. Most of the schools either require or strongly recommend that students meet together in study groups outside of the classroom to handle the voluminous work load. In addition, informal socializing is well organized (would you expect otherwise?) at most of the schools. Thus group effort becomes a critical endeavor at most of the top business schools. And since cooperation is the basis for almost all business activity, it is a skill and experience not to be underestimated.

Faculty

The persons you thought never existed, whose names you may have seen in business books and journal articles, are actually alive and well and teaching at the top ten business schools. The overall quality of the faculty at the top business schools is excellent. Many of these professors are engaged in "frontier" research, and teach basic or advanced courses for MBAs. They appear to teach quite well. Most of the schools emphasize teaching (as opposed to research) very strongly, and most professors take their teaching very seriously.

University

Behind every great business school is a great university. The university generally has the resources, the reputation, and the commitment to excellence that carries over to its business program. In one sense, the business schools operate their programs fairly independently. But in another sense they operate within the confines of the university, which offers business program administrators, faculty, and students exposure to other ideas and educational programs.

Recruiting and Placement

The ultimate measure of success of any MBA program — the bottom line, so to speak — is its placement record. By this measure, the top ten business schools all have achieved unparalleled success. Graduates of these schools are highly sought after by major and minor companies, earn starting yearly salaries of $60,000 or more, and move quickly up the ranks of the organization to positions of power and influence.

DISTINGUISHING CHARACTERISTICS

Chicago

Chicago's program is renowned for its rigor. Maintaining primacy in the field of finance is Chicago's lodestar; however, the entire MBA program is uniformly robust. Chicago does not attempt to simulate real-world business experiences in the classroom through the case method. Rather, Chicago unabashedly sets out to create critical, analytical, problem-solving decision makers. Whether one plans a career in finance, marketing, or consulting, the analytical discipline one develops is essential. The GSB's preeminent faculty, ardent belief in a laissez-faire economy, and gifted student body give the Chicago MBA its underlying value.

Columbia

Columbia Business School has recently undergone dynamic changes. Spearheaded by a new dean, Columbia has established a new curriculum stressing the importance of ethics, human resources, quality, and globalization across all disciplines. It has been called a program for "poets as well as physicists." Given the school's

New York City location, Columbia is well positioned as the premier school for international business. New York also provides Columbia's diverse student body with access to original research, business leaders, world-class employers, and social opportunities second to none.

Darden

Darden was established in 1954 and has risen quickly to the ranks of the top ten business schools. The program is designed to educate the next generation of business leaders. Since the school utilizes the case method of instruction exclusively, students are trained primarily as general managers with exceptional analytical and problem-solving skills. Other valuable qualities, such as strong interpersonal skills, the spirit of teamwork, and effective time management are also emphasized. All of this is achieved in Mr. Jefferson's university, established in 1819. Darden has become one of the nation's finest institutions of business education.

Harvard

Harvard is the academic equivalent of marine boot camp. Through a rigorous program of more than eight hundred cases and mandatory classroom participation, future general managers are trained to assimilate large amounts of data quickly and to make difficult decisions with confidence. Harvard demands the full energy of its students and faculty, so no one goes to Harvard part-time. It is arguably the premier business school in the country and has more graduates at the head of Fortune 500 companies than any other school. While slavishly dependent on the case method of teaching, Harvard is adjusting its curriculum to the changing business environment of the nineties, breaking new ground in entrepreneurial management and international business. Harvard is defined by its intensity and its leadership.

Kellogg

Traditionally, when people thought of Kellogg, they thought of marketing. However, the school is developing a strong reputation in organizational behavior, real estate, transportation, and management policy. While other schools train functional specialists through highly quantitative programs, Kellogg uses a more humanist approach to develop competent general managers. The program emphasizes group work in almost every course. Kellogg is held in high esteem by its students and those who recruit them.

MIT

Mention MIT to an educated person in Japan, India, or Mozambique and he or she will undoubtedly have heard about the university to which you are referring. In terms of name recognition outside the United States, MIT holds an esteemed position as a world-class American institution. In the increasingly international world in which we live, the high brand-name recognition of MIT is a key selling point of the degree given there, and a key reason why Sloan is a favorite choice of international business students wanting to study in the United States. The consequent cosmopolitan flavor and plethora of distinguished faculty are two other powerful drawing cards of the MIT Sloan School of Management. And don't let the quant-jock image of the MIT program scare you. With the exception of a couple of fairly number-intensive first-year core classes, a Sloan MBA is only as quantitative as you make it.

Michigan

Michigan's strength lies in its hands-on, no-nonsense approach to business. Known best for its emphasis in general management, Michigan boasts numerous departments that are considered among the strongest in their fields, with unmatched educational facilities. Innovation is a trademark at Michigan, with experimental learning and flexible teaching methods leading the way in corporate business education. With a new program in place that guarantees all students access to corporate field consulting projects, the Business School is giving its students invaluable experience that executive recruiters seek. Most important, however, the diversity and strength of fellow students enhance this highly interactive learning environment.

Stanford

The Stanford Graduate School of Business is tops from admissions (the most selective) to average starting salaries (highest in the country). The school offers an excellent general management education and is making a concerted effort to integrate international business into the curriculum. The Stanford campus and surrounding northern California area cannot be beat as places to enjoy yourself during graduate school. In fact, the real world has a tough time matching the level of excitement Stanford students enjoy during their two-year stay on "the Farm."

Tuck

Founded in 1900, Tuck established the first graduate school of business. Today its distinguishing characteristic is its excellent general management program supplemented by a strong emphasis on group projects. Tuck concentrates on developing practical business knowledge and interpersonal and leadership skills. In addition, its small size and its location in Hanover, New Hampshire, promote a supportive community of faculty, students, and staff. The rural location also provides the opportunity for engaging in a multitude of sports, including skiing, hiking, and skating as well as other typical outdoor athletics. What makes Tuck unique? Most Tuckies would do it all over again.

Wharton

Wharton offers a top-quality graduate management education program that shouldn't be overshadowed by its reputation as a finance powerhouse — especially since the school responded to the changing needs of business and business students by rolling out an innovative new MBA curriculum. The program emphasizes integrative learning and practical managerial skills without losing analytical rigor and in-depth functional training. The flexibility of the program and the many choices available appeal to a diverse and large (750 per class) student body. Wharton's goal is to educate the next generation of business leaders. This ambitious agenda makes the program demanding and an excellent preparation for any business career. Despite the intensity, students manage to have time for fun, while the school encourages this balanced perspective.

Any major investment involving two years and tens of thousands of dollars merits long and careful consideration. Once the decision has been made to go to business school, the choice among the top schools is difficult. While you can't go wrong with any of the top schools, not every school is right for every person. It is necessary to weigh individual needs and interests carefully. It is important to look beyond the academics and the reputation of the program to the cultural and social environment and to the personality of the school. Each school has its own identifiable strengths and weaknesses. Choose wisely and well, and be prepared for a demanding two years. It is one investment that will certainly pay off throughout your career.

II

TOP BUSINESS SCHOOLS' ADMINISTRATORS' INSIGHTS

An MBA represents an investment of more than $100,000 and two years of intensive study. Therefore, most applicants first want to know, Is it really worth it? What will I learn? What will it prepare me for? And then if the decision is made to get an MBA, the next set of questions are, What kind of students are the top programs looking for? How do I increase my chances of getting into a top program?

Surprisingly, the answers are relatively straightforward. Top business schools have clearly defined their mission and demonstrated their value. While getting in is not easy, programs do have a profile of both the individual and the class they are trying to recruit. Understanding the mission, the value, and the student/class profile of top MBA schools should prove useful in deciding whether an MBA program is right for you and what can be done to get into the best school possible. Following, three top business school administrators provide the answers and the insights prospective students seek.

Chapter 12

AN MBA PROGRAM LOOKS TO THE FUTURE*

AN observer of our recent graduation exercises noted that the ceremony was "a truly down-to-earth experience." In many respects that is the essence of Columbia Business School. To describe this institution with fifteen hundred students, three hundred faculty and staff, and nearly thirty thousand alumni and alumnae in another manner would be misleading. The school is a rugged, intense, and greatly rewarding experience that is, in many ways, a very traditionalist one.

Feedback about our being down-to-earth comes from students, recruiters, alumni and alumnae, visiting professors, and even the media. Our students are from the group that sits forward rather than leans back in their chairs. Our students represent our roll-up-your-sleeves, hit-the-ground-running philosophy. He or she is someone who is always ripe for a new experience. The people who come to Columbia Business School are smart, talented, and diverse. Though we teach what many consider to be a stringent curriculum, at the end of the day we place our faith in the talent, education, creative enterprise, and individual initiative of our students.

Columbia Business School leads management education because of the way we use the complex environment that is New York City, the world's greatest living laboratory. We are a vital part of a great research university — and the only Ivy League school on Manhattan Island. New York City means Wall Street, SoHo, Broadway, and Fifth Avenue; the world's financial capital; global corporate headquarters; and the United Nations. Every day, our students work on field projects in corporate home offices and public sector centers located a short distance from the campus.

* BY MEYER FELDBERG, DEAN, COLUMBIA BUSINESS SCHOOL.

Our mission is to educate leaders, builders, and managers of enterprises who create value for all stakeholders and constituencies. These are the managers and leaders of the future. The population who graduate here at the approximate age of thirty have had several years of work experience, and after they leave Columbia Business School they will make quantum leaps in their professional careers.

At the school we often talk about the future, about "the world of the twenty-first century." The manager of the future is facing a shrinking economy, one in which recessionary pressures are forcing downsizing throughout all levels of a corporation. Yet increased competition from abroad necessitates maintaining high standards, even as the work force shrinks.

The Columbia Business School MBA program has been restructured to represent these changes. It addresses not only the traditional discipline-based education but also the skills that need to be taught, such as computer proficiency and a sensitivity to the global environment, learning to take cultural differences and complex moral and ethical situations into account.

The group we educate at Columbia Business School consists of men and women who, whether they concentrate in finance or accounting or management, must include in their knowledge a tremendous series of new sensitivities.

A business leader of tomorrow will need to think multinationally. That person will need to understand how to work with governments as well as with the public sector and nonprofit institutions.

Our new curriculum, introduced in the fall of 1992, meets these challenges by focusing on four central themes: globalization, quality, human resource management, and ethics. These concepts are the key to the future of American graduate management education. We call this a program for poets and physicists. Rather than describe a series of seminars, the four themes represent fundamental philosophical foundations of the entire program:

Globalization. Today's manager operates in a shrinking world, one where national boundaries are becoming increasingly irrelevant to the movement of capital, goods, and services to whichever market offers optimum opportunity. In this dynamic economic context, different languages and cultures are troubling boundaries.

Business educators must offer students a thorough understanding of the global economic environment. At Columbia Business School, the Jerome A. Chazen International Business Institute will prepare students to compete in the global marketplace. We've drawn on the help of New York's top CEOs in our curriculum redesign and are making use of their skills and experience in ongoing symposia and lectures targeted for faculty and students. In addition, we're sending faculty members overseas to study our trading partners' economies firsthand.

It's no longer enough to think of foreign trade as "vacation activity." Global thinking has become central to the effective management of America's economy.

But globalization isn't confined to international trade. A student in a recent incoming class asked if our new curriculum had room for someone who wanted to work in Boise, Idaho. My answer was brief: the manager in Boise is living in the same competitive international environment as the manager in Berlin. It's no longer possible to do business domestically without being aware of the larger picture.

Quality. As the recession places greater pressure on companies to streamline operations and improve efficiency, quality has often become the forgotten virtue in the American enterprise. If we lose our commitment to quality, we lose the very advantage that has made the American business world competitive.

Management education must find ways to promote the notion of quality — quality in every aspect of the production, distribution, and promotion processes. Only by committing to quality can enterprises survive in a global marketplace.

Human resource management. Just as quality is the key to competitiveness, so the effective management of people is the key to quality. Today's manager faces a diverse work force encompassing a wide range of attitudes, skills, levels of training, and cultural backgrounds. Modern managers must be able to inspire a cohesive, unified effort from this diversity.

Ethics. After the Wall Street scandals of the 1980s, business has gotten a bad name. What many people don't realize is that this "bad name" wasn't just bad publicity — it was also bad for business. At Columbia Business School we believe it's impossible to teach ethics by confining it to one course. Instead, we've integrated the concept of business ethics into every aspect of the new curriculum.

To create a curriculum we were happy with, we gathered data from alumni/alumnae, students, recruiting companies, Columbia

Business School faculty, faculty from peer institutions, and from a series of focus groups with senior executives. Our studies, conducted under the auspices of the Strategic Planning and Curriculum Review committees, revealed that diversity of approach to business is alive and well in the United States. Businesses, large and small, have unique perspectives. Opportunities for creative and quirky entrepreneurs and managers are pervasive.

Many of these changes came about through the fall of national boundaries. National boundaries gave everyone the same rule book — how France operated, how Japan operated, how the United States operated. Now, as national boundaries change constantly, doing business means getting your hands on many different rule books and remembering that the rules are constantly changing. Because of this, the educators of tomorrow's managers must ensure that our future leaders have the flexibility and training that allow them to think quickly on their feet and cope with our acceleratingly uncertain environment.

MBA programs are often criticized as being outmoded, even unnecessary. I went to a dinner party recently where someone dropped one of many magazine stories "bashing" the MBA into my soup. He asked me what I thought of the story. I said I liked it — when I read it some fifteen years ago.

For some time now the nation's media have published several cogent critiques of graduate business education, faulting MBA programs for a host of reasons, ranging from focusing too much on research and theory to tending toward the "trendy" — teaching the hot skills and concepts without regard for the needs of future managers. Too little practical training, they've said, too little hands-on experience.

There is no doubt that curricula at the major business schools needed to be revised to meet the ways of the new world in which we live. The twenty-first-century manager will have to deal with a different set of problems than did those executives and entrepreneurs who rose to prominence in the 1950s and 1960s.

But, to paraphrase Mark Twain, reports of the death of the MBA have been greatly exaggerated. At Columbia Business School, the MBA is not only alive and well but also is headed for the new century with a revised curriculum firmly in place.

As we move forward in a fiercely changing world, American

business faces tough times and exciting challenges. To remain effective, Columbia Business School feels it must look ahead while still remaining responsive to the demands of today. By revising our curriculum and through other bold initiatives, we ensure that the MBA we offer will continue to serve both the business community and the nation as a whole.

Chapter 13

*WHAT MAKES A SUCCESSFUL BUSINESS SCHOOL APPLICANT**

It has been said that the world is an untidy place. Cartographers chart new country boundaries, company CEOs weather storms of mergers, technology enables us to pack more into a twenty-four-hour day, and the size and diversity of the work force change at all levels. Clearly, the only constant is change, which means that there are no prepackaged, magic solutions to problems facing today's managers. No one can predict with any certainty what the business landscape will look like in the future. Managers of the nineties and beyond will need to understand the forces of change, thoughtfully analyze and strategically allocate both financial and human resources, and lead confidently toward the intended goal. Management is both an art and a science, and business schools believe that graduate education should incorporate elements of both. It should enhance knowledge and skills in functional areas such as finance and accounting, and develop the student's personal effectiveness as a leader and visionary.

This is what the Stanford Business School is all about. The school provides a conceptual framework to help MBA students understand business as a total enterprise. Its interdisciplinary approach means that students will not learn finance without learning about decision models, that a complete understanding of product manufacturing cannot be had without an appreciation for the effort of designing the product. The school's emphasis is as much on why things are done

* BY MARIE MOOKINI, DIRECTOR OF MBA ADMISSIONS, STANFORD GRADUATE SCHOOL OF BUSINESS.

as on how things get done. Efforts are made to achieve a balance of analytic reasoning skills, interpersonal skills, and knowledge of business practice. As important as it is to be able to tell time, it is more important to teach how to build the clock and understand what makes it tick. Therefore, having the "big picture" and an appreciation of its interconnectedness are vital so students can begin to ask "Why?" and "Why Not?"

The Stanford Business School acknowledges that its students are making an enormous sacrifice in time, energy, and money to return to graduate school. The school's goal is to ensure that the "value added" to human capital during the program continues to grow, that the $60,000 education does not become obsolete or outmoded in five or ten years. Although it cannot be predicted with 100 percent accuracy what the business world will look like in ten or twenty years, there is one certainty: if a manager has a theoretical understanding of how business works as well as a finely tuned, broad-based problem-solving strategy, he or she will be able to tackle any management problem successfully.

Therefore, the focus at the Stanford Business School is less on teaching "best current practice" than on broadening the understanding of business concepts and sharpening analytic reasoning skills. A systematic approach to problem solving is timeless and versatile and will equip students to develop specific tools to deal with specific situations. Core courses teach basic principles of how markets work, how people behave, and how political and social processes work. The electives offer the opportunity to apply many of the concepts taught in the core. (One alumnus describes the rigorous course work of the core as being like medicine: "It didn't taste very good going down, but it was good for me in the long run.")

Most business schools are looking for the same characteristics and qualities in applicants. A quick glance at any business school viewbook will show that business schools share the same basic criteria for admission: (1) solid academic aptitude; (2) demonstrated managerial potential; and (3) special contribution to the business school community and beyond.

To begin, schools actively seek candidates who have a commitment to learning and who present solid records of achievement in college. Many schools also require the GMAT, which can be an important part of the equation. Thoroughly preparing for the examination is highly recommended (this includes a good night's sleep before the test). The higher one's score the better, but a stratospheric performance is not a guarantee of admission, any more than a modest score assumes that an "I regret to inform you" form letter will be in the mail.

Because the mission of the Stanford Business School is to prepare MBA students to become good senior-level managers and leaders, the strongest candidates have demonstrated success (and potential) in leading and managing people and projects. In the application, readers look for the acquired skills and personal qualities that are the hallmarks of a good manager. Applicants who have worked for great managers should think about the qualities and skills most admired and respected in those people. These are the very attributes the admissions committee looks for: initiative, good interpersonal skills, perceptiveness, patience, and excellent oral and written communication skills, to name a few. Those who haven't had a chance to lead a team at work or supervise a unit should not worry. Remember, potential is weighed as well as the record of achievement.

While strengths in one area can compensate for weaknesses in another, the Stanford Business School favors candidates who present as many strengths in as many different areas as possible. With about 350 places per class, the school simply cannot admit all the qualified candidates — those who can handle the course work and who have something special to contribute to the GSB. The admissions committee does not sort out those who are not qualified and admit all the rest. To do that would create a class many times its intended size.

The job of the admissions office would be very cut-and-dried if it simply admitted candidates by adding one's GMAT and GPA and taking the "best times." But the admissions process at the Stanford Business School is not a contest of "best times." The process is designed to build and shape a community of people who are more than constellations of test scores and grades. That is why candidates are asked to tell us more about themselves, to go beyond the numbers, and to share their interests, values, and ideas of what really matters most. Because Stanford does not provide interviews, the essays become the applicant's paper alter ego. The most common mistake applicants make is in telling too much of what they've done and not enough of who they are as people.

One of the best pieces of advice about essay writing comes from a former colleague who recommended, "Tell a story, and tell a story that only you can tell." Why tell a story? Everyone loves a good story — including admissions committees. Stories have themes. Stories can be revealing. And well-written stories are evocative, creating vivid images of characters and events. That is what application essays should accomplish.

Admissions officers also advise applicants to tell a story "that only you can tell." The details of the latest IPO or LBO the applicant has worked on may be informative and somewhat interesting, just as a narration of travels to faraway lands may be fascinating for those without frequent-flier miles. But anyone can tell those stories — many people have traveled, many people have conducted due diligence. Telling a story only you can tell means telling more about *why* the financial transaction was so interesting, *what* was learned from the team experience, *how* travel influenced an outlook on life.

Many spend too much time trying to figure out how to "market" themselves to stand out from the other four thousand applicants — a futile task, since aspiring MBAs don't know who else will be applying and what they'll be presenting. Too often this tactic results in unnecessary and gimmicky "extra stuff" such as videotapes, audiocassettes, annual reports, and photographs that are rarely reviewed by the admissions committee. The best plan of attack is to share *you* with the committee in a sincere and compelling way. This can be the very thing to set successful applicants apart. When the committee gets a good sense of the person who has applied, and the applicant articulates well his or her passion for management and how Stanford can help realize goals, it is easier to determine a fit between potential students and the GSB. And "fit" is what admissions is all about.

The GSB is a microcosm of the real world, a community of people from many different countries, coming from different industries, and with a unique set of experiences, personal values, and strong convictions. An appreciation of differences plus learning to work with people with varying backgrounds are two aspects of the informal curriculum that are vital to management education. The ability to work cooperatively with others, and the desire to participate actively in study groups, class discussions, and extracurricular events are of utmost importance.

Three pieces of advice to applicants:

(1) *Applicants should take some time to think about who they are as a person, and the various roles they play — brother, sister, son, daughter, wife, husband, caretaker, parent, teacher, board member, tennis doubles partner. What they bring to each of these roles (attitudes and energy) and the quality of that interaction say a lot about how applicants spend their time and a lot about what they value. It is also interesting to discover how the people with whom applicants interact have helped shape attitudes and beliefs and helped the aspiring MBAs define who they are.*

Why is the process of self-discovery so important? Effectiveness as a leader and manager is shaped by core beliefs and by the value put on interactions with others. Does this mean that an introvert can never become an effective manager of people? Does this mean that the person voted most valuable player will always be the most reliable manager? Yes and no. What it means is that each applicant should know well his or her strengths and weaknesses, likes and dislikes, "I'd rathers" and "I'd rather nots," so that when they find themselves thrown into an ambiguous situation or a conflict, they are in a better position to "do the right thing," however it is defined — to do what is consistent with individual ethics as well as those dictated by the situation. Basically, if you don't know who you are or where you are going, it's hard for others to follow your lead.

The admissions committee is as interested in learning more about each applicant as a person as it is in knowing what he or she has accomplished. Many applicants say that the essay question that asks them to describe themselves has led to some insightful introspection. Two of the fundamental values of the GSB are that students learn from one another but also engage in thoughtful reflection. The essay questions on the admissions application are designed to lead to the first step on the path of self-discovery, which is part of the process of becoming a more sensitive and effective manager.

(2) *Having given some thought to who he or she is, each applicant must ask why he or she wants to go to business school. Why give up the wonderful job (read: salary) to live the life of a pauper for the next two years, with no guarantee of a lucrative*

job on graduation? It is certainly reasonable to want to go back to school to fill in the gaps in knowledge, but it is another thing to believe that the MBA is the Holy Grail of business.

This leads to a second piece of advice, which is to temper expectations with realism. There is no question that the two-year experience at the Stanford Business School will be rewarding and enjoyable. It is an interactive process through which to learn theories of management, gain tangible skills, refine problem-solving skills, forge great friendships, and develop a renewed self-confidence. As with anything else, the more effort put into the experience, the greater the reward. However, the MBA degree will not necessarily land each student a job as CEO of a company right after graduation. The diploma is not a magic potion to guarantee that each new business idea will put another new name on the Fortune 500 list.

(3) *The final piece of advice is to apply to more than one business school. For those applying to several highly selective schools, there is an outside chance of not being offered admission at any of them. Reapplying to the first-choice school is always an option, but the odds of acceptance do not necessarily increase with successive applications. Those who reapply to a program are encouraged to call or write the admissions office for honest feedback to address any concerns the admissions committee may have had. Again, it is important to keep in mind that there are usually more qualified candidates than spaces available in the first-year class, and more often than not there is nothing negative an admissions committee can point to that was the reason for not admitting a candidate. Sometimes the committee can point to tangible reasons — for example, a low GMAT or lack of managerial experience. But "fixing" these areas does not guarantee admission; it simply makes a more competitive candidate for admission. Overall, admissions committees tend to look for reasons to admit a candidate rather than reasons to deny. A fair amount of professional judgment goes into making admissions decisions. The committee does the best it can, based on limited information.*

The special value of the Stanford MBA is the "balanced excellence" sought in all facets of the Stanford Business School community: a balance between fundamental theory and practical skills in the curriculum, a balance in teaching methods (no one method dominates), and a balance students strive for between their personal and professional commitments.

Students as well as faculty find the Stanford Business School a very special place because of the cooperative and noncompetitive culture of the school. Students spend two years learning to work together in study groups, to refine their leadership skills through extracurricular clubs, and to absorb and distill tremendous amounts of knowledge without the pressure of grades. Not only do students work hard (they spend more minutes in class than do students at any other top business school), they also play hard (witness the more than forty clubs and extensive public service outreach). And the result is that students not only enjoy their two years at the GSB, they also leave with a network of close friends, a breadth of perspective, and a healthy appreciation for balance in their personal and professional lives. They know that they will never again have the opportunity to be with a group with as diverse a set of backgrounds and perspectives, and in a supportive environment that actively encourages sharing of ideas and self-growth. For that reason a wonderful energy radiates throughout the GSB, energy that is channeled in many directions when graduates embark on their new careers.

Every business school brags about the quality of its faculty. The Stanford Business School is proud of the quality of its teaching and faculty research. Faculty members are free to use whatever teaching method suits them, whether it be lecture, case studies, field research, or a combination of all three. Because the Stanford Business School is relatively small, there are many opportunities for team teaching, development of interdisciplinary courses, and cross-fertilization of ideas among faculty in the various disciplines. Among the faculty are accounting gurus, a Nobel Laureate in economics, successful entrepreneurs, former government leaders, and experts in international finance.

Many alumni and alumnae look back on the Stanford MBA program as a two-year experience and process, rather than viewing it as simply a way to get their career tickets punched. They leave the GSB with a solid skill set, a broad-based perspective, and a renewed self-confidence in managing people and resources. After spending two years in Silicon Valley reaping all the benefits of being in a small community and having the advantages of a world-renowned university "across the street," graduates leave feeling energized (despite a $30,000 average debt) and ready to take on the world!

Chapter 14

WHAT TO CONSIDER WHEN APPLYING FOR GRADUATE MANAGEMENT STUDY*

VIRTUALLY every top business school now realizes that the needs of today's executives are very different from those of the past.

The needs that the Tuck School has defined for business and management in the next five to ten years include

- a more thorough understanding of the international realm;
- a greater emphasis on empowerment within organizations;
- a movement away from simple skills-building in communication toward a more strategic approach at both the individual and corporate levels;
- a movement away from basic accounting toward value chain analysis;
- a new paradigm for corporate strategy toward back-to-basics core competencies and understanding about (1) leveraging intellectual assets and (2) how organizations learn.

All of the topics listed above are covered thoroughly in the Tuck curriculum through our International Business Environments, Management Communication, Organizational Behavior, Strategic Cost Management, and Business Policy courses. Tuck's faculty are on the cutting edge of research and application of new knowledge in the classroom. All this is part of the Tuck School's central mission: to provide theory that can be directly applied to the practice of management.

* BY HENRY F. MALIN, DIRECTOR OF ADMISSIONS, THE TUCK SCHOOL OF BUSINESS.

About our MBAs, who take theories our faculty develop and apply them to real business situations, Tuck tends to attract people who have demonstrated leadership in undergraduate school or at work or both and who feel comfortable in leadership roles. In addition, a track record of effective teamwork, at work or outside of work, is highly desirable because the ability to function well in groups is essential for academic and social survival here. Applicants must also articulate, in person and on paper, why an MBA is essential to their career progress. Finally, applicants need appreciation for cultural diversity in all its forms.

Most Tuck students have either lived abroad or had significant experience in international business or cultures. Further, applicants should demonstrate awareness of Work Force 2000 issues and how demographic changes will affect the workplace throughout this decade and beyond.

As much as it might sound like a cliché, Tuck's admissions committee tries to keep in mind that we are an office of admissions, not rejection, in distinguishing candidates from a large pool of highly qualified applicants. Our readers evaluate applications not by finding what's wrong with them but rather by focusing on what's right.

In admissions terminology, this approach of focusing on what's right with an applicant is referred to as the "hook." We look for a hook with which to pull the applicant into a class. In some cases the hook is simply all-around excellence: solid work experience, good personal qualities, high GPA, and high GMAT score. In other cases there may be one or two specific hooks, such as highly unusual or nontraditional work experience, a set of outstanding recommendations, or a passion for a particular extracurricular pursuit.

However, our first and foremost consideration is academic readiness for Tuck's curriculum. Are we convinced that this person can do the work? If not, clever essays and compelling interviews won't be enough. We do look for good grades and test scores, but there is a broad range of acceptability in this definition.

Beyond the obvious "search for excellence," the Tuck admissions committee has the luxury of being able to define what a perfect match is in its decisions to admit one candidate over another. We carefully examine the following:

- Does this person believe in teamwork, the participatory management style that Tuck teaches?
- Is this someone who strives for balance in his or her life, or who at least appreciates the need for balancing one's professional and personal lives?
- Has the candidate done his or her homework on the Tuck School?

Another, often underestimated, question we ask ourselves when evaluating an application is: "Would this person be an alumnus or alumna of whom Tuck could be proud?" Our pride in that person would be measured in terms of the positive impact the graduate has had on his or her employer rather than in salary or title.

We would offer three pieces of advice to an applicant to Tuck's MBA program:

First, a bad essay can ruin a good interview. Remember that an application for admission to business school is reviewed by a committee. Applicants frequently assume their interviewer is the person who will also be evaluating their written application. Most admissions offices have several people making many of the final decisions on applications.

We cannot even begin to count each year how many denied applicants telephone to say, "But I thought you and I got along so well during the interview. How did I get rejected?" Our reply, unfortunately, is often, "Your essays are just as important as your interview." You may be charming and persuasive in person, but if you don't measure up in your essays, it's unlikely you'll be admitted. At Tuck, the interview report is the last piece of paper into an application folder, which means that whoever reads your file already has a strong sense of your candidacy by the time he or she reads that report.

Second, commit wholeheartedly to the admissions process. Applying to business school is not to be taken lightly. You will probably receive even more advice now than you did when you applied to undergraduate school, so accept it but recognize that it's ultimately your decision where to spend your education dollars. Once you've narrowed down your list of potential schools, conduct extensive and thorough research about each program: visit campus when schools are in session, talk with students and alumni/alumnae, and talk with friends of friends who attended those schools.

At the same time, view each communication with your prospective schools as an opportunity to make a good impression. Don't underestimate the perception and power of the receptionist who greets you when you visit the admissions office. Put the time into your applications so you are proud of the final product. Never allow a bad presentation to be a reason for denying your application.

Third, don't make excuses for lackluster past performances. If your grade-point average in college was marginal because you simply didn't work hard enough, tell the truth rather than narrate a rambling account of personality conflicts with professors and administrators or how you "just weren't focused."

If you're concerned that a lack of interests outside of work will detract from your application, don't dismiss this point by saying you're too busy. If you are too busy, tell us why. We often use the phrase "Give explanations, not excuses." It's pretty easy for admissions officers to detect the difference in either interviews or essays.

Although we believe that the most important aspect of the Tuck MBA is still the experience itself in total, the following aspects are what most of our alumni and alumnae would agree make this the best business school in the world:

A *strong, loyal alumni/alumnae network.* Tuck MBAs are the most loyal among the nation's top business schools. Annual giving rates over the past decade have consistently been more than 90 percent for the most recent classes. In addition, Tuck's class notes section in its alumni/alumnae magazine is the longest and most thorough of any school in the country. And Tuckies become friends for life, which leads to lots of social and business interactions among graduates.

A *safe, accessible environment.* During the two years that a student attends Tuck, he or she lives in a beautiful, safe environment free from the stresses and strains one associates with city life. In addition, because this is a real community of students, faculty, and staff, students get to know each other and the faculty, who are accessible to them both day and night.

A *first-rate learning experience.* Tuck faculty members are among the best teachers in the world. In addition to focusing their attention on research to stay on the forefront of business and management issues, faculty work very hard to put their research into language that managers can understand and use.

A team orientation that goes beyond the "ropes course." Although our students receive the same kind of "outward bound" experience that students get at other business schools, we carry on this team orientation throughout the entire Tuck experience. Students work in teams in their first term on consulting projects, in study groups for virtually all first-year classes, and in the first-year business simulation for the business policy course. But most of all, the Tuck experience itself is based on teamwork within a competitive environment.

III

BUSINESS SCHOOL TIPS

Chapter 15

TEN TIPS ON GETTING INTO BUSINESS SCHOOL

(1) *Make sure that business school is right for you.*

(2) *Get as much information as possible on the schools to which you are applying.*

(3) *Build up your college grade-point average.*

(4) *Study for the Graduate Management Admissions Test (GMAT).*

(5) *Get a solid grounding in math, economics, and English.*

(6) *Pursue leadership roles in college and community activities.*

(7) *Apply early.*

(8) *Use any connections you have.*

(9) *Work for two to four years before you apply.*

(10) *Make the most of whatever opportunities you have in college or on a summer or regular job.*

1. MAKE SURE THAT BUSINESS SCHOOL IS RIGHT FOR YOU

BUSINESS school requires a major investment of time and money. For two years you will earn no money, work twelve to fourteen hours a day under enormous pressure, and, to top it all off, pay dearly for the privilege. Is it worth it?

This is a question you must ask yourself and be able to answer to your full and complete satisfaction. Is it worth it for me to forgo two years of income? Given my previous skills, training, and experience, will I learn enough to make it worthwhile? Will I be significantly better off in my first or current job if I get an MBA? How much will an MBA help me in my future career or chosen line of work?

The facts are clear. MBAs from the top ten schools generally earn starting salaries averaging over $60,000 a year. They usually have more than one job offer. They succeed in advancing within corporations or in starting up their own ventures. The MBA degree, like the American Express Gold Card, is a readily accepted credential. Finally, an MBA gives you a personal sense of confidence and security in whatever you do. It is something you have rightly and proudly earned.

However, like anything else worth having, it requires long and arduous hours. The process is sometimes enjoyable, but more often than not it is just hard work. But in the end, you taste the thrill of victory.

An MBA is not for everyone. To get in, you have to decide that you really want it. You must spend a lot of time, effort, and money in the application process alone. And that's only the beginning. Therefore, make sure that an MBA is right for you. Once you have made the personal commitment, be prepared to go all out for it. It is worth the effort.

2. GET AS MUCH INFORMATION AS POSSIBLE ON THE SCHOOLS TO WHICH YOU ARE APPLYING

CHOOSING an MBA program is an important decision. Whatever program you choose will occupy the next two years of your life and could well determine your future career path. Therefore, it is critical to get as much information as possible on the different schools and their programs to make an informed decision.

First, send for the catalog and read it carefully and thoroughly. Next, contact the school or its alumni office and ask to speak to recent graduates. Most of the schools will accommodate you by providing some names. MBAs from the school know more than anyone else about the program and its pluses and minuses. Finally, go to see the school, sit in on some classes, talk to current students, and interview with its admissions staff. In most cases these interviews are for information only. But it is worth the time and effort to learn more about the place where you may spend the next two years of your life.

After you have gathered all this information, use it. First determine if the program meets your needs. If it does, then try to figure out what the school is looking for in its applicants. Depending on the orientation of the program, the school may be interested in applicants who want to be general managers, or if the school is strong in finance, it may favor candidates who want to go into investment banking. The more you can tailor your application to the specific strengths and interests of the school, the greater the likelihood you will be accepted.

3. BUILD UP YOUR COLLEGE GRADE-POINT AVERAGE

IF you have graduated or are a senior and have just taken your final exam, forget about improving your undergraduate grades. However, if you are a sophomore or a junior, read on. Grades are important to graduate business schools. They are tangible data that admissions officers can use to predict how well you will do in business school. While grades are not everything, they do count.

The higher the grades, the better the chance of getting in. Try to do well in all courses, but excel in some. Don't figure you can let your grades slide in math or English, assuming that they wouldn't count that heavily. All the top business schools require students in their program to take both the highly quantitative statistics or economics course and the nonquantitative human behavior or interpersonal relations class. The top schools are looking for the applicant who does well in both, and stands out in some areas. Someone who has had little business experience can favorably impress the admissions board by submitting excellent grades.

4. STUDY FOR THE GRADUATE
MANAGEMENT ADMISSIONS TEST
(GMAT)

WHILE it is often too late when applying to business school to affect college grades, it is usually possible to improve your business boards. They count heavily for every school except Harvard (which neither requires nor considers the GMAT) and can be a major factor in the decision process. They are the one standardized test all applicants take and, therefore, are useful in comparing the abilities and potential of an overabundance of all seemingly highly well-qualified applicants.

There are a few very talented people who could score 800 on the GMAT without doing anything. But for most of us a good score requires some work and study. Most people can improve their scores either by using a do-it-yourself book or by taking a prep course for the GMATs. In either case, it pays to do something.

If by chance you don't do as well as you hoped you would, take the boards again. It can't hurt you (unless you do worse) and most likely will help you.

5. GET A SOLID GROUNDING IN MATH,
ECONOMICS, AND ENGLISH

No one ever said it was going to be easy. The top business schools have very difficult programs. They require highly developed skills in math, economics, and English. Regardless of which school you go to, you need to be able to crunch the numbers (i.e., be able to analyze and use quantitative formulas and data) as well as an accountant and still be able to express yourself as well as an English major. While very few of us are equally adept with numerical figures and figures of speech, the more facile you are in both, the easier business school will be for you.

Therefore, if you can demonstrate extensive training or experience with numbers and can express yourself clearly, your chances of getting in are improved. The top schools recruit heavily among engineers and numbers types, especially those who can speak and write as well as they can express themselves quantitatively. While it is not necessary to get an engineering or accounting degree, it doesn't hurt to take courses that will help you get in and also prepare you for the rigors of a top-flight business program.

6. PURSUE LEADERSHIP ROLES IN COLLEGE AND COMMUNITY ACTIVITIES

ALL businesses are continually searching for good leaders because the essence of good management is the ability to lead or to motivate people. Therefore, a major purpose or function of business school is to train and to develop good managers or leaders. As a result, business schools look for applicants who have the potential to be good leaders.

The best way for an applicant to demonstrate this potential is to show leadership experience in college or community activities. This can be done in a number of ways: by holding office in a student organization, being elected captain of an athletic team, sitting on the board of directors of a local nonprofit corporation, and so forth. Being elected head of an organization gives you the opportunity to try out various management skills and to prove your leadership potential. It also shows that you are well thought of and respected by your peers and/or associates.

You don't always have control over being elected to a leadership position, so pursue those activities where you can exercise some control. For example, if you were captain of a football team in college, you might coach a midget football team after you graduate. It also shows that you have a variety of experiences and can lead in any type of situation. This is the type of individual business schools seek.

7. APPLY EARLY

SEVERAL thousand applicants apply to each of the top business schools. Each applicant sends in approximately ten or more pages of information for the admissions committee to evaluate. This means the committee must read, digest, and evaluate over a thousand pages for each hundred students who apply. That is the equivalent of reading Clavell's *Shōgun*. By the four hundredth application, a committee member has read the equivalent of Clavell's oriental quartet. And to think that process has just begun. When do you want your application read?

While there are no hard-and-fast rules and schools will vehemently deny it (at least officially), logic dictates that it is easier to get in the earlier you apply. Since most schools use rolling admissions, more places are open in the beginning of the process. Admissions officers probably take this into account somewhat. But when fewer and fewer slots are available, judgments tend to be more critical. In addition, there is not as much time pressure on admissions officers early in the process and they may tend to be more open than they will be in later months, when they may tire of the arguments and essays. While the edge in applying early may be small, in many cases the difference between being accepted and rejected is equally narrow. Therefore, apply early.

8. USE ANY CONNECTIONS YOU HAVE

BUSINESS schools often rely on connections and contacts for alumni/ alumnae contributions and job placements. The top schools encourage the informal network and often boast of the widespread influence of their alumni in the business world. Given this orientation, it is reasonable to ask whether contacts can help you get into school.

The official answer is no. In an ideal world, admission to the top schools should be based solely on merit — on what you know, not whom you know. And in one sense, it is probably true that if you are clearly unqualified for admission, no contacts in the world (short of a father who will contribute a library in your name) can get you into a top school. On the other hand, if you are qualified and competitive, a good reference letter from a heavy contributor or an alumnus or alumna who knows you will probably help.

9. WORK FOR TWO TO FOUR YEARS
   BEFORE YOU APPLY

BUSINESS schools, unlike the armed forces, want experience. It may seem curious that an institution established to give experience also requires it. But business schools are looking for well-qualified applicants who not only can benefit from the MBA program but also can contribute to it. Someone who has had a few years of work experience is more likely to be able to do this. In addition, business schools prefer students who are more mature and more likely to have developed a sense of who they are and where they are going. And an applicant with work experience can make a better case on his or her application when asked to state his or her three greatest accomplishments and career goals.

The number of students coming to business school directly out of college is extremely small (2 to 4 percent at most schools). Given this propensity to favor applicants who have had work experience, does it make a difference what that experience was? The answers are yes and no. On one hand, positions in accounting, banking, and product management provide excellent preparation for business school. Jobs in these fields may make it easier to justify your decision to apply to business school. On the other hand, the schools are looking for a well-rounded student body and, therefore, accept their share of college professors, musicians, army officers, small retailers, and so forth. It is more important what you accomplish on the job than what job you do. (See the next tip.)

Generally, business schools prefer students with two to four years of work experience. It is difficult to determine whether schools purposely desire this precise amount of experience or whether the majority of applicants happen to possess that amount. Regardless, it makes sense for both the schools and the students. The schools benefit by getting experienced yet not inflexible students. Students with two to four years of experience also benefit because they can leverage their degree more than their classmates who have a lot of or no work experience.

Some schools also offer deferred admission, an option that lets applicants have their cake and eat it, too. Under deferred admittance, some schools grant acceptance to highly promising college seniors on the condition that they work for a few years before entering business school. Thus a deferred admittee can work after college yet still be secure in the knowledge that he or she will enter a top business school a few years later. It's great if you can do it.

10. MAKE THE MOST OF WHATEVER OPPORTUNITIES YOU HAVE IN COLLEGE OR ON A SUMMER OR REGULAR JOB

WHAT sets successful applicants apart from their rejected counterparts is not so much specific grades or references as it is a total record or picture of achievement. Almost everyone who applies to the top schools has good grades, good recommendations, and some work experience. In short, most applicants to the top schools are qualified. The difference is that the applicants who are accepted have done something special, unique, or outstanding and have achieved distinction or honor in doing it.

For example, it is not enough simply to have worked for IBM or General Foods. During your employment you must have demonstrated your management potential by doing something that helped the company and that was unusual for someone at your level. And if you don't have business experience, your college record should contain a similar accomplishment. Perhaps during your time at school you were president of the school's community service society and were instrumental in doubling the size of the program.

To set yourself apart, you generally have to create your own opportunity. Most of the time during college or on the job it is very difficult to do something outstanding. Great ideas and record-breaking success are not common occurrences. But these achievements can enhance the likelihood of acceptance to a top business school.

Chapter 16

TEN TIPS
ON FILLING OUT THE BUSINESS
SCHOOL APPLICATION

(1) *Market yourself as a valuable addition to any MBA program.*

(2) *Be aggressive in both style and content.*

(3) *Identify what you have done that is unusual, unique, or outstanding.*

(4) *Be justifiably proud of your accomplishments.*

(5) *Communicate that you are right for the school and the school is right for you.*

(6) *Keep essays short, interesting, and to the point.*

(7) *Make the application look professional: typed, neat, and error-free.*

(8) *Use professional references and recommendations.*

(9) *Take your time, and take it seriously.*

(10) *Be honest and candid.*

1. MARKET YOURSELF AS A VALUABLE ADDITION TO ANY MBA PROGRAM

APPLYING to business school is the classic marketing or strategic planning problem. What do you as the applicant have to offer that makes you more attractive or better than the thousands of other applicants? Why should they choose you? The path to acceptance is good marketing — that is, showing your competitive advantages.

First, you must offer a good package — good grades, boards, recommendations, essays, etc. Second, you must offer something special that sets you apart from the crowd (see tip 3). Third, you must show how you can contribute to the program or why you are a more desirable candidate than others. This is important because business schools are often viewed solely as places where students learn or receive training — that is, a one-way relationship. This ignores the fact that good business schools also expect a lot from their students in terms of classroom participation, group projects, informal interaction, etc. Therefore, your ability to contribute to this learning environment is as highly valued as your ability to learn. As a result you must demonstrate in the application that because of your experience, analytical abilities, or leadership capabilities, you can contribute to the program.

2. BE AGGRESSIVE IN BOTH STYLE AND CONTENT

THE one common and shared characteristic of MBA students at the top schools is that they are aggressive. They know what they want, and they go out and get it. While they all have a significant record of achievement, the aggressive attitude distinguishes them. How do you show aggressiveness in an application?

First, carefully focus the content of your essays. They should portray you as a go-getter — that is, someone who not only did well academically but also played sports, held office in a major campus organization, and earned all his or her spending money for four years. Your major limitation was that you had to sleep for four hours a night. While this may be a bit exaggerated, you must communicate to the admissions office that you work hard and can accomplish whatever you set your mind to. Business school is difficult and not for the weak of heart or those lacking endurance.

Second, your writing style should also be aggressive. Use active verbs. Use short sentences and paragraphs. Use exciting words such as "manage" and "accomplish." The application is the only place where you can really show how aggressive you are. Don't blow it.

3. IDENTIFY WHAT YOU HAVE DONE THAT IS UNUSUAL, UNIQUE, OR OUTSTANDING

IMAGINE that you are an admissions officer for one of the top ten business schools. You have to read a couple of thousand applications. Then you have to accept a couple of hundred students. Seventy-five to 85 percent of the applicants are clearly qualified with good grades, boards, and recommendations. How do you choose?

It's obvious that you cannot make a judgment based strictly on grade averages, board scores, and favorable recommendations. So you review the applications and try to decide which one has something unusual, unique, or outstanding to offer the program.

As the applicant you must determine what that something is. It does not have to be previous employment at a Fortune 500 company or honors from Harvard. Perhaps it's a small business venture that may even have made a little money. It still shows that the applicant has the initiative and drive to do something that probably few of the other applicants have done. If you didn't start a business, maybe you had an unusual job. People from such diverse areas as television reporting, nonprofit performing arts, government research, architecture, and other fields can make very attractive candidates.

Even if you had a mundane job, you can still highlight significant achievements or responsibilities. If you worked as a supply clerk for a large company but were responsible for millions of dollars' worth of inventory, that's significant. If you were an accountant but saved the company some money, you should highlight it. And if you didn't work and have just graduated from college, you can still pinpoint an unusual or outstanding accomplishment. You might be the foremost Latin scholar in the nation. You might have run student services for a campus of ten thousand students. The key is to position what you have done so it sets you far apart from a madding crowd of MBA applications.

4. BE JUSTIFIABLY PROUD OF YOUR ACCOMPLISHMENTS

THE application to business school is no place to be modest. You are trying to convince admissions officers at the top schools that you are the greatest thing since sliced bread. Therefore, you must blow your own horn.

Whatever you have done, build it up and make it sound important. If you won the college debating tournament or were the youngest marketing executive at ABC Company and you feel that those were important accomplishments, say so. Never lie, but don't be reluctant to give the most self-enhancing interpretation of any job or accomplishment.

On the other hand, avoid the flagrant and egregious statements that cast doubt on your credibility. Case in point: one top business school applicant described a *summer* job as the strategic planner for GM. While this might be believable for a tiny company, it sounds ridiculous for a major multinational corporation. Just avoid straining anyone's belief.

5. COMMUNICATE THAT YOU ARE RIGHT FOR THE SCHOOL AND THE SCHOOL IS RIGHT FOR YOU

THE top schools differ greatly in academic strengths, teaching methods, general orientation, etc. Therefore, it only makes sense when filling out the application to tailor your responses to each particular school.

For example, Harvard is noted for its general management orientation. Therefore, you should stress in the application that you want to be a general manager and highlight what you have done that demonstrates general management potential. Chicago, on the other hand, is more quantitative. Thus you might want to say that you're interested in the more quantitative side of management and that Chicago is perfect for you.

While it is not necessary to be a general manager to apply to Harvard or a finance jock to apply to Chicago, it is necessary to say why that particular school is right for you. Generally, the more you can tailor your application to each individual school, the better are your chances of getting in.

6. KEEP ESSAYS SHORT, INTERESTING, AND TO THE POINT

ADMISSIONS officers have to read thousands and thousands of pages. Moreover, they read the same story over and over again. They know all the reasons why applicants want to go to business schools, what each hopes to do after graduation, and so forth. Keep essays short, interesting, and to the point if you want to break through this paper logjam.

If the essay is short and interesting in both content and style, admissions officers are more likely to read it carefully. If it is long-winded with a lot of extraneous material, they are more likely to skim over it. Try to differentiate your essays in some way from the "typical" responses they receive. You might want to study short stories, advertisements, or other documents that strive for an economy of style.

7. MAKE THE APPLICATION LOOK PROFESSIONAL: TYPED, NEAT, AND ERROR-FREE

IT would seem obvious that the application should look professional. However, it is surprising how many fail to satisfy minimum criteria of acceptability.

First, the application should be typed. Do it on a good typewriter or computer printer with a good ribbon. Rent one if you have to. Second, be neat. Left-hand margins should be aligned. The overall presentation should look clean. Finally, make sure there are no mistakes in the application; check spelling, grammar, and typing for errors. Typos indicate that you're careless and indifferent. Proofread the application a couple of times yourself and then have a friend or family member look it over. Remember, since you are presenting yourself in the application, it should reflect the way that you want to be evaluated.

8. USE PROFESSIONAL REFERENCES AND RECOMMENDATIONS

MANY applicants submit personal letters of reference from senators, congressmen, and heads of corporations that begin "As a friend of the family I have known John [or Sally] since he/she was a child and I can unequivocally state he/she is a fine, upstanding human being." While these letters are nice and show that you are well connected, they generally carry far less weight than professional references from former employers, teachers, and anyone else who knows you in a professional capacity.

When asking people to write a recommendation, give them an updated résumé. Discuss it with them. Tell them why you want to go to business school. Explain to them why you feel that their recommendation will help you get into business school. Ask them to be as specific as possible. Request that they highlight an accomplishment, such as the competitive marketing analysis that you did that everyone felt was outstanding and benefited the company.

The key is to get your reference to write more than just a perfunctory "Johnny did a good job" letter. Try to get a letter that tells why what you did was good and why it was useful. Try to get your reference to write as if your admission depended on his or her letter, because it does.

9. TAKE YOUR TIME, AND TAKE IT SERIOUSLY

FILLING out the application may seem to take forever. But wait till you get to business school, when the real work begins. Remember that you will be spending two years of your life and tens of thousands of dollars at this school. It's worth putting in the effort on the application. Take time to think through each question in the essay section. Carefully consider who you want to write your recommendations. Study for the GMATs and take them twice if necessary. If an additional couple of hours are required for acceptance at a better school, they're worth it.

Although filling out an application is a pain in the neck and very time-consuming, take it seriously; after all, it's your career and future. If possible, speak to graduates of the program, visit the school, discuss the application with your college professor or boss. While some people can fill out the application over a couple of beers during *Monday Night Football* and get in anywhere, for the rest of us it takes a lot of time.

10. BE HONEST AND CANDID

AFTER marketing yourself and your accomplishments in the application, remember Shakespeare's immortal words, "And this above all else, to thine own self be true." Look over what you have written. Does it make the strongest possible case and still accurately represent you?

This is important, because generally admissions officers can tell whether your essay is consistent with the rest of your file, or whether you are only trying to get in. For example, if you say that your one and only ambition in life is to be in finance, and yet you are twenty-eight and have never held a finance position, it's obvious you're lying. You should have a good reason for wanting to go to business school. State what it is. As in the rest of life, truth is always more powerful than fiction.

Chapter 17

TEN TIPS ON SUCCEEDING AT BUSINESS SCHOOL

(1) *Be aggressive and take the initiative.*

(2) *Learn to manage your time; don't fall behind in your work.*

(3) *Form study groups.*

(4) *Get to know your classmates both academically and socially.*

(5) *Take advantage of the opportunity to know and work with faculty.*

(6) *Know where to get help if you need it.*

(7) *Get involved in school clubs and activities.*

(8) *Learn to write and speak clearly, concisely, and logically.*

(9) *Think conceptually.*

(10) *Keep it all in perspective.*

1. BE AGGRESSIVE AND TAKE THE INITIATIVE

THE meek may inherit the earth, but not the nation's top business schools. The top business schools are tough and demanding. They seek students who are tough and demanding. To succeed at business school, you, too, have to be tough and demanding.

Being aggressive means doing the work and more. It also means participating in class and taking the initiative in group projects, clubs, and activities. While being aggressive is usually a virtue, some students practice it to a fault. In other words, you must be aggressive but still cooperative — that is, take the initiative without being domineering. Business school, like business, is in many senses a cooperative venture. Students are constantly working together to do a tremendous amount of work no one individual could do by himself or herself. Therefore, most students learn to channel and control their aggressiveness into accepted cooperative ventures. Those who don't will soon learn the downside of going it alone when everyone else is working together.

Business schools reward aggressive students who show initiative. To survive and succeed, use your aggressiveness both wisely and well.

2. LEARN TO MANAGE YOUR TIME; DON'T FALL BEHIND IN YOUR WORK

WORK is to business school what winning was to Vince Lombardi: it's everything. Almost all the top business schools require ten to fifteen hours of work a day. It's not humanly possible to do all the work that is assigned. Therefore, the key to success at business school is learning to manage your time.

Time management means prioritizing the work and then doing it. There is no way around putting in the time. One friend spent all his time studying or attending class except for Saturday night and one afternoon during the weekend. While this is an extreme example, you will be amazed at how much time most people put in, even the superbright.

Time management also means working harder and working "smarter." This involves forming study groups, letting recommended readings slide, looking for shortcuts in the readings or assignments, and so forth. Study hard early in the semester and learn the basics. This will make the rest of the semester much easier.

The cardinal rule at business school is never fall behind in your work. The work is cumulative, and it piles up fast. Once you fall behind, you will be playing catch-up the rest of the semester. Do the work on a daily basis; it's the only way.

3. FORM STUDY GROUPS

IF business schools have one redeeming feature, it's study groups. Study groups are great.

(1) *They help the student understand difficult concepts and material.*

(2) *They make it easier to cope with an overwhelming amount of work.*

(3) *They provide emotional support for the pressure-filled, anxiety-ridden aspects of the program.*

(4) *They provide a social group with whom you can share and enjoy the business school experience.*

Study group members quickly become compatriots and close friends whom you can call at midnight when you are having problems figuring out tomorrow's 9:00 A.M. assignment.

Most study groups meet frequently, if not nightly, for the first semester and then taper off. They can be extremely helpful to new students during the first semester, when the work load and pressure are the greatest. After that, most groups continue to meet on a social basis throughout the two years.

It's best to form study groups early in the semester. Pick class members with whom you feel you will be personally compatible. Select individuals with a variety of skills and experience (e.g., accounting, computer, economics, and marketing), so that each can contribute something different. Don't hesitate to use the study group for help with nightly assignments. Most of the top schools expect and encourage it, because most business organizations, by definition, are cooperative efforts and the experience of working in informal groups is invaluable.

4. GET TO KNOW YOUR CLASSMATES
BOTH ACADEMICALLY AND SOCIALLY

THE skills and training notwithstanding, the business school experience is meeting, getting to know, and establishing lifelong friendships with your classmates. Social contact and interaction are at the heart of the business school program.

It is often said, and justifiably so, that you learn as much both in and outside class from your classmates as you do from the professors. Your classmates form the basis for study groups, group projects, and early-afternoon, late-night, and weekend discussions. These classmates also make the rigors of business school tolerable by sharing the ups and downs of the program. Finally, these fellow students become valuable lifelong friends and contacts. Many of them will become heads of major corporations. Others are useful for jobs, information, and advice.

Actively pursue friendships and contacts with your classmates. Informal socializing is as important as more formalized interaction or study groups. Take the time and make the effort to get to know other students. Short of having dinner with Thomas Jefferson, you will probably never meet a brighter, more interesting group in any one place at any one time.

5. TAKE ADVANTAGE OF THE OPPORTUNITY TO KNOW AND WORK WITH FACULTY

WHILE professors are not the fount of all knowledge, they do know something. They are generally well read and knowledgeable in their field. They are a good source for advice and job contacts. In many cases, they are even nice and interesting people. Many are highly approachable and enjoy student-faculty contact.

Use the faculty. You might as well, because you are paying dearly for the opportunity. If you have questions about the course, consult the professor. If you have questions or concerns about grading, again talk to the professor. If you are interested in a field either academically or careerwise, faculty can provide guidance and stimulate your own thinking. Many have contacts in the field and will recommend someone to talk to about the industry or specific jobs.

While most professors are available and quite willing to help, avoid "brownnosing" them. They know as well as you do when you are just trying to impress them. It doesn't work. On the other hand, the faculty is an integral part of the educational process at business school and should be used whenever needed.

6. *KNOW WHERE TO GET HELP IF YOU NEED IT*

BUSINESS school can be very Dickensian — that is, it can be both the best of times and the worst of times. It is the best of times in that you probably will never learn as much in such a short period of time, meet as many bright people in one place, and make as many friends. On the other hand, it is the worst of times in that you will never work as hard again while paying for the privilege, and be under such great pressure to perform or achieve against admittedly somewhat arbitrary standards. Most people can cope with it most or all of the time. But if you can't, don't hesitate to seek help.

Business school is tough. Everyone needs help, some people more than others. If you are having trouble academically, seek help from your professors, friends, or classmates. If necessary, hire a tutor. Don't wait until the last minute. The cost of employing a tutor is minuscule in comparison with the cost of the entire program.

If you are having trouble adjusting or coping with any part of the program or life in general, seek help. All the schools provide counseling or referral services. And you would be surprised at how many students and faculty take advantage of them. Remember that the bottom line is getting your MBA. Whatever can help you do that is worth the additional cost or effort.

7. *GET INVOLVED IN SCHOOL CLUBS AND ACTIVITIES*

IT's very easy just to work at business schools. There certainly is more than enough to do, and those who put in incredibly long hours are often amply rewarded by professors and peers. However, business school is more than work and classes; it is a total experience. A valuable part of this experience is school clubs and activities.

First, school clubs and activities can expose you to another side of the business world through seminars, get-togethers with business leaders, and so forth. Second, these clubs can be valuable sources for job contacts, information about specific industries, new developments, etc. Third, clubs and activities are good ways to meet fellow students with like interests. Finally, these clubs and activities often provide a welcome respite and diversion from the intense pressure of the classroom and the work load.

Select a few activities or clubs in which you are interested. Devote a certain amount of time to them. Expand your horizons and enjoy the activities.

8. LEARN TO WRITE AND SPEAK CLEARLY, CONCISELY, AND LOGICALLY

BUSINESS school programs are two years long. During that time, you take at least twenty-five to thirty courses. Each course has a final exam. Most have midterms. Classroom participation is also graded in most schools. To get through the fifty to sixty exams plus the daily verbal challenges, two skills are necessary. First, you must be able to crunch the numbers and analyze the data. Second, and equally important, you must be able to express yourself both orally and on paper. This latter communication talent is sometimes overlooked by the more quantitatively oriented business school students.

Most business schools have a writing or business communication course. Generally these courses are not highly regarded. However, the communication skill being taught in these courses is critical. This is often learned painfully in class and on exams during the semester.

If you are not a clear and logical writer or speaker, get help and practice. Take courses either prior to entering business school, or seek some kind of help from the professor, the university counseling service, or friends during business school. Then practice, practice, and practice. Take the time to think through what you are going to say or to write. The same logical thought processes that go into analyzing a business problem should be applied to your writing and speaking skills. While out of necessity these communication skills will improve during the two years at business school, the earlier you start and more time you devote to improving them, the easier those two years will be.

9. THINK CONCEPTUALLY

NEVER lose sight of your goal. Business school problems, like real business problems, are confusing and full of numbers and contradictory data. In analyzing these problems, students, like businesspeople, often find safety in numbers. Numbers beget numbers. As a result, the original problem and goals you were seeking become obscured.

If you were a major company and had a couple of thousand dollars to spend each day, you would call in a consultant. If you are a student and can't afford high-priced help, stand back, think, and try to view the "big picture." Try to identify the real problem and the concept or theory being examined.

Conceptual thinking and big-picture planning are done primarily by top management in corporations. However, a big advantage of an MBA over a non-MBA is the ability to think in larger terms — that is, to transcend the numbers and to think about the overall problem. The more you can develop this skill in business school, the more successful your career will be both in business school and in business later on.

10. KEEP IT ALL IN PERSPECTIVE

AFTER you have overworked yourself to the bone, relax and enjoy. Keep repeating to yourself, "It's only business school, it's only business school, it's only business school." Keep it all in perspective. It's true you're going to have to work hard and put in more hours than you ever imagined. However, it's also true that you will learn a lot, make new friends, and even enjoy yourself sometimes. Plus you get an MBA, which should not be undervalued in a highly competitive marketplace.

If you are admitted to a top business school and you accept, you are in for two long, hard years. Few students flunk out. The failure or flunk-out rate averages less than 2 percent at almost all the top schools. While this may provide small comfort to you when you have five exams the next week and your entire grade for the course rests on those exams, from the overall view, these exams are merely interim hurdles that must and can be overcome.

Getting through a top business school program is an accomplishment. Like most achievements, you have to work for it. The school certifies that you passed the rigors of the program. That in essence is why employers are paying top MBAs more than $60,000 a year as a starting salary.

During the heat of the academic battles, keep the "big picture" in mind. Admissions and alumni/alumnae opinions notwithstanding, business school is not the only place to begin one's career. However, it is a very good place to start. Make the most of your business school years: work, learn, and enjoy.

Chapter 18

TEN TIPS ON GETTING A GREAT JOB AFTER BUSINESS SCHOOL

(1) *Determine what you feel will be a great job for you.*

(2) *Interview with numerous companies to learn what is available and what is best for you.*

(3) *Experiment with a summer job in an industry that interests you.*

(4) *Take full advantage of the school's recruiting facilities and programs.*

(5) *Use whatever contacts you can.*

(6) *Write a résumé that highlights achievement.*

(7) *Be knowledgeable in the interview about the company, its markets, its products, and industry trends.*

(8) *Don't go only for money; keep in mind flexibility, future opportunity, and personal fit with the company.*

(9) *Be aggressive and confident.*

(10) *Be persistent.*

1. DETERMINE WHAT YOU FEEL WILL BE A GREAT JOB FOR YOU

THE primary reason for getting an MBA is to get a great job. And most graduates of business schools certainly are not disappointed. Consulting firms, the current rage at most top business schools, now pay new MBAs a starting salary of more than $70,000 a year. Investment banks, a more traditional source of employment for MBAs, also pay well above the $60,000 starting salaries that new business school graduates now command. While these fields are lucrative, fast-paced, and prestigious, they may not be right for you.

You must determine what a great job is for you based on your career interests, financial needs, geographical preferences, and personal priorities. Carefully think through your career goals, rank order and weigh your needs, and then evaluate each field and position in relation to your goals and needs. Investigate a number of fields early in the recruiting process. Then select a few areas in which to concentrate.

Too many new MBAs go for the almighty dollar or are swayed by the opinions of their classmates. While some students are willing to give their eyeteeth for offers from McKinsey and Booz Allen or Morgan Stanley and Goldman Sachs, you may be happier in another field or even out on your own. You will be faced with many options and offers upon graduation from business school; only you can and should decide which to take.

2. INTERVIEW WITH NUMEROUS COMPANIES TO LEARN WHAT IS AVAILABLE AND WHAT IS BEST FOR YOU

WHEN you are not at business school, looking for a job is a hassle. It is expensive and time-consuming. You may send out two hundred letters and get five responses. Then you may have to pay for a trip to an initial interview for a job that may or may not exist. Additional months may pass before the company contacts you again. The whole process is neither encouraging nor enjoyable.

Now consider the situation facing top business school graduates. First, the companies come to you — not five or ten, but hundreds. Moreover, all these companies have jobs to offer at high starting salaries. Your problem is to decide which offer to accept. While this description is a bit overstated, there are tremendous recruiting opportunities at the top business schools. Students have to work hard for offers, but it definitely is a seller's market. Take advantage of this opportunity. Recruit with numerous companies to sharpen your interviewing skills and to explore different career fields. Broaden your search as much as possible at the outset and then focus in when you can eliminate careers and companies that are not right for you. The advantage of looking at numerous areas is that you might uncover a good position or company you may not have initially considered. It also makes you feel more comfortable in the job you accept knowing you have considered all the options and picked the best one for you.

3. EXPERIMENT WITH A SUMMER JOB IN AN INDUSTRY THAT INTERESTS YOU

STUDENTS often go to business school to switch fields. Sometimes they know what they want to do. At other times they just know what they don't want to do. Classes may provide some help in picking a field, but really to know a job or industry, it is necessary to work in it. While a full-time job after business school is probably the best way to learn, you may want to try out a field during a summer.

Summer jobs represent good opportunities to experiment with limited risk and commitment. You can work for three months and familiarize yourself with a basic knowledge of the industry, the company, and career opportunities. If you don't like the field, nothing is lost. If you like it, then you have a leg up on the other students with no experience in the industry.

Summer jobs are difficult, if not almost impossible, to get, especially if you have no experience in the field. The best way to get a summer position is to start early, be aggressive, send out numerous job inquiry letters, seek out as many potential job openings as possible, enlist the aid of professors, use alumni/alumnae contacts, use family contacts, and then hope. It may take time to get a good summer job, but it's worth it if it helps you select a future career.

4. TAKE FULL ADVANTAGE OF THE SCHOOL'S RECRUITING FACILITIES AND PROGRAMS

THE recruiting facilities and programs of the top business schools would make many top executive recruiting firms jealous. The business schools have extensive libraries, job and company files, company contacts (alumni/alumnae), and the influence and prestige of the school itself. The business schools run extensive recruiting programs in the spring, and two hundred to five hundred companies visit the campuses in search of MBAs.

The spring job search is almost a ritual at the top business schools. Going through company files in the library, meeting recruiters at company-sponsored cocktail parties, and getting haircuts are all part of this process. However, too many students stick to the traditional paths and therefore miss out on other job opportunities. Because so many companies eagerly recruit on-campus, not enough students seek out the smaller companies that don't come to visit. The schools' recruiting offices generally keep files on all companies, both those that come to the campus and those that don't. Placement offices are normally more than willing to help students in nontraditional job searches. Faculty, whose school and consulting contacts are invaluable, are also often ignored by many students seeking jobs. Faculty are generally more than willing to help if asked.

5. USE WHATEVER CONTACTS YOU CAN

WHILE in many ways the growth of MBA programs embodies the rise of meritocracy, contacts never hurt. Many businesses still utilize personal contacts, especially in filling jobs. The top schools recognize this and do everything to try to strengthen their alumni/alumnae contacts.

Use these contacts whenever you can. Speak to alumni/alumnae in those areas you are interested in pursuing. They can be very helpful in providing information, the occasional job, or referring you to other people who are knowledgeable in the field.

Never neglect family or friends' contacts. Don't be embarrassed about asking for their help. After earning an MBA, you are more than a friend or a relative, you are also a trained professional. Contacts are especially helpful if you have a nontraditional background. Contacts may provide you with an opportunity to talk with people you ordinarily would not have gotten to speak with. Contacts also may be better able than the placement office to put you in touch with people in slightly nontraditional areas who can appreciate your own nontraditional background and experience.

6. WRITE A RÉSUMÉ THAT HIGHLIGHTS ACHIEVEMENT

A good résumé is like a good doorbell. If it rings loud and clear and people pay attention to it, it should get you in the door. After that, it's up to you. Since you are getting an MBA from a top school, you have one item on your résumé to differentiate yourself from the competition. However, since your classmates also will have an MBA from a top school on their résumé, you need to distinguish yourself from them.

One way of doing this is to highlight your achievements. Do not merely list jobs, dates, and responsibilities on your résumé; also show what you have accomplished that helped the company. Instead of stating that you conducted a marketing analysis, show how that analysis increased sales or cut expenses. Even small improvements or ideas that show accomplishments will enhance your value to prospective employers.

There are plenty of good résumé-writing books available. Some of the schools even publish their own guides. Use them.

7. BE KNOWLEDGEABLE IN THE INTERVIEW ABOUT THE COMPANY, ITS MARKETS, ITS PRODUCTS, AND INDUSTRY TRENDS

THE interview can make or break you. Before your first meeting, the company has very little data on you. It has had a chance to look over your résumé briefly. But that's about it. The initial screening takes place in the first half-hour interview. At this point the company decides to grant a second interview and invite you to the company headquarters or else to send you the well-known bullet (rejection letter).

While your résumé may be great (see the preceding tip), you are competing against other great résumés, namely those of your classmates. To differentiate yourself, you must show an interest in the company and the field. You can do this by extensive preparation for each interview. This means reading the company's annual report, collecting information on the industry and future trends, talking with professors and classmates, and whatever else you think will help. This tells the interviewer whether you are really interested in the company or merely gaining experience with the interview process.

The interview is not only an opportunity for the company to evaluate you; it also gives you a chance to evaluate the company critically. The more knowledgeable you are about the company and the industry, the better able you will be to make an informed choice.

8. DON'T GO ONLY FOR MONEY; KEEP IN MIND FLEXIBILITY, FUTURE OPPORTUNITY, AND PERSONAL FIT WITH THE COMPANY

ONE of the primary reasons people go to business school is to earn more money after they graduate. Therefore, it is only natural that money plays a key role in the job decision. After all, who would not be swayed by the $70,000 or more some top consulting companies are paying new MBAs? This is especially true when you have just invested tens of thousands of dollars to get the MBA. The investment should pay off.

However, despite the happiness that money buys, don't go only for the almighty dollar. Jobs that pay a lot demand a lot. Burnouts are common in consulting and investment banking. Look at your own personal interests. Decide what kind of life you want to live and what kind of work you want to do. Think about where you want to be in five or ten years. Certain companies with lower-paying jobs may be far more suited to your interests and needs. Remember that most of your waking hours will be spent at work, so you might as well enjoy them and find them rewarding.

9. BE AGGRESSIVE AND CONFIDENT

BUSINESS school students are often thought of as being very aggressive. In most cases it's true and in most cases it helps. To get through the rigors of the top business school programs, you need to be aggressive. In the job search, aggressiveness is also seen as a positive trait. Companies look for the archetypal business school grad — one who is young, bright, willing to work, and a go-getter.

Being aggressive means being enthusiastic and taking the initiative in the interview. Ask questions that show you are interested in the company and the position. Answer questions fully, but don't pad your answers. Show them the interview is a two-way process and that you are evaluating them as much as they are you.

Be aggressive but not obnoxious. There is a fine line between the two, but generally it is easy to tell by someone's reaction which category you are in. Be confident. You are getting a degree from a fine institution and most likely will have more than one job offer. Sell yourself, but don't overpromise or oversell. Companies want bright and aggressive people, but they also are interested in employees who will fit into the overall organization of the company.

10. BE PERSISTENT

THE recruiting process is like a roller coaster ride with incredible ups and downs. There isn't a business school graduate who has not gotten his or her share of rejections or bullets. Some schools even keep track of the more notorious ones. If you are really interested in working for a company or in a particular field, don't let a few bullets stand in your way.

Write to companies that rejected you and tell them you are still interested in them. Give them a reason to reconsider your application. Seek out smaller companies that may not recruit on-campus but that may offer plenty of opportunity for the right person. Call alumni/alumnae to seek information and possible job openings. Read the trade press, looking for major industry and personnel changes. Write the companies and individuals involved and offer them your skilled services.

Never take no for an answer, and never settle. Business school graduates from the top schools are highly valued and over the long run will do very well. Take charge and be persistent. After all, it's your future.

Appendix

COMPARISON CHARTS
OF THE
TOP TEN BUSINESS
SCHOOL PROGRAMS

School	No. of Applicants	No. of Students	% Women	% Minority	Median Age	% Directly out of School	Academic Strength	Teaching Methods
1. Chicago	3,000	460	23	18	27	2	Finance, general management, marketing, economics, quality management	Combination
2. Columbia	2,651	518	30	23	27	10	Finance, accounting, international business	Combination
3. Darden	1,889	240	31	17	27	0	General management	Case primarily
4. Harvard	6,000	803	28	15	26	0	General management	Case primarily
5. Kellogg (Northwestern)	4,373	440	28	16	27	1	General management, marketing, finance, organization behavior	Combination
6. MIT Sloan	1,750	240	25	12	27	1	Finance, economics, technological innovation, information technologies, operations, organization behavior	Combination
7. Michigan	3,000	420	23	26	26	4	General management	Combination
8. Stanford	4,592	342	31	25	28	0	General management	Combination
9. Tuck (Dartmouth)	2,627	168	33	9	27	3	General management	Combination, consulting projects
10. Wharton	4,865	736	27	13	27	4	Finance, general management, marketing, entrepreneurship	Combination

| School | Average Class Size | | Admissions Requirements | | | | Tuition |
	1st Year	2nd Year	GMAT	Ref.	Grades	Other	Annual (Approx.)
1. Chicago	43	31	Yes or GRE	2	Yes	Personal essay and letters of recommendation are required; interviews strongly encouraged	$19,250
2. Columbia	60	40–60	Yes	Yes	Yes	—	$19,000
3. Darden	60	10–65	Yes	2	Yes	Essays, work experience, and interview encouraged	$6,855 in-state; $14,227 out-of-state
4. Harvard	85	85	No	3	Yes	Two yrs. work experience or equivalent, essays	$18,550
5. Kellogg (Northwestern)	60	30–50	Yes	1–2	Yes	Interview	$18,700
6. MIT Sloan	50–60	25	Yes	3	Yes	Economics (micro/macro) and calculus	$19,500
7. Michigan	65	45	Yes	2	Yes	College Calculus I	$11,550 in-state; $18,200 out-of-state
8. Stanford	60	20–50	Yes	3	Yes	Essays, work	$19,236
9. Tuck (Dartmouth)	55	20	Yes	2	Yes	Interview strongly encouraged	$18,750
10. Wharton	55	15–80	Yes	2	Yes	Interview encouraged; college quantitative course	$18,800

School	Course Requirements		% Courses or Areas		Waive Courses	% of Students Who Do Not Complete Program
	1st Year	2nd Year	Required 1st Year	Required 2nd Year		
1. Chicago	Leadership Exploration and Development (LEAD) is the only required course. Students must also select one from a variety of courses in each of the following three subject areas: Microeconomics, Cost Accounting, Statistics. In addition, one course in four of the following six areas is required: Financial Management, Human Resources Management, Marketing Management, Production and Operations Management, Macroeconomics, Managerial Accounting	Business Policy	9	Student discretion	Substitute electives either inside or outside GSB	Less than 1
2. Columbia	Global Economic Environment, Managerial Economics, Managing Human Behavior in Organizations, Accounting I, Managerial Statistics, Decision Models (½ semester), Accounting II (½ semester), Business Finance, Marketing, Operations Management	Strategic Management of the Enterprise	70	10	Yes	Less than 1
3. Darden	Accounting, Analysis and Communication, Business and the Political Economy, Ethics, Finance, Marketing, Operations, Organizational Behavior, Quantitative Analysis	Directed study, Leadership and Strategic Management	100	40	No	2–3

SCHOOL	COURSE REQUIREMENTS		% COURSES OR AREAS		WAIVE COURSES	% OF STUDENTS WHO DO NOT COMPLETE PROGRAM
	1ST YEAR	2ND YEAR	REQUIRED 1ST YEAR	REQUIRED 2ND YEAR		
4. Harvard	Finance; Marketing; Control; Production and Operations Management; Organizational Behavior; Business, Government, and International Economics; Introduction to Financial Statements; Managing Information Systems; Competition and Strategy; Human Resource Management; Management Communications	Management Policy and Practice	100	15	No	2–3
5. Kellogg (Northwestern)	Accounting, Management Strategy, Organizational Behavior, Mathematical Methods, Economics, Statistics, Operations Management, Finance, Marketing	None	75	None	Yes, and substitute	1
6. MIT Sloan	Applied Microeconomics, Applied Macro- and International Economics, Statistics, Decision Models, Managerial Behavior in Organizations, Accounting, Information Systems, Industrial Relations and Human Resource Management, Marketing, Finance, Operations Management, Strategic Management, Communications	Concentration in one area and a thesis	90	20 (thesis)	Yes	1
7. Michigan	Financial Accounting, Organizational Behavior, Computer, Statistics, Applied Microeconomics, Managerial Accounting, Financial Management, Marketing Management, Operations Management, International Business, Multidisciplinary Field Project in a Company, Corporate Strategy I	Corporate Strategy II, Business Law, or Ethics	90	10	Yes, and substitute electives	2

SCHOOL	COURSE REQUIREMENTS		% COURSES OR AREAS		WAIVE COURSES	% OF STUDENTS WHO DO NOT COMPLETE PROGRAM
	1ST YEAR	2ND YEAR	REQUIRED 1ST YEAR	REQUIRED 2ND YEAR		
8. Stanford	Economic Analysis and Policy, Accounting I, Decision Support Models and Information Systems, Organizational Behavior, Accounting II, Finance, Marketing Management, Decisions and Data, Operations, Strategic Management, Business and the Changing Environment, Human Resources Management	Business and the Changing Environment	80	8	Yes	3
9. Tuck (Dartmouth)	Applied Statistics, Business Policy, Decision Science, Finance, Financial Accounting, International Business Environments, Management Communication, Managerial Accounting, Managerial Economics, Marketing, Operations Management, Organizational Behavior, Political Economy and the Business System	None	100	0	Yes	1
10. Wharton	Accounting, Finance, Marketing, Management, Managerial Economics, Macroeconomics, Quantitative Methods and Statistics	Business Policy, five major courses	80	30	Yes	2

School	1992 Top Three Job Areas	1992 No. of Companies That Recruit On-Campus	1992 Average Starting Salary	No. of Days per Week Classes Held
1. Chicago	Commercial banking (16), investment banking (12), consulting (15)	230	Varies	6
2. Columbia	Consulting (16), corporate finance (15), marketing (15)	325	$56,300	4
3. Darden	Finance (37), marketing (20), consulting (15)	206	$55,252	5, with a few exceptions
4. Harvard	Consulting (24), investment banking (13), real estate (8)	400	N/A	5
5. Kellogg (Northwestern)	Consulting (25), finance (25), product management (21)	375	N/A	4
6. MIT Sloan	Consulting (29), financial services (24), high tech (20)	160	$62,900	4, with a few exceptions
7. Michigan	Finance (35), marketing (23), consulting (17)	361	$57,600	4
8. Stanford	Consulting (28), marketing (13), finance (8)	211	$65,000 (median)	4
9. Tuck (Dartmouth)	Finance (N/A), consulting (N/A), marketing (N/A)	100	N/A	5 first year, 4 second year
10. Wharton	Investment banking (27), consulting (24), marketing (16)	270	N/A	4

School	Academic Pressure	Social Environment	Reputation/Mentality
1. Chicago	Intense	Cohort-oriented	Analytically rigorous
2. Columbia	Intense	Individualistic	Cosmopolitan/financial capital
3. Darden	Intense	Group-oriented	General management excellence
4. Harvard	Intense	Section-oriented	West Point of business schools
5. Kellogg (Northwestern)	Moderately intense	Relaxed	Marketing-driven/group perspective
6. MIT Sloan	Intense but friendly	Relaxed	Analytical/international, technological focus
7. Michigan	Moderately intense	Group-oriented	Innovative excellence in general management
8. Stanford	Intense	Team-oriented	Balanced excellence
9. Tuck (Dartmouth)	Moderately intense	Close-knit groups	Well-balanced generalists
10. Wharton	Intense	Informal	Finance forte/professional management

NOTES ON THE CONTRIBUTORS

PROFILES

K. PAGE BOYER — *Chicago*

Page was awarded her MBA with Honors in Finance and Marketing from the University of Chicago Graduate School of Business in 1988. Prior to entering the GSB, she was a financial consultant with Merrill Lynch. Page graduated as a Rufus Choate scholar from Dartmouth College, where she earned her BA in Economics in 1984. Currently she is working on her first novel and plans to pursue a doctorate in Industrial Organization.

DAVID RAY — *Columbia*

David graduated from Columbia Business School in 1992 with a degree in International Business and Management of Organizations. He did his undergraduate work at Brown, graduating with a BA in American Literature in 1984. Prior to his MBA, David worked as an image and identity consultant to Fortune 500 companies. He currently works in this field.

FREDERICK STOW, JR. — *Darden*

Fred is a 1987 graduate of The Darden School at the University of Virginia. Prior to going to business school, he owned and operated his own business providing petroleum land services to independent exploration and production companies. He received his BA in Business Administration in Petroleum Land Management from the University of Texas at Austin in 1982. Fred currently works in Houston for Dexco Polymers, a joint venture between Dow Chemical Company and Exxon Chemical Company.

N. THOMPSON LONG — *Harvard*

Tom is a 1988 graduate of Harvard Business School. He did his undergraduate work at the University of North Carolina at Chapel Hill. Before starting business school, he worked in marketing for Kaiser Roth Hosiery and McCann-Erickson. He currently is employed by the Coca-Cola Company in Atlanta in sales management.

SANDY ZUSMANN — *Kellogg*

Sandy is a 1987 graduate of the Kellogg Graduate School of Management. He received an AB degree from Duke in Economics and an MS in Communication from Georgia State University. Prior to starting business school, he worked as a field auditor for a bank. Since graduation, Sandy has worked in the magazine industry for *Southern Homes*. He currently works in marketing for Coca-Cola.

JULIE SELL — *Kellogg*

Julie graduated from the Kellogg School with an MBA in 1993. Her major areas of concentration were International Business and Marketing. Prior to business school she was a journalist. She did her undergraduate work at Mount Holyoke, receiving a BA in political science in 1983.

JOHN KRAFCIK — *MIT*

John received an MS in Management from MIT in 1988. Before going to business school, John worked for Xerox and NUMMI, a joint venture between General Motors and Toyota. He did his undergraduate work at Stanford in mechanical engineering. John currently runs his own consulting business, Competitive Manufacturing Research.

ANTONY SHERIFF — *MIT*

Antony received an MS in management from MIT in 1988, with concentrations in Marketing, Technological Innovations, and Corporate Strategy. Prior to attending the Sloan School, Antony worked as an advance and international product planner for Chrysler. He received a BA in economics and a BS in engineering from Swarthmore College. Antony now works as a management consultant for McKinsey & Co. in New York and London.

DAVID ARDIS — *Michigan*

David is a 1992 graduate of the University of Michigan Business School. He received a BA in History and Religion from the College of William and Mary in 1982 and worked for the next seven years as General Manager for one of the largest independent restaurants in the Washington, D.C., area. He currently works for Morrison Restaurants, Inc., based in Mobile, Alabama.

DAVID HESSEKIEL — *Stanford*

David graduated from the Stanford Graduate School of Business in 1988. Prior to business school, he worked as a journalist, first as a free-lance writer in Mexico City and then as a newspaper reporter in New Haven, Connecticut. David received a BA in government from Wesleyan University in 1982. He now works in magazine management for the Meredith Corporation.

FRANCIS W. HUNNEWELL — *Tuck*

Frank graduated from the Amos Tuck School at Dartmouth in June 1988. He received his AB from Harvard in 1982. Prior to starting business school, he worked at J. P. Morgan, Inc., in New York City, where he was responsible for client relationships in Colombia, Ecuador, and Panama. Frank is now a consultant at Bain and Company, Inc., in Boston.

CHRISTY KALAN — *Wharton*

Christy received her MBA in Management from Wharton in 1992. After receiving a bachelor's degree in English from Colgate University in 1982, she worked for seven years in student travel and cultural exchange programs. While at Wharton, Christy worked with the Vice Dean of the Graduate Division on developing, implementing, and troubleshooting their new curriculum. She now works as a free-lance consultant to small businesses.

BURNETT (JODY) HANSEN — *Wharton*

Jody received his MBA in Finance and Decision Sciences from Wharton in 1993. He completed his bachelor's degree at Yale University in 1985 and worked in commercial banking and fund-raising for six years. After earning his CFA designation, he taught financial statement analysis before pursuing a business degree. He currently works in management consulting at the Center for Applied Research in Philadelphia.

INSIGHTS

MEYER FELDBERG

Meyer is Dean of Columbia Business School at Columbia University. Since 1989 he has overseen the initiation of several institutional policies, including the development of a revised curriculum. Feldberg also serves as a consultant to numerous American and European companies and is on the board of Federated Department Stores, Inc. Meyer received his BA degree at the University of Witwatersrand in Johannesburg in 1962. He earned his MBA at Columbia University in 1965 and his PhD at the University of Cape Town in 1969.

HENRY MALIN

Hank is Director of Admissions at the Amos Tuck School at Dartmouth College. He received his AB from Dartmouth in 1982 and his EdM from Harvard in 1985. In addition to teaching for six years at independent schools in Massachusetts, Hank served as Assistant Dean of Admissions at Union College (N.Y.) and Associate Director of Admissions at Tuck.

MARIE MOOKINI

Marie is Director of MBA Admissions at the Stanford Graduate School of Business. She previously worked in the Undergraduate Admissions Office at Stanford for eight years, where she evaluated applications of high-school seniors and transfer students. Marie received her Master's and PhD in Education from UCLA, and her BA in Psychology at Stanford.

EDITOR

Tom Fischgrund

Tom is a 1980 graduate of Harvard Business School. He has a PhD in political science from MIT and a BA from Tufts University. He has directed a graduate program in Public Administration and done government research. He then spent six years in advertising. He currently is working as a senior marketing manager for Coca-Cola. His latest book, *Barron's Top 50: An Inside Look at America's Best Colleges*, was published in 1991.